BRING BACK MY STRINGBAG

BRING BACK MY STRINGBAG

Swordfish pilot at war 1940-45

LORD KILBRACKEN
formerly Lieutenant-Commander (A)
John Godley DSC RNVR

LEO COOPER · LONDON

First published in Great Britain in 1979 by Peter Davies Limited.

Republished in this revised edition in 1996 by LEO COOPER
190 Shaftesbury Avenue, London WC2H 8JL
an imprint of Pen & Sword Books Ltd
47 Church Street, Barnsley, South Yorkshire, S70 2AS

ISBN 0 85052 495 4

A CIP record for this book is available from the British Library

Printed in England by Redwood Books.

CONTENTS

ACKNOWLEDGEMENTS

My flying logbooks, in which I recorded details of every flight made, have been my most important source, supplemented by my memory, as amplified and corrected by such contemporaries as I could contact, in particular the late John W ('Jake') Bennett, Brian Walsh Atkins, Arthur T. ('Bertie') Ingham, David B. ('Doc') Moffat and Charles S. ('Charlie') Simpson. I am particularly grateful to David Brown, head of the Naval Historical Branch at the Ministry of Defence, his colleagues Alan Francis and Robert Coppock, and Miss Reilly of the Naval Historical Library, for their patience and help; and to the staff (and the computers) at the Public Record Office, Kew.

Of the books I have consulted, I would mention in particular *Find, Fix and Strike* by Terence Horsley; *Aircraft and Sea Power* by Admiral Sir Arthur Hezlet; *The Catafighters* by Kenneth Poolman; *Fairey Aircraft* by H. A. Taylor, and *Chronology of the War at Sea* by Dr G. Hümmelchen and Dr J. Rohwer.

Finally my former wife, Penny, who has kept a day-to-day diary for over fifty years, was able to supply forgotten details of those we shared and for this too I am grateful.

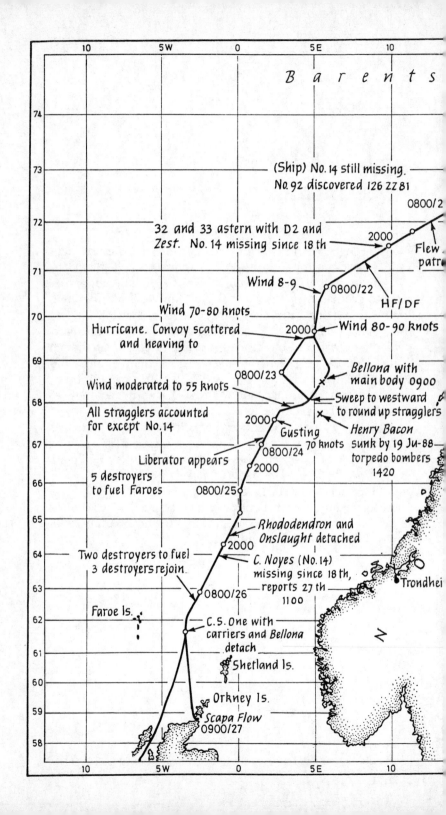

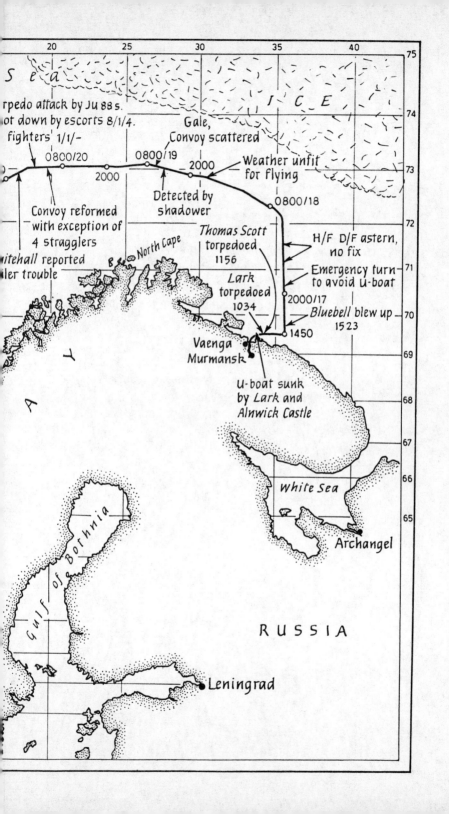

_S e a_

I C E

rpedo attack by Ju 88 s.
ot down by escorts 8/1/4.
fighters' 1/1/–

0800/20

0800/19

Gale,
Convoy scattered

2000

2000

Weather unfit
for flying

0800/18

Convoy reformed
with exception of
4 stragglers

North Cape

Detected by
shadower

itehall reported
ler trouble

Thomas Scott
torpedoed
1156

H/F D/F astern,
no fix

Emergency turn
to avoid u-boat

Lark
torpedoed
1034

2000/17

Bluebell blew up
1523

1450

Vaenga
Murmansk

U-boat sunk
by _Lark_ and
Alnwick Castle

A Y

White Sea

Archangel

Gulf of Bothnia

R U S S I A

Leningrad

The Swordfish relies on her Peggy,
   The modified Taurus ain't sound,
So the Swordfish flies out on her missions
   And the Albacore stays on the ground.

Bring back, bring back,
   Oh bring back my Stringbag to me, to me!
Bring back, bring back,
   Bring back my Stringbag to me!

THE SONG OF THE ALBACORE PILOT c. 1941

I

CHARON LEADS THE WAY

I only just caught the train. Sprinted along the platform at Waterloo to throw myself as the guard's whistle blew into the last packed-full carriage. Wearing grey slacks and a sports jacket, my hair newly cut to approved length for the Navy. Sailors passed out and dishevelled after a night of shore leave in London, one with his girl's scarlet lipstick still smudged across his mouth. And another seeing it wipes his own lips with the back of his hand although not needed. And evacuee children with their gas-masks in cardboard boxes, screaming with anxious mothers, to be disgorged at safe stations on the way. And Wrens with their black cotton stockings and little round hats with turned-up brims reading Tit-Bits and Reveille.

I examine a sleeping sailor, mouth open, sprawled in a corner. Big black boots, bellbottoms, cap tipped over his eyes, anonymous HMS ribbon. Can it be that's how I'll look tomorrow, even tonight? How do you tie that ribbon, put on that collar, fix up that black silk scarf with such nonchalance, ensure the tilt of the cap at just the authentic angle? The only service to fight the war in nineteenth-century fancy dress.

The train wheezing at last into Portsmouth Harbour station, where I'm to take a ferry to Gosport. Never before been there. Spying a wizened bluejacket with a *St Vincent* cap-ribbon, shouldering a kitbag. *St Vincent* – a barracks, not a ship – that's where I'm going! He doesn't know it and I'll not tell him but within an hour I'll be his shipmate! Meantime, if I follow him he will lead me there: Queequeg showing Ishmael the way, or could he be Charon? Down the ramp behind him to the ferryboat, then swaying across the harbour on this sun-bright first of July morning in 1940 with grey-blue warships at anchor, not knowing a cruiser from a sloop. A tuppenny ride in a green double-decker bus through prim suburban streets to great gates on the right, a mast with a White Ensign, a mammoth parade ground. Charon descends, I follow.

Descends also overwhelming shyness, worse by far than joining a new school and no consoling mother. Standing for five minutes, little brown suitcase in hand, plucking up courage to enter. My last moments in Civvy Street. Beyond the gates, bands of hulking bluejackets going about their business. Parties of them drilling, officers shouting orders. How many hundred sailors, initiates, old hands, waiting to mock me with all their known mysteries? Gazing across the parade ground to the red brick dormitory blocks. Are all those stories true of sodomy in the Navy, with the many weeks at sea without the sight of a woman? What nameless acts behind those walls at lights out? I am nineteen, I have come from Ireland beyond conscription, to fly and fight in the clouds. What has this red brick and asphalt to do with it?

A last deep breath. Crossing the road and saying what I'd been told to say: I've come aboard to join.

All would-be naval pilots, apart from the few who already held RN commissions and volunteered for flying, joined the service through *St Vincent* in batches of fifty to sixty every four weeks. Mine was the sixteenth course, so the first must have been well before the war. Your course number always stayed with you:

– What course were you on then?
– Sixteen.

At first this would be greeted with disdain, you were a makey-learn pilot, but by the time ten more had gone through it was respectable, and towards the end of the war, when the seventieth or eightieth course must have been starting, there weren't all that many left flying from an earlier one.

– You said *sixteen?* Jesus!

We joined as Naval Airmen 2nd Class, lowest of the low, bell-bottoms and all, the same as Ordinary Seamen, and got fourteen bob a week all found. Broke after nine months at Balliol, I'd live on my pay alone for the seven weeks of the course. Helped by cigarettes at a shilling a hundred. And a cup of tea in the NAAFI was one old penny. We could afford to go ashore, as we were taught to call leaving the barracks, once or twice a week for a round of beers, a pass at a girl or two.

Something over half of us would eventually get our wings after nine months of training, when virtually all (unlike the RAF boys) would become officers. The rest would fall by the wayside somewhere along the line. They were said to have dipped. Very few indeed would yet be killed. Perhaps they were found to be LMF (lacking in moral fibre) or deficient in OLQ (officer-like qualities). But mostly it became clear they'd never make pilots. Then they found themselves still in the Navy, but as plain Ordinary Seamen, hauling on a rope somewhere – who had joined only to fly, for the glamour of the air, marooned on the lower deck.

Seven weeks at *Vincent* learning things that had no connection with flying whatsoever. Square-bashing under Chiefy Wilmott. Seamanship. How to tie knots, the reef, bowline, clove hitch, sheepshank. Flags and pendants, the Morse code, even semaphore. And the Traditions of the Navy. Never whistle. Say 'Aye, aye, sir', never 'Yes, sir.' Salute with palm turned downward. The three white stripes on the collar for Nelson's three great victories. Wear your cap straight across your eyes, never tilted or flat-a-back. Tie a tiddly bow.

The day after joining, getting to know one another, not yet issued with uniform, all acting tough, we are to be addressed by the Commander. In he strides, three gold stripes, looks us over, speaks without preamble.

– How many of you went to a public school?

Jesus what a question! When we are busy playing sailors! I

raise my hand instinctively, then in horror see too late I am the only one.

– And what school did you go to?

– Eton, I say hopelessly, the shame of it rising inside me. The only one and, worst of all, from Eton. The stigma will never leave me. But the Commander is only playing. His eyes move round the room.

– Well where did *you* go then?

Well actually Winchester. Feeling a little better.

The Commander simply showing off how easily he can pick us. Four or five more follow: each time he is right. Then a homily about Officers and Gentlemen, the Nelson Touch, Sailors of the King.

Which was worse, to have admitted it or been found out?

Next week the bombing started. It was already the Battle of Britain though no one knew it till long afterwards. The first lot came over high, taking everyone by surprise. Seeing them silver in the sky overhead, Heinkel 111s, ten or twenty in formation, then hearing the whistle of the bombs just before the sirens. Throwing ourselves, we rookies, flat on the ground, heads covered, waiting for the crunches.

Looking up to see old hands in trained discipline moving to action stations or allotted shelters, mocking us as they passed. The bombs falling harmlessly on open ground a hundred yards away.

Getting worse each day. Soon the first Stukas. With so many major targets nearby, why did they bother with *St Vincent?* JU87s, gulled wings, fixed undercarts, diving on us out of the sun to under 300 feet. Doubling to our shelter two or three times a day, sometimes false alarms, sometimes only distant crunches. Or the rattle of machine-gun fire as our own ill-armed positions opened up, then crunches all around that you could feel. All of us singing like fools: the Siegfried Line, the Quartermaster's Stores. But sudden silence when the near ones fell, the shallow shelter visibly moving and shuddering, the smell of high explosive. A direct hit on a shelter fifty yards away, a dozen seamen killed, more injured, an officer calling for volunteers to dig out bodies. Red-faced Chief Wilmott, till then no more than a parade ground martinet, suddenly a hero in action, claiming a Stuka 'probably destroyed' from his Lewis gun position on the roof of G Block, coming laughing down the stairs, everyone pummelling him.

– I *got* the bugger, I think I *got* the bugger.

That's all we had, two or three Lewis guns on the roof, about as good as pea-shooters. Unless you were Chiefy Wilmott. Not a Spitfire or Hurricane in sight.

Later that evening, sirens and back to the shelters. *Eggs, eggs, walking on wooden legs,* we sang. Going on much the same the rest of the time we were there. *Have you any dirty washing, mother dear?* Once I said a fervent prayer while the bombs fell all round us and everyone else was singing.

– If I have to die, I can accept it. But God do me a favour. Give me a bloody chance: let it be in the cockpit of a warplane, not cowering underground.

He gave me the chance and I took it. And I lost count of the times I'd remember that prayer I'd made, thinking Jesus is this the pay-off.

We left *Vincent* on August 19th to start our flying training. Anchors on our sleeves as Leading Naval Airmen. Together by train to London, where the serious bombing was starting, then split into two parties: one to Luton to fly Magisters, one to Elmdon to fly Tigers. It was of no special significance which party you were in, but we who went to Luton thought we were the lucky ones. The Tigers were easier to fly but the Maggies more of a challenge and far more fun. Sleek streamlined monoplanes, you could pretend they were Hurricanes. Arriving, singing, at twilight at the airfield. And there they were, dispersed at intervals in the grass of the perimeter, yellow toys waiting our pleasure.

Flying had always been a passion, an ecstasy, first known when I was a schoolboy at Ashdown House in Sussex. The Hannibal airliners of Imperial Airways, great four-engined biplanes, floated over it like stately queens as regular as clockwork on their $2\frac{1}{4}$-hour flight between London and Paris. And the day came when I was twelve, in 1933, and went with my mother on a Sunday during term-time to see a flying circus. They were giving five-bob flights in a Hannibal and I said please mummy oh please. And the rickety airliner soared skyward in the brightness of the evening with at least twenty passengers, the Sussex patchwork spreading flattened under me. And, when the pilot banked, the plane stayed horizontal and the miniature fields slanted up towards me. And my mother with her spectacles and fussy Sunday dress must have been standing there in the field, never taking her eyes from me for a second, desperately fearing that something might go wrong. And the sheer delight of cleaving the brilliant air, the sudden silence when the pilot throttled back.

From then I'd save for joy-rides whenever possible. Or, if I couldn't get two half-crowns together, on the bike to Croydon to watch. Where I managed to scrape acquaintance with Captain Bill Ledlie, one of my boyhood heroes, a pilot with a charter company, Olley Air Services. I could sometimes get Captain Ledlie to give me a flip for nothing, say if he was taking his Leopard on a test flight. Or he would let me go along, sitting up-front beside him, on short hops to Hendon or Brooklands.

– Here, take a feel of the joy-stick, lad. Then, putting his man's hand over mine, he would let me share the craft's delicate response to each small movement he made, to each he made me make. Quiver of a wildbird, swooping and turning to our command. I was ensnared for ever, his slave.

Most holidays I'd go home to Killegar in the remote depths of Ireland, where herons flew and kingfishers but no aeroplanes. But my parents' marriage was ending and soon with my brother and sister, both younger than me, I was sent to each of them for whatever period was allotted by court order. My mother, always on the move, had a succession of houses or furnished rooms, sometimes in London and sometimes in Rottingdean, still an unspoilt fishing village, with the slot machines on Palace Pier and a vagrant pilot who gave joy-rides from Windmill Hill, out to seaward across the cliffs.

And when I was fifteen, for some forgotten reason, she took a house near Reading for her half of our summer holidays, worked out exactly to the day. The first evening, on my maroon racing bike, up to the airfield at Woodley. I couldn't believe my luck, they had a flying school, it cost a pound an hour. The joy-ride pilots took pride in making the five-bob flights so short that the wheels were still turning from the takeoff when they landed. Here, for the price of four joy-rides, a full hour in the sky and at the same time *learning to be a pilot*. It was just too good to be true.

The aircraft were Miles Majors, low-wing monoplanes, two open cockpits one behind the other. I took out all I had in the Post Office and had four hours' instruction. The pure delight, the unimagined sense of power, when this silver swallow dipped and slanted to my finger tip!

And this was the year of the Flying Flea, the Pou-de-Ciel as its young French inventor, Henry Mignet, had named it. A brilliant genius! He planned to bring private flying to every-one with this tiny, lath-and-fabric single-seater, powered by a two-stroke engine. A wonderfully simple design: no ailerons, no elevators, but two mainplanes one *behind* the other and a rudder. You could buy an assembly kit for £25 complete with elaborate blueprints and pay what you could afford for a second-hand engine out of a motor-bike. Everyone was building them on both sides of the Channel and it seemed the skies would soon all be buzzing with Fleas. On the bicy-cle to Heston to see the first one built in Britain: its con-structor, Stephen Appleby, had just landed but took off again and made a circuit for my sole benefit.

Naturally I decided at once to a build a Flea, using the facilities available at the School of Mechanics at Eton. I was barely sixteen. I soon had enough saved to buy the bits and pieces for the rudder. The extremity of excitement when they arrived! I had already worked out in my school atlas the route I would follow to fly her home to Killegar – she would just have the range, I reckoned, for the shortest sea crossing from the Welsh coast to Dublin – and chosen the field where I could land her. I wasn't too great a carpenter but with much help from the instructors I did actually build that rudder. And started saving for the fuselage.

This wasn't easy because there was also the little matter of learning to fly, which I also had to save for. By the following Easter I had enough for three or four more lovely hours and started on landings. But then disaster struck when I was almost expelled from Eton. I'd become the school book-maker with well over a hundred clients and a turnover of some £30 a day, getting on for £1000 in today's money, which might soon have earned me enough to buy a Flea ready assembled and to complete my flying training with something over. But my sins came to light in Ascot Week when I was discovered with the day's takings in a Wool-worth's cash-box and could invent no explanation for the possession of such wealth. I was swiped by the headmaster and had my leave stopped for weeks. Worse still, I had no time to hedge half-a-dozen sizeable winning bets and lost more on that one day than all my previous profit. And then my mother, usually my trusted ally in such crises, punished me even further by forbidding me to fly. There seemed no point in going on with the Flea even if I could have afforded it. That beautiful rudder, silvery and shining, was as far as I ever got. It languished alone in the School of Mechanics for ever.

I don't know what happened to all the hundreds, maybe thousands, of other Flying Fleas that were abuilding as the craze swept over Britain. Maybe enthusiasm waned, maybe money ran out, or more than likely it was found, as would almost certainly have happened with mine, that their would-be builders had insufficient skill and knowledge to construct a flying machine that would be well enough built to get its essential C of A (Certificate of Airworthiness). It's possible that some dozens did actually fly but I never again saw one after that breathtaking Brooklands day.*

Much later I realized that my mother had been scared silly by my flying and used this heaven-sent pretext for putting an end to it without having to admit her fears to me.

---

* A cleaned-up version of the Flea has now (1996) reappeared in Britain, designed by Mignet's grandson, Alain. The bits and pieces for the air-frame are again available for DIY fanatics from Ian Harwood of Flea-planes, Hitchen, for around £1,000, much the same after inflation as in the thirties.

For these she had reason. Her first husband, Wing-Commander Neville Usborne, had been killed in a flying accident in 1916. As her second marriage disintegrated, she increasingly idealized her first, treasuring each memory of her lost hero. With whom, at least in recollection, their four years had been perfect: the gentle lover, the wise father, the brilliant man of invention. And I do believe that Neville, of whom she so often spoke to me, was indeed more than an outstanding naval officer. A visionary with an eager mind as well as great charm and magnetism, he had been one of the very first sailors to specialize in flying. As early as 1909 he was appointed to superintend the building at Barrow by Vickers of *No. I Naval Airship*, known less formally as *Mayfly*, the first aircraft (though a failure) in any navy in the world. She was completed in 1911, the year before his marriage, but never flew more than a few feet and was wrecked on the ground by high winds in that September.

By then Usborne was perhaps the most experienced airship pilot in the Navy, and was given command of the French-built *Astra Torres*, the first successful naval airship, when she arrived in the spring of 1913 from France. He once flew my mother over Paris in her, an event she often described to me in childhood, eyes shining. At the outbreak of war, still captain of *Astra Torres*, he was in charge of Kingsnorth Naval Air Station and had qualified as an aeroplane pilot. His death was on a trial flight before members of the Cabinet of an anti-Zeppelin craft, which he himself had invented and built. I never realized it but I was taking over from my father, long before the divorce, the impossible task of replacing her vanished lover.*

So was it a mere coincidence that I too became a naval pilot? Or was I seeking to follow in the slipstream, to match or surpass the record, of this long-dead but still-strong rival for my mother's love and admiration? I believe it was a coincidence, whatever the psychiatrists may say (to whom there are few coincidences). I may have been drawn to flying by the stories my mother told me, but not to naval flying in par-

---

* For details of Usborne's work with airships, see Appendix 1.

ticular. When war came, why did I fly, why did I fight? I was at home at Killegar, not yet nineteen, just finished with Eton, about to start at Oxford. My father wanted me to change my plans, to switch to TCD, stay safe in Ireland. But I set forth for Balliol. And then by chance as I stepped from the train on arrival at Oxford seeing a poster: BE A MAN! FLY WITH THE RAF! And deciding suddenly to hell with it. Never stopped to think I might be killing, very probably killed. Not considering war's ethics, the futility of violence, why I should involve myself. I'd be taking a chance but why not? Why not be a man? I'd be learning to fly for nothing, in fact be paid for learning! The opportunity seemed too good to miss, the bargain fair enough.

Nor law, nor duty bade me fight,
Nor public men, nor cheering crowds:
A lonely impulse of delight
Drove to this tumult in the clouds. *

So I went the same day to a recruiting office, to join the Air Force not the Navy. Where they told me they could put me on the waiting list and I mightn't get in for a year. Queueing up to die. But how could I wait so long? By then the war might be over.

– If you're in such a hurry, join the Fleet Air Arm. You'd be flying in the Navy. In less than a couple of months.

I at once put my name down, surrendering my early manhood and very probably my life without a moment's reflection. I went to Balliol all the same but naturally did no work. I was supposed to be reading Greats but would hardly complete a term and Plato seemed irrelevant. Word came soon that I wouldn't be called up before Christmas. From then there were postponements every couple of months, so in three full terms it never quite seemed worth starting to work seriously. But I had a fine time, I broke with my Irish girl, I met Angel.

* W. B. Yeats, *An Irish Airman Foresees His Death.*

10

Meantime the Air Force must have been getting more air-craft than anticipated. So boys who put down their names for it after I volunteered for the FAA to get into the air more quickly were well on their way to action before I reached Luton to start flying training.

Naval pilots until awarded their wings were trained by RAF instructors in RAF aircraft at RAF stations. And so it came about that I made my first flight in the Navy with Flight-Lieutenant Cudemore in Miles Magister N3823 from No. 24 Elementary Flying Training School at RAF Luton on August 21st 1940.

Of those who dipped, many never even went solo, the greatest single hurdle, which wasn't long coming. They reck-oned on having a good idea, often on knowing for sure, whether a pupil had the makings of a pilot within the first week. Many of the Tiger-boys went solo after five or six hours of instruction. Maggies took rather longer but after ten or twelve hours you were sweating.

My log-book says I took eleven hours but I've an excuse. On September 5th, with seven hours behind me, I took off with a new instructor, Pilot Officer Parr, to have another go at landings. Circuits and bumps we called them. They were much the most difficult part of early training though once you'd got the knack you could put a kite down blindfold; it's like learning to ride a bicycle. If you made a hash of it, the instructor would take over, yelling on the intercom that he'd 'got her', jamming open the throttle and taking her round again.

What did you do in the war, Daddy?
How did you help us to win?
Circuits and bumps all day, laddie,
And how to get out of a spin.

This day, with Parr, my first landing was OK. Approaching for the second, 500 feet, 300 feet, concentrating like crazy, eyes flicking back and forth between the spot I'd chosen, the ASI, the altimeter, no planes near by, everything fine. *Come on now,* three more good ones and you'll be flying solo.

Suddenly Parr's urgent voice on the intercomm.
– Oh Jesus Christ, I've got her.
For God's sake what have I done? Everything was just fine. Height, airspeed, attitude, glide angle. And now why doesn't the bugger *say* anything?

Pilot Officer Parr was too busy taking avoiding action. Overhead a squadron of Heinkel bombers, one-one-ones. Spitfires after them. A stick of bombs crunching across the airfield. A Maggie parked below us instant matchwood. Two more sticks, a terrible tongue of flame from the Vauxhall Works alongside. A little soon to be in action. Steep turn to starboard. Get the hell out. Hedgehopping to safety.

It was over in less than ten minutes. Returning to the circuit, a red light from flying control, not safe to land. Of course no radio so we couldn't know it then but there were many UXBs (unexploded bombs) which could have delayed-action fuses, might go off at any moment. Parr finding his way to a small airfield nearby, Barton-in-the-Clay. Landing there after a total flight of seventy minutes, all to be included in the eleven hours I took to solo.

Coming back by car, the Maggie collected next day. Everyone shaken, cheering and singing. 'Vauxhall Works badly hit' says my logbook. The spurt of flame from a direct hit on the paint store; twenty or thirty killed. A pupil on my course, Hugh Popham, injured and in hospital. Amazingly the only one; a twelve-foot crater obliterating our dispersal point where we waited when not flying, but there'd been three minutes warning, everyone dived for the hedge. One by one the UXBs are detonated. All hands to filling craters.

Some time in the small hours, all asleep, a shattering explosion rocks and buffets our tent. Out and into the ditch. A UXB beside us hadn't been noticed. Sometimes they went in plunk and buried themselves several feet down without disturbing the surface especially in long grass. Must have had about a twelve-hour delayed action fuse. Not much more sleep that night.

The airfield back in operation ten hours later. Red flags marking filled-in craters. Fifty minutes with Parr, circuits and bumps.

– Three or four more like those and you'll be on your own.

Christ, I thought. Christ, I'm going to make it.

Pilots get killed before they get their wings, though very seldom, through carelessness or panic or disobeying orders – or, most often of all, through simply showing off. I never heard of a death on a first solo. You are concentrating for every second.

Taxiing circumspectly round the perimeter to the chosen downwind position – of course no runways. Checking controls, looking to leeward for other aircraft, lowering goggles. Throttle and rudder to turn into wind, pick up a point to aim at. Right, this is it, open her up full throttle. Gathering speed, bumpity bump over the grass, keep her straight, now ease the stick very gently forward, up comes the tail wheel. Hold her a few more seconds, keep her straight for Christ's sake. You can't yet tell when she's ready just by the feel of the stick, without checking on the airspeed, though that will come quite soon, so just a quick glance. Now, *now:* ease back imperceptibly, the nose rises, the last little bump. Jesus we're airborne, airborne. Keep full throttle, keep straight, keep the correct climbing speed. I'm on my own, totally detached, unattainable, on my own in the sky. The airfield perimeter flashing under my wing-tip, the whole world stretched before me.

Laughing and cheering aloud. Inarticulate cries with no one to hear them, bouncing up and down, the need to express somehow the exhilaration and joy, the release of tension, the relief. Off goggles, whole face into the slipstream, still cheering and singing, feel the clear air rushing on my face till tears run a tenth of an inch and are swept away astern of me.

Reaching 500 feet. Throttle back, level out, medium turn to port through ninety degrees, open up again, continue climbing. Luton a toy-town below. Stay on this crosswind course to 1000 feet, throttle back to cruising revs. Now look around. Relax. Check everything.

I'm allowed ten minutes of soaring and climbing. Then

back into the circuit. Downwind, crosswind, then upwind for the landing. Parr will be watching me, now's the time to show him. There goes the perimeter fifty feet below me. Level out, close throttle, now back with the stick, come on back, come on back, we've *done* it. Bumpity-bump as we run across the field, keep her straight, brake her ever so slightly, come to a joyous standstill. Taxi back to dispersal. Grin and wave to waving grinning comrades.

OK now let's start flying, you reckless birdman.

II

CASSANDRA AMONG
THE PIN-TABLES

We were eight weeks at Luton, flew fifty or sixty hours, half of it solo. To say we were good boys who always obeyed orders would be inaccurate. Some were but not most, including me. You get no sensation of speed when flying at normal height but at fifty feet it's different and low flying was a perpetual temptation to which we were known to yield. Some of the boys would rendezvous out of sight to carry out formation flying (strictly forbidden) – on one occasion so close, they boasted afterwards, that they touched wings. We were meant to stay within ten miles of the airfield except on navigation exercises but the temptation to fly home and show off to parents or girl-friends was no more resistible than low flying. By now (not yet twenty) I was engaged to Angel (a few months younger) who had left Somerville in post-Dunkirk patriotic fervour to make bombs at Brock's Fireworks Factory, Hemel Hempstead, which was conveniently nearby, only just outside the permitted radius, and I should have been practising steep turns when I was zooming over her chimneys showing how clever I was; look at me, I'm flying. Just the way to get killed.

I can't say on which day, since I'd hardly put it in my log-book, but it must have been towards the end of September that I came very close indeed to writing myself off in such an act of recklessness. And what a spectacular death! Let me explain about spinning. A spin occurs basically if you make a turn with insufficient speed. Simplest way: reduce speed to just on stalling, pull back on the stick and apply full rudder, either way but let's say starboard. The plane then whips sharply over to starboard and falls vertically earthwards (or it seems vertically) spinning clockwise like a top, one or two revolutions a second. A strange illusion: once you're spinning you feel you're suspended motionless, with the earth rising to meet you, and it spinning rapidly about that central point below you where you would plunge into eternity if you didn't know what to do about it.

It's quite possible to spin off a turn by accident and you're dead if this happens at under 500 feet. But with enough altitude you can get out of it, so every pilot is taught the drill and carries it out half-a-dozen times at safe height before flying solo. I loved aerobatics, and soon started spinning, as well as loops and rolls, when flying solo, though this was forbidden at EFTS. I was totally self-confident. On this particular morning I first broke the rules by map-reading my way to Eton: look at me, I'm flying. Then I climbed five or six thousand feet till I was precisely over Windsor Castle, throttled back, full port rudder and over into a spin. The whole world revolving about the Round Tower, with College Chapel a bit off-centre.

But now I made the most appalling error. Always previously, with or without an instructor, I'd let her spin for not more than half-a-dozen revolutions. Today in case anyone was watching I kept her in it for over 2000 feet. OK, let's come out. I went through the usual drill and absolutely nothing happened.

Let there be no mistake, if I'd panicked I would quite certainly have plunged vertically into Windsor Castle, writing off not only myself but maybe most of the Royal Family if they happened to be at home. I gave the situation about three seconds of cool deliberate thought (the earth was rising towards me at about 200 feet a second). The only possible explanation was that I was now descending much faster than ever before and spinning much more rapidly; the only hope was to go through the whole drill again, very slowly and calmly, very deliberately, exaggerating each stage of it.

Below 3000 feet now. Starboard rudder every inch she would go. Hold her there a full five seconds. For the love of Christ don't panic. The spin slowing at 1200 feet, centralize controls, wait, wait, I'm in a straight vertical dive. At 700 feet, haul back on the stick as hard as I dare, don't pull the bloody wings off, she's coming out. Nearly brushing the oaks of Windsor Great Park, slinking away to westward, hoping no one had taken my number, a long slow turn for home.

Never a word to anyone.

We remained Leading Naval Airmen from leaving *Vincent* till we got our wings seven months later. Our pay was six-and-six a day, of which three-and-six was danger money for flying (whether or not we flew on any particular day) but we now had to pay the full price for cigarettes, ten for sixpence. Half-a-bitter was about the same, and remember, please, I'm talking in old pence. I had £100 a year from my father, soon paid off most of my debts and therefore considered myself in a state of great financial security. So Angel and I were planning to marry around my twentieth birthday. Somehow my parents and her mother (her father had died in her early childhood) didn't seem wholly to share our confidence.

London was now getting it every night, and every night we could clearly see the red glow of its burning in the sky twenty miles away. Yet on our free weekends we would leave without a moment's thought on Friday evenings to hitch towards that glow, where the bombs might be dropping but the fun and the girls were. It seems crazy now but millions were living through it night after night so why should we worry about a weekend? A couple of years earlier I had read with amazement that the buses in Barcelona went right on running through the air raids and thought: How the hell can they do it? With bombers right overhead? Yet now like everyone else I was doing it myself, hitching rides into the blitzed city for an evening out with Angel – in those days even engaged couples didn't automatically sleep together –

and moaning like crazy if we had to queue overlong for a 19 bus after the theatre when the West End was burning round us.

We could always hitch anywhere in bellbottoms. Almost everyone, not only nice girls, really did seem to like a sailor, especially if he were far inland and standing by a roadside. Elsewhere we were bought drinks, people all called us Jack and dear old ladies came smiling up to us: Touch a sailor's collar. We wore plain HMS cap-ribbons as everyone did in wartime except those in barracks, so for all anyone knew we were on shore leave after months of reckless daring at sea. It was only other sailors who could tell at once we hadn't been in a dogwatch, from such giveaways as the colour of our collars (not yet faded), the swing of our bellbottoms, the way we wore our caps. But there was a shop in London where you could buy ready-faded collars, just like jeans today. They also sold cap-ribbons with the legend FLEET AIR ARM, which were completely unauthorized but some thought them a better line than plain HMS. Switching ribbons as we left the airfield.

We left Luton on October 12th for the RAF's No. 1 Senior Flying Training School at Netheravon, where we rejoined the other half of our course who had been flying Tigers at Elmdon. Now the major decision was taken: would it be fighters or bombers? We had no say in the choice. I had somehow always assumed I'd be a fighter-boy, which was supposed to be much more dashing, and was somewhat mortified to find the assumption mistaken. I was among those chosen to fly Hawker Harts, as a prelude to Swordfish and Albacores, rather than Fairey Battles, which would lead to Skuas and Fulmars. This seemed the wrong way round because Harts handled like fighters, whilst the Battle, though admittedly a monoplane, was relatively sedate, much more like a bomber. It meant I had the infinite pleasure of aviation in the Hart – and its variants, the Hind and Audax – for the next five months.

Wonderful kites! No one who flies today can ever know the joy they were. Swordfish in miniature to look at, strutted biplanes with wide-open cockpits, but faster and totally aerobatic. There was nothing you couldn't do with a Hart except pick gooseberries, we used to say. They were almost impossible to spin. Shove on full rudder with the nose held vertically upwards at below stalling speed and she would just gently roll over on her back and fall in a slow spiral, coming out the moment opposite rudder was applied.

The enormous airfield, an amorphous, ill-defined expanse of Salisbury Plain, was grazed by errant flocks of sheep. These, with its rolling undulations like a green Sahara, made landing interesting. There were no runways. At the end of your chosen sheepless approach, it was disconcerting to find the ground falling, or perhaps on the other hand rising, as much as fifty feet just as you reached it. Good preparation, perhaps, for touching down on a storm-tossed carrier, though it can hardly have been planned as such and came rather early in training.

Our status changed significantly at Netheravon. Though still Leading Naval Airmen we lived in the Officers' Mess, had WAAFs to make our beds and were supposed to wear white bands covering our cap-ribbons to show we were future officers. Hated the damned things. We knew we'd be commissioned as soon as we won our wings, automatic unless we were very bad boys and got found out, but for now we were busy being jolly jack tars and the white bands came off like lightning the moment we went ashore (as we were still taught to describe leaving the airfield). The worst of both worlds if we wore them.

Two of our number were in fact bad boys and paid a greater than usual penalty. Petrol was strictly rationed and there were these huge mobile bowsers bringing thousands of gallons of fuel to our aircraft. I had a car called Diana which I had bought for £5 and I'm bound to admit I topped her up, let's say once or twice, from a bowser. But the two baddies, who both happened to come from very distinguished families, got into much deeper water, milking bowsers daily and flogging the petrol in Salisbury for at least two bob a gallon. They did fine for a while but it was dyed red to discourage such enterprises and they were just about certain to cop it in the end. They each got six months in jug. As it happened, both became exceptionally fine pilots in the end but they flew for years as petty officers.

Our progress was slow because we had so few aircraft. Day after day we would arrive at dispersal to find only one, sometimes none at all, for the half-dozen pupils in our flight. And we would play pontoon all morning. I flew only twelve hours in November. Next month was better, but January reached an all-time low with less than six hours logged. Then it improved again. Our course couldn't be extended, so we'd have done less flying than planned when we got our wings on leaving Netheravon, in my case only eighty-eight solo, including Maggies. And we'd a lot to learn.

Formation flying, aerobatics, night flying, divebombing, navigation, instrument flying. Also shooting at towed targets with a fixed machine-gun mounted in the cockpit, firing through the propeller blades. I knew quite well this worked all right, you never shot the prop off, but I could still never quite believe it and always felt a qualm when I pressed the tit. The prop was turning thirty times a second and to this day I can't understand how such marvellously, incredibly accurate timing was achieved with such unsophisticated equipment. Yet it had already been possible in World War I.

We most of us bent the rules on frequent occasions. On an overcast day in December, my duty was a navigational exercise – fly to Peterborough, land there, fly back. Coming home I ran into this sudden patch of bad weather, got somehow lost and put down in a field. On inquiring of an amazed local – it never ceased to astonish when a bluejacket climbed out of the cockpit – I was told I was five or six miles from Bedford (not *too* much off course). By an amazing coincidence Angel, now an Aircraftswoman 2nd Class in the WAAF, was in Bedford on Christmas leave, because her stepfather, Wing-Commander Luck, a World War I balloonist, was Commanding Officer of the RAF station at Cardington nearby, which made it that little bit more dicey.

Angel's mother joining us for drinks that evening, then the Wing-Commander.

– Well, me boy, got a bit of leave then?

– No sir, duff weather, got lost on a navex. Put down in a field.

– Lost on a navex, eh? And where was this field?

– A few miles out of town, sir.

We looked one another very straight in the eyes. A broad grin spread across his face.

– Yes, yes, I know. Can happen to anyone. I remember in 1916...

He never split on me.

My twentieth birthday had just gone by and we weren't yet married. I was a ward of court and the learned judge had offered no opposition – successive judges had always decided, ever since I was twelve, in favour of whatever course I myself wanted whenever my parents disagreed on a major issue involving me, which was almost always – but Angel's mother was resolutely stonewalling and her consent was indispensable. Her first name chanced to be Patience. A reputed versifier, I sent her some doggerel accepting the situation, ending with the line:

With Patience Luck will come my way.

It never did though. Not that particular luck anyway.

I was to get my wings, in official language 'authorised to wear the flying badge in accordance with King's Regulations and Admiralty Instructions, paragraph 811', on the day we left Netheravon, March 29th 1941, along with all those who had lasted the course. Two of those who hadn't were in prison, one had been wounded by enemy action, the remainder simply dipped. Nobody had been killed and I don't remember an aircraft being seriously damaged. With our happy indiscipline and general recklessness, the low standard of aircraft maintenance and the lack or absence of safety equipment and procedures now taken for granted, this approaches the miraculous.

We didn't even have radio, let alone radar. If pilots wished to communicate, it could only be visually. Formation flying was ordered by the simplest possible manual signals for echelon starboard, line astern or whatever. A wing-waggle from the leader was the sign to re-form vic formation. We could 'talk' to each other only by signalling in Morse with our free hand in a series of long or short up-and-down strokes, a procedure known as zigging. If the weather was closing in, there was no way base could recall us.

Flying control was almost non-existent. If we had to land at another airfield, they wouldn't be told to expect us. We would just turn up hopefully and join the circuit on an 'After you, Claud' basis. Same when landing at Netheravon. Choose an approach line more or less into wind, free of sheep and taxiing aircraft, make sure no one else coming in nearby, go on ahead and land. The only safeguard: if anyone in the control tower happened to notice two Harts approaching in close proximity and apparent ignorance, or a Battle about to take off as an unseeing Hind was about to land on top of him, all he could do was grab a pistol and fire a red Very light (something like a Roman candle) through the window.

Even the most basic precautions were often not taken. For instance at the end of the course we flew for two weeks of advanced bombing practice at the RAF's Bombing and Gunnery School on the coast at Newton Down in south Wales. Out targets were located in the sea some four or five miles offshore. Yet we flew without a dinghy or even a Mae West, and had no radio. This could well have cost my life. On one such flight I was on my own and had to drop my bombs after a dive from 8,000 feet. I pulled out at low altitude and the elastic broke – my Rolls Royce Kestrel simply stopped. I'd be swimming in a minute.

By luck (if luck exists) I located the cause within five seconds. You have to weaken your mixture as you climb into thinner air – there was a lever alongside the throttle – and reverse the process descending. The latter, with suicidal carelessness, I'd completely forgotten to do. I shoved the lever forward and my Kestrel burst back into life.

But for me there'd have been no return to life if I'd noticed my error a very few seconds later. No one would have known I'd be ditching and I couldn't have swum five miles in cold rough water without a life jacket – especially in flying gear. And yet, as I clearly remember, I thought nothing of it afterwards – though this is the first time I've ever admitted the fact to anyone.

Somehow we all survived though I don't know how we managed it. We flew with panache and abandon, seeming to court disaster. For we thought we knew it all, which was very far indeed from being the case.

We were rewarded with a full week's leave, our first since joining nine months earlier, when we finally said farewell to Salisbury Plain. Our commissions would date from the day it ended, April 7th. Because we were serving 'for hostilities only', these would be in the RNVR, known as the Wavy Navy from the wave in our gold stripes, in contrast to the broad straight stripes of career officers. With a gold A in their loops to tell the world we were aviators. From which we were known as A-boys. Those over twenty-one became Temporary Sub-Lieutenants. Those aged twenty (as I was) would be Temporary Acting Sub-Lieutenants, a nice distinction, till our twenty-first birthdays. Whilst those under twenty were mere Temporary Midshipmen.

Diana had gone the way of all £5 cars, so I planned to hitch to Andover and take the train to London. Neatly folded on top of my kit-bag was the shiny new uniform I'd ordered some weeks earlier from the representative thoughtfully sent by Gieves, who guaranteed our money back if we should dip at the last moment. By far its most important feature was the pair of golden wings on its left sleeve, above the single wavy stripe and much more valued. Also packed handily were the peaked cap, white shirt, stiff white collar, front stud, back stud, cufflinks and black tie. In some ways it would be a comedown to look like a chauffeur, sometimes mistaken by short-sighted old ladies for a porter, instead of being a bluejacket loved by everyone, but the wings were what made the big difference and I simply couldn't wait, though strictly speaking I still had a week to go on the lower deck.

Arrived at the station with time to spare, I headed for the heads (as the jacks are known in the Navy), found one empty, paid my penny. There in its bleak confines took place my metamorphosis to gold-winged black butterfly from wingless blue chrysalis. Off for the last time with my well-worn bellbottoms, my now well-faded collar, so often touched for luck. On with the creased trousers, a wee bit of trouble with unwonted collar and tie (first time for nine months), then the reefer with all its brass buttons. I emerge, face the mirror, adjust my dress before leaving. Thence to the outside world on the station platform, pretending to feel not the least conspicuous, not to be awaiting my first salute.

It was thus in the shit-house of the up platform at Andover station that I became an officer of His Majesty's Royal Naval Volunteer Reserve (Air Branch).

We aviators of No. 16 Pilots Course could claim without too much presumption to be lineal descendants of the first four RN officers who learned to fly aeroplanes (as distinct from balloons and airships) in the summer of 1911. It had been only eight years since the first-ever flights of heavier-than-air flying machines by the Wright brothers and to fly at all was an achievement. No one had yet even dreamt of the aircraft-carrier as we have come to know her. The main role of naval aircraft was seen as operating from shore bases in support of the fleets, spotting for their guns or flying on reconnaissance ahead of them. But late the previous year a civilian pilot, Eugene Ely, had managed to take off from a small wooden platform constructed in the bows of the US cruiser *Birmingham* and a few months later to land on a similar platform in the stern of the battleship *Pennsylvania,* a most remarkable feat. The possibility of operating aircraft from warships had therefore been established, and this was strengthened when an RN pilot, Commander Charles Samson, took off in January 1912 from the bows of the battleship *Africa* as she lay at anchor in Sheerness, and in May from the battleship *Hibernia,* again using a platform, whilst she steamed at ten knots. And research was in progress to develop successful 'hydroplanes' (as seaplanes were known), which were correctly foreseen as an important component of early naval aviation. Meantime the numbers engaged in this infant branch of the Navy were steadily growing. When the Royal Flying Corps was constituted by Royal Warrant in April 1912, it was divided into a military wing and a naval wing, with RN officers and men constituting the latter. But they were soon calling themselves the Royal Naval Air Service, though this did not exist officially till July 1914.

The RNAS and the RFC then developed independently till they merged in 1918 to form the new-born Royal Air Force. During those years, however, officers of the RNAS though an integral part of the Navy were already given such future RAF ranks as Wing-Commander (instead of Commander).

Even in the earliest days before World War I, the Navy's attitude towards flying was ambivalent, to say the least, and would always remain so, as I myself would soon find out. There were factions for and against flying, both in the Navy and in Parliament, at every level: the air-minded and the ship-minded. The latter were very much in the majority, those who regarded aircraft as useless toys, who declined or were unable to modify the existing concepts of naval warfare that were so deeply engrained in them, to find room for the whole new vistas that aviation should have been opening. And it was they who were responsible, their successors who would remain responsible, for the relatively slow development of naval aviation in Britain through the coming decades, compared with the United States and Japan. Of those with the vision to foresee its full potential, let there be written in gold the names of Churchill among the politicians, of Fisher among the admirals, of Sueter and Samson among the flyers.

During World War I, most operations by naval aircraft – whether landplanes, seaplanes or airships – were indeed flown from shore bases. But by 1913 the concept of the seaplane carrier had already become a fact with the conversion of the ancient cruiser *Hermes* (to be sunk by a torpedo the following year) with a platform from which up to three 'hydroplanes' could take to the air. On completion of their missions they would come down on the sea nearby for hoisting inboard. Alternatively she could fly off landplanes, which could land ashore if this was within their range or ditch alongside, when the aircraft would inevitably be lost. By the end of 1914 four more seaplane carriers were in service, all of them conversions: the former merchantman *Ark Royal* and three former packet-boats, *Empress, Engadine* and *Riviera*.

All these vessels were small and slow. There came a considerable advance with the commissioning in April 1915 of the former passenger liner *Campania* as a seaplane carrier. Not only was she large enough to carry no fewer than six aircraft and have a 'flying-off deck' with a length of no less than 120 feet, but with a maximum speed of twenty-two knots she could nearly keep up with the fleet. She was even more effective after further modification a year later, with twice as many aircraft, the flying-off deck extended by eighty feet and the ability to recover her seaplanes after each sortie and hoist them inboard without having to heave-to, as had always previously been unavoidable.

Meantime *Ben-my-Chree*, another converted packet ship, had been commissioned along with *Vindex*, and her seaplanes became the first aircraft to take off from a carrier to attack enemy shipping with torpedoes.

It was the arrival on the scene of *Furious* in June 1917 that led to a revolution in thought on the operation of shipborne aircraft. There had previously been no question of landing back on board the carrier, though the American experiment had shown this to be possible as early as 1910. *Furious* had been laid down as a battle-cruiser but the decision was taken before her completion to convert her to a carrier by removing her forward gun-turret to make way for a flying-off deck ahead of her superstructure. Because this, like the modified *Campania's*, was 200 feet long and the ship's maximum speed in excess of thirty knots (which could be used to reduce the aircraft's groundspeed), several of her pilots thought it might be possible to land on.

The extraordinary hazard involved cannot be exaggerated. Not only did the deck slope downwards and of course had no arrester wires,* but the pilot would have to dodge

* See below, page 43.

around the superstructure before a last-moment turn to windward for his landing. This astonishing feat was accomplished by Wing Commander Edwin Dunning in a Sopwith Pup on August 5th.* Next day he pushed his luck, tried again and was killed.

But the vast possibility had been demonstrated of fast landplanes taking off *and returning to land* in mid-ocean, with the carrier at full speed. All that was required was either an after landing deck running from the superstructure to the stern, or better still an uninterrupted flight deck the whole length of the ship. *Furious* was at once modified in accordance with the former principle and *Argus,* which had been laid down as an Italian passenger liner and was now being converted for use as a carrier, in accordance with the latter. When they came into service in the last year of the war, pilots found little difficulty in landing over their sterns, which would thereafter become the universal practice in all the world's great navies.

Argus became the first and only carrier with a completely flush, unencumbered flight deck running the whole length of the ship. All those that followed had the 'island' offset to starboard housing the bridge, which it was more than possible to hit when landing or taking off. Putting down on the *Argus* tabletop was such a piece of cake that she was still being used for training in World War II. I myself landed on her in 1942, when *Furious,* once again modified, was also still in service.

Throughout the first war the number of naval aircraft grew steadily. Airships, especially the blimps†, put in thousands of hours on submarine patrols. Apart from the landplanes and seaplanes operating from shore bases and carriers, almost all battleships, battle-cruisers and cruisers had been equipped with a platform from which at least one seaplane could operate by 1918. And several more packet-boats were turned into seaplane carriers. When the RAF was formed, some 55,000 officers and men were transferred

* See plate 1.
† See plate 2 and Appendix 1.

from the RNAS, together with almost 3000 aircraft, a prodigious number at that time.*

Four more carriers came into service in the next dozen years. *Eagle* (1920) had been laid down as a battleship and converted. A second *Hermes* (1924) was the first-ever designed as a carrier from the start. *Courageous* and *Glorious*, laid down as battlecruisers, were completed in 1928 and 1930 respectively. Nothing more till a new *Ark Royal* was at last commissioned in 1936. *Argus* and *Furious* meantime soldiered on. So on the outbreak of World War II the Navy would have only these seven carriers, two of which were antiques and two obsolescent. (The total would revert to six when *Courageous* was torpedoed and sunk on the fourteenth day of the war.) And they carried so few aircraft – a maximum total establishment, which they seldom reached, of barely 200 between them. This should be compared with US Navy figures: *USS Enterprise*, commissioned in 1938, alone carried seventy-six, yet even from HMS *Illustrious*, which was still on the stocks, only thirty-three could be operated.†

This deplorable state of affairs resulted largely from the bickering that had continued intermittently between the Navy and the RAF over the control of naval aircraft ever since their transfer to the Air Force. This began to grow more bitter in 1935 when the admirals increased their pressure for the complete return to the Navy of all Fleet Air Arm personnel and aircraft.

It was a ludicrous squabble because the two services were competing for a responsibility that neither of them really

* Yet among Neville Usborne's papers I have found a document in his handwriting dated November 1914 with the heading: 'Notes on the Construction of a Supreme Air Fleet. ' Its aim was 'to put in the field a force of 2000 gun-carrying aeroplanes' and it set out in much detail how and why this should be done. It must have seemed to Their Lordships the impossible dream of an amiable madman, but in less than four years the target had been reached.

† The later ships in her class, *Victorious* and *Formidable*, carried the same number. The main reason for their operating so few aircraft was the great weight of their armour. Later, by adopting the use of a 'deck park', i.e. by having nearly half their aircraft permanently parked on the flight deck, they could carry up to fifty-seven.

wanted. The RAF had neglected naval aviation: apart from being under strength, the FAA was equipped, as it would always be, with aircraft no self-respecting pilot in the Air Force proper would consider. When control did eventually return to the Navy in 1938-9, thousands of RAF personnel who had been flying and maintaining the naval aircraft were transferred with equivalent rank to the Senior Service. They included some who had switched from dark blue to light blue in 1918 and now switched back as Captains and Commanders, as Petty Officers and 'Chiefs'. But there was no magical improvement in aircraft and certainly no change in the attitude of many straitlaced, straight-ringed officers who regarded aircraft and those who flew them with grave suspicion or active distaste. Whilst naval aviation had been an RAF sideline, it had been the Cinderella of both services. Now it became just the Cinderella of the Navy.

It was somehow symptomatic of the ambivalence felt for us that we went ever afterwards under at least three names and no one knew which was the right one. We were nobody's children, never properly christened. I still don't know if the Fleet Air Arm ever really existed. It was what most people called us and what we most often called ourselves, but was really an illogical hangover from the years between the wars when those in naval aviation, this much was certain, had been called the Fleet Air Arm of the Royal Air Force. Many RN officers certainly held there had been no FAA since control of its aircraft and aircrews had been handed back to the Navy. We were sometimes described as the Air Branch of the RN, or the Branch for short. Others preferred the Royal Naval Air Service, a reversion to pioneer days. You could take your pick but it didn't help *esprit-de-corps*.

Right up to the end of the Second World War there was still an occasional RAF sergeant or aircraftsman to be seen in the squadrons, probably forgotten through some administrative oversight, but otherwise the change over had been complete, except that our early training was still in Air Force hands.

It was now when we were newly winged and commissioned that we returned to the Navy's not very ample bosom for our operational training, to fly specialized naval aircraft from Royal Naval Air Stations with Royal Navy instructors. Specialized naval aircraft meant mainly that they were far slower and more ancient than anything an Air Force pilot would look at. The fighter boys went off to Yeovilton and there converted to Skuas, Rocs and Fulmars, caricatures of warplanes but all the Navy could offer. Our lot, at Crail and then at Arbroath, was the Stringbag, as the Fairey Swordfish was always known, and occasionally the Fairey Albacore, a tarted-up version with a closed cockpit and flaps, and even a VP airscrew. Both were biplanes with fixed undercarriages.

The top speed of the Stringbag was officially 135 knots, but that must have been going downhill without a load. A more realistic figure would be nearer 120 knots (136 mph). Their main functions as maids-of-all-work had been regarded as torpedoing enemy shipping, 'spotting' the fall of gunfire and reconnaissance for the fleet. They were therefore known as TSR aircraft, those who flew them as TSR pilots. This was soon out of date, with bombing more important than spotting, and TBR was substituted.

My happy marriage to the Stringbag was consummated soon after I reached Crail, near St Andrew's in Fifeshire. And lasted four years almost exactly, during which I would be wholly faithful to her (I hadn't any alternative), apart from a bit on the side with that flashy Yankee hussy, the Vought-Sikorski Chesapeake, a *coup-de-foudre* that was fairly shortlived like so many such extramarital affairs. I was quickly forgiven without recriminations. When it ended by mutual consent on April Fools' Day 1945, I was Commanding Officer of the second last operational Swordfish squadron (apart from 836, which didn't fly as a single integrated unit).*

* For a brief account of the development and early history of the Swordfish, which originated from an Air Ministry specification issued in 1930, see Appendix 2.

The very first time we had it off together was on April 8th 1941, the day after we began our ten weeks' training on these fearsome front-line aircraft. With a grand total of 150 hours solo, no more than an airline pilot now logs in a couple of months, we were then supposed to be ready to go forth into action. When you convert to a single-engined operational aircraft, there can be no dual instruction. You just study the manual, take a look round the pilot's cockpit, climb aboard and fly the thing. Which for me happened on this fine April morning at RNAS Crail.

How to convey the experience of piloting a Stringbag, which certainly ranks among the most remarkable aircraft ever invented? A makey-learn pilot converting to any other operational type at once knew he was handling a lethal, steely machine that meant business, at least if compared with training aircraft. Not so the Stringbag, bless her dear old heart. She seemed to have been left in the war by mistake, to belong to another age, though she'd been in production for only six years. It was almost impossible to believe that it was with *this*, though she might be a great lark to fly, that we'd soon be expected to go tearing into action. Yet she had the most wondrous virtues. Was almost totally foolproof. You could take nearly any liberty, fly her far beyond textbook capability. The willingness and ability to do so was a major part of being a worthy Stringbag pilot and she always saw you through. She was absolutely stable and even at almost the lowest speeds the controls were firm and positive. Scream down from an immense height in a dive, the speed would stay well below 200 knots and you could haul back on the stick for all you were worth: a fast, firm pull-out with no fear of that old enemy, the high speed stall. No one ever wrenched the wings off a Stringbag though on the ground they could be folded fore and aft with an amazingly simple manual mechanism to reduce the space they'd take up on a carrier.

Cut back speed and the slots would come out on the leading edges of the mainplanes, to decrease wing-loading and thereby the speed of stall, at about sixty-five knots. Slower still and she would waffle ever so slightly but full control was maintained. When at last stalling speed was reached at fifty-eight or so, even if at this moment you pulled back hard on the stick, her nose would drop sedately, very gently earth-wards and she would fall in relative equilibrium through perhaps 100 feet until flying speed was regained. She'd come home though riddled with bullets like a colander.

There was just nothing to go wrong so long as the Pegasus III engine kept ticking over. My Peggy, as it happened, was twice to let me down, but such ill luck was exceptional. She could keep going with two cylinders shot away.

Faithful though I may have been, I cannot deny the Stringbag's appearance was against her. All those struts and wires, the fixed undercart, the frail fuselage. And then the little matter of having two wings. Really quite embarrassing to land at an RAF station with its Spitfires or Beaufighters (later Whirlwinds or Fortresses). She just didn't look like a warplane, not remotely. But her low speed had pros as well as cons. It took at least two ME-109s to shoot down a String-bag – if the pilot knew the tricks and kept his head. The basic tactic was to wait till the enemy fighter nearly had you in range, then cut right back on speed and go into the steepest possible turn at around sixty knots in the appropri-ate direction. The 109 or any other modern fighter simply couldn't keep with you, couldn't bring guns to bear. A six-pence inside a half-crown.

Shore-based gunners bluntly refused to believe your speed was eighty-five or ninety whatever their radar might indicate. Shells or tracer would (with any luck) be fifty yards ahead. By the time they'd cottoned on, you hoped to have jinked your way to safety, probably to sea level.

The absurdly low landing speed of a Stringbag made it possible to operate when even the birds were walking (as we used to put it). The carrier could be pitching all over the Arctic but, if the wind over the flight deck was fifty-five, the Stringbag's forward speed relative to the deck would be a mere five knots, no more than a fast walk. Sometimes I've had to motor her in and touch down above stalling speed to keep up with the ship. Indeed a Stringbag in my squadron was patrolling some way astern of the convoy when a gale blew up; the convoy was steaming into the wind at only ten knots but the pilot ran out of petrol before he could catch up and was never seen again. We were completely exposed to the elements. I need hardly mention that our cockpits were unheated, though the pilot (but not his observer and gunner in their separate cockpits behind him) derived some little benefit from Peggy's close proximity. This did indeed make it chilly on the Murmansk run at below zero Fahrenheit, but to feel the wind in your face is a joy seldom known to today's flyers. And you could get out in a hurry.

There, my Stringbag, I've given you my say. God love you, it's the best testimonial I can write you.

And despite everything I remember with perfect clarity that my chief impression as I first flew a Stringbag, over springtime Fifeshire fields and out across the Forth, was of her enormous size and power. Flying this damn great thing all by myself! (NB: wingspan forty-five feet, engine 690 hp.) And the feeling of total stability as she seemed to sail skywards of her own personal volition.

Our operational training: seven weeks at Crail learning to drop torpedoes and three weeks at Arbroath for our initiation to the gentle art of deck landing (though we didn't get so far, at this stage, as actually landing on a deck). These interspersed with formation flying, night flying, divebombing, depth charge dropping and all that. Also the Stringbag was in those days still equipped with a fixed forward-firing 303 Vickers machinegun, though there were no conceivable circumstances in which it would ever be possible to use it when every other warplane was twice as fast at least. But so long as it was there we had to learn to use it. There was also a moveable Vickers or Lewis gun fired by the air-gunner from the aftermost cockpit.

Dropping a torpedo is an extremely tricky business. It weighs getting on for a ton and should be dropped into the sea from a height of fifty to seventy feet. After entering the water, it runs under its own power at twenty-five knots a few feet below the surface for over 2000 yards unless anything gets in its way, in which case it goes off bang with devastating effect. A single torpedo (known to us as a tin-fish) can sink a large merchantman. The trickiness lies in the fact that you have to be flying at the correct low speed, and as straight and level as possible, and at the right altitude, at the moment you release it and for several subsequent seconds, if it's going to run accurately or indeed to run at all. This is none too simple if your target is the friendly *Brigadier*, our usual target vessel in the pacific Firth of Forth. It's quite a different matter if the tracer is coming at you from a heavily defended enemy fleet or convoy.

Another little matter is that over a minute will elapse, if you drop from 1000 yards, before the tin-fish reaches its target, which will meantime have travelled 800 yards if steaming at twenty knots. So you must judge her speed, aim the right distance ahead and guess what avoiding action she may take. At this the *Brigadier* was most adept: attack too fine on the bow, for instance, and she would at once alter course towards you, presenting an impossibly small target and 'combing' the torpedo.

Our attacks would start from several thousand feet, whence we would dive seaward, spend not more than ten seconds at sea level if possible, then climb steeply away for home. Our first efforts were made light, then we'd fly with a dummy torpedo weighing 1600 pounds. In both cases a camera automatically took a picture at the moment you pressed the tit, from which could be computed your altitude, attitude, range – and, given the speed of the target vessel, whether you would have hit her. Later we dropped 'runners', which were the same as real torpedoes but without the explosive charge, set to run deep so that they would pass under the target vessel and then rise to the surface for recovery. Otherwise the tin-fish, worth several thousand pounds, would be badly damaged on impact and very probably lost. They were so scarce and valuable that we were rationed to three drops each.

I was a dab hand with tin-fish and passed out top. In twenty-three attacks I scored nineteen hits and all four misses were by less than thirty yards. That's not counting one unforgettable occasion when I never got as far as pressing the tit. It was my first real brush with that old enemy, death. And I can still only guess how I survived.

Airborne on that brilliant May morning towards the end of the course, for once flying an Albacore. Climbing with two others for a synchronized attack on *Brigadier*, steaming eastward up the Firth at twenty knots. At 5000 feet our leader gives the signal.

The usual drill. Airscrew to fully coarse. Cut back to one-third throttle. Then in a screaming seaward dive, steep as I can make it, jinking like crazy to avoid the imaginary flak. Always keeping an eye on *Brigadier*. I'm to approach from the starboard beam. If she alters course towards me, switch to her quarter. Switch to her bow if she alters away. I hope to reach dropping height, sixty feet, some 1200 yards from her. Begin easing her out at about 800 feet, target fine on my port bow and starting to alter course away, violent turn to starboard to bring me ahead of her, then to port for a perfect approach on her starboard bow, speed falling to 130, airscrew to fully fine, altitude OK, open the throttle before taking final aim....

And nothing whatever happens. My unloved Taurus engine is as silent as death. At seventy feet, flying directly down wind.

I know I've about ten seconds. Immediate, instinctive check of the mixture control. Petrol tank nearly full. All the time jiggling the throttle, nothing. Slam back the glasshouse roof, ditching inevitable, no time to turn to windward, no time to lower flaps. Back on the stick, for Christ's sake. Get the bloody tail down. A split-second recollection of water thrown up around me, of being violently thrown forward, smashing my face into the instrument panel. Silence and darkness.

But it can only have been for moments that I lost consciousness. Dead downwind and flapless, I'd have hit the water at a far higher groundspeed, maybe forty knots higher, than when landing in a more conventional manner. And the Albacore, having shuddered in a spray-storm to a standstill, tilted abruptly forward to an angle of forty-five degrees and at once began sinking. I revived very rapidly as the water reached me.

Just in time for a last salty air-gulp before going under, strapped firmly into the cockpit and bleeding profusely from two head-wounds. Right, let's get out of here. Just got to release the safety harness. Its four straps, two from above and two from below, crossed my body to form an X, held in place by a four-inch pin. Pull out the pin, back with the straps and you're free. I couldn't see underwater but it should have been easy blindfold, the dozens of times I'd done it. Felt for the pin, couldn't find it. Now for Jesus' sake don't panic: three feet under water, panic and you're dead. Looking up, the white light of the sun, a column of brightness above me, air and life those few hard inches distant. But where in hell's the pin?

Feeling the webbing of the harness-straps from my shoulders down to the central metal boss, just above my navel, where the pin held all four straps together. Lungs beginning to burst now. Finding the central boss, feeling for the pin. Just bloody well not there. Involuntarily taking the first choking mouthful of salt water down to my lungs. A million images crowd into my mind. My mother, I remember, smiling from the shining sunshaft above me. Must, must get out of this grave. A great gulp of water. So there's only one way to do it. I've got to break the straps.

A madman's decision. Totally impossible to break them for the strongest man on earth. And I know it perfectly well. But this the straw I cling to after a full minute under water. Reaching with both hands to grasp the top of the windscreen above me. Pulling upwards like hell. And shooting up to the surface like a cork.

How to explain what seems a miracle? I've wondered a hundred times. No question of it, the harness was unbreakable. But there has to be a rational explanation. All I've been able to come up with: in those first stunned seconds, had I already pulled out the pin, an automatic, instinctive action, knowing in semi-consciousness it was the first step I'd need to take to survive? So then after full revival was I searching for a pin that was no longer there? The straps would stay in place until pressure was applied. But why did I think of even trying such a desperate, hopeless remedy – which, however, certainly saved my life?

The Albacore was never popular. Despite its more modern appearance, it never had the guts and manoeuverability of the Swordfish and, as I'd just shown once more, its Bristol Taurus II engine wasn't a patch on its stablemate, the much-loved Peggy. It must have been at about this time that someone wrote a new song, to be sung to the tune of Bring Back my Bonny. It soon became a FAA favourite and has been bawled out round wardroom pianos ever since – not only by Albacore pilots looking back with nostalgia on Stringbag days:

> The Swordfish relies on her Peggy,
>   The modified Taurus ain't sound,
> So the Swordfish flies out on her missions
>   And the Albacore stays on the ground
Chorus
> Bring back, bring back,
>   Oh bring back my Stringbag to me – to me!
> Bring back, bring back,
>   Oh bring back my Stringbag to me!

I sang it with special fervour that night. I never flew an Albacore again. I was back in the air, in a Swordfish, four days later with a part-shaven head where the stitches had gone in. Two more attacks on *Brigadier*. Two more hits amidships.

Rational explanations. There's a pendant to the story. This time I can offer no explanation at all, other than coincidence, the last refuge of rationalism.

A few weeks earlier, on leave in London with Angel, swinging our way down Coventry Street, arm-in-arm, I in my shiny new uniform, she wearing my ring. A gypsy fortune teller in a neon-lit amusement arcade. Cassandra among the pin-tables, bangles and golden ear-rings outside her curtained booth. Let's have a laugh, let's hear our fortunes!

One-and-sixpence each, deary. Palms, cards, crystal ball or tea-leaves. But, oh no, not together. Has to be one at a time. Sorry, deary, that's the way it is. No, not even for five bob.

It spoiled the fun but she was adamant. We tossed and I went in first. Palms, I said. One hand then the other. And out came the usual vague banalities, perhaps even more banal than usual. A long sea voyage and so on – I forget. Nothing about Angel. Well what could you expect?

Angel's turn. She was longer in the booth or so it seemed. I played one of the pin-tables. A tarty blonde in black stockings watched me, made a suggestive gesture. Angel unsmiling back through the curtains, Cassandra remaining inside.

– Well? Well? What did she tell you?

Was there an imperceptible pause?

– Nothing, said Angel. Really she told me nothing. All the usual stuff about dark strangers.

– Just how it was with me. And she didn't even mention you.

– She said you were so happy.

– And so I am, my darling.

Angel was quiet that evening, complained of a headache, went back early to her mother's. A couple of days later she saw me off to Scotland.

The years went by, I didn't marry Angel, I married Penny, we had Christopher. The war ended, I returned to Oxford leaving Penny and Christopher in Alverstoke. A few months later I heard the news, Angel's back, married to someone called Bohm, who however was never visible. Like me she'd got a grant after four years as a WAAF to finish her degree. We met, we became friends again, we took out boats on the Cherwell, we talked till three in the mornings about the old days, about the new days, about our already-failing wartime marriages. And one night, after an unusual silence, Angel asked did I remember her? The fortune teller among the pin-tables? I'd just the vaguest memory.

– She told us nothing.

– She told you nothing. And I told you nothing.

– Whatever do you mean?

Angel inclined her head. She supposed she could tell me

now. It had been a terrifying experience. The fortune teller wouldn't take her money, ignored her palm, used no paraphernalia. Just looked at her and looked at her.

– You and your boy-friend were arm-in-arm, deary, you're wearing his engagement ring, he's so pleased and happy. It would be easy for me to tell you what you expect of me, that you and him will be married and raise a family. And I know this is all just a joke for you. But you'll never marry him, deary. How can I tell you lies?

Angel was finding it less of a joke. The gypsy grew even more serious and said nothing for a minute beyond murmuring that she didn't know what to say, didn't know whether to tell her. But finally she came out with it.

– Well I'll just have to warn you, deary, though I don't want to vex you but it's something that I know. Not too long from now, that boy of yours is either going to be killed or will only escape death by … by something nearly a miracle, something never fully explained. There, deary, now I've told you. But don't ever mention it to him, so long as his life's at risk. He flies in the Navy, doesn't he, I know from his new golden wings.

Angel had been stunned, had waited to recover her composure, smoked a cigarette. And it had indeed been an extraordinary decision to tell such things, however certainly our Cassandra knew them, to a young girl in wartime about her sweetheart. But tell her is what she did. And what she told her was true.

III

CHEESECAKE DAYS

The Branch had many songs of its own, bawled out in the evenings with countless pints of beer round out-of-tune wardroom pianos. Our favourite at this time, to the air of 'Home on the Range', had maybe a dozen verses but I remember only the chorus:

High, high in the sky,
Where the Swordfish and Albacores fly;
Now we've all got our wings
We'll be doing such things
That Taranto will seem like small fry..

What a hope! What fearful presumption! The victory at Taranto, owed entirely to the Stringbag, had been arguably the greatest in the history of the Navy. I have to include a reference to the Stringbag's finest hour. I remember the incredulity, then the great lift to our own spirits, the cheers and joyful pride, that its astonishing news aroused in us. The Stringbags to which we were almost certainly destined must be aircraft after all!

Here are the bare facts. Taranto, in the curve of Italy's instep, was the main base of the Italian Navy, the most important, most heavily defended port in the Mediterranean. In November 1940 it was sheltering a fleet of enormous strength and firepower, which (at least in theory) gave the Italians command of the sea, of their Mare Nostrum: no fewer than six battleships, nine cruisers, seventeen destroyers, a multitude of smaller craft. Apart from their own guns, which ranged up to the fifteen-inchers of the two Littorio-class battlewagons, they were protected by innumerable shore-batteries. Besides this, twenty-two barrage balloons stretched their deadly cables from barges and breakwaters encircling the harbour. And all six battleships were protected by anti-torpedo netting.

To attack this fortress, which should have been impregnable, My Lords of the Admiralty sent twenty Stringbags. Two officers in each.

It is hard to understand how such a decision was ever made. The Charge of the Light Brigade simply wasn't in it. Can it really have been foreseen that the entire mad venture would be anything but a disaster? It had been necessary to scrape the barrel to get together even those biplanes. The newly-commissioned *Illustrious* was the only serviceable carrier in the Med, owing to boiler trouble in *Eagle*. She carried a few fighter aircraft (Fulmars) and two TBR squadrons, 815 and 819, which boasted twenty-two Stringbags between them. But seven of these were written off in a series of unfortunate accidents in the days before the attack, though without loss of life: two in a fire in the hangar, three through ditchings caused by dirty petrol, two in a flight-deck collision. The number was brought up to twenty by the addition of five from *Eagle*. It was absolutely on the cards that all twenty would be lost, leaving the Mediterranean Fleet without a Swordfish to its name. And that the raid would achieve nothing.

With all this at stake and the tiny numbers involved, it might be thought axiomatic that the two squadrons would join forces in one attack. But no; each was to go in alone. First would be 815: twelve Stringbags, six carrying torpedoes and six with bombs. Two of the latter also carried flares to illuminate the harbour before they themselves attacked. Then, exactly an hour later, the eight of 819, five of them with tin-fish and three with bombs including a flare-dropper. Thus the Italian gunners could concentrate their fire to the fullest possible extent on the two separate little waves and would have ample time to recover from the first assault and collect themselves for the second. Moreover *Illustrious,* with her screen of four cruisers and four destroyers, must stay for an extra hour in the take-off area. This was near Corfu, about 100 miles from Italy's heel, within very easy range of shore-based bombers.

Both squadrons pressed home their attacks with unbelievable gallantry and skill. An 815 Swordfish arrived fifteen minutes early by mistake, so the gunners were alerted and a devastating curtain of fire was waiting to greet the biplanes as they bumbled in at all of ninety knots. The Italians had just one problem. The torpedo-carriers came in so low, at less than twenty feet, that the gunners would be firing at each other, at their own ships and the town of Taranto itself, once the Stringbags had entered the harbour. But how could they possibly miss such sitting targets?

The outcome of the raid was little short of miraculous. Two battleships were sunk and a third so heavily damaged that she took no further part in the war. Three cruisers and a destroyer were put out of action. Shore installations, including the seaplane base and an oil refinery, were very severely hit. Since the capital ships must have received two or three tin-fish each, it means that almost every pilot scored a direct hit. And here, perhaps, the most remarkable fact of all. An average of about 5000 shots was fired at each of the Stringbags. Yet only two succumbed; and the crew of one of these survived, to be made prisoners of war. None of the other aircraft received even a single hit. So the total loss of life to the Navy amounted to two officers. And the entire balance of power in the Med was reversed in a single night.

We left Crail on May 24th and reported after three days leave to RNAS Arbroath for our deck-landing training course. Taking off from a carrier, even when a heavy sea is running, presents no real problem: open up the throttle, release the brakes, keep her straight down the middle and wait till you're airborne. But 'landing on' needs discipline and skill. The smallest flight decks were sixty-two feet wide and 414 feet long, but even on a fleet carrier, more than half as long again, there was little room for error. And this small floating platform on which we had to land would be steaming steadily away from us at ten to twenty knots, often pitching like crazy. At Arbroath, to prepare us for this, a section of one of the runways was painted to look like a flight deck, so that we could learn the technique without the risk of going over the side.

The pilot throughout his approach was completely in the hands of a gentleman known as the batsman, officially the Deck Landings Control Officer, stationed on the port side near the aftermost end of the deck. In each hand a circular yellow disc with a short handle. With these so-called 'bats' he gave signals to the pilot and they had to be obeyed *totally*, whether or not you agreed with them: come higher, slower, faster, lower, to port, to starboard. If you were making a hash of it, an imperious circling motion with a bat above his head meant go round again for Christ's sake.*

When he judged you were in exactly the right position – a few feet off the deck, directly fore-and-aft – he signalled 'Cut!' by lowering both bats and crossing them in front of him. Whereupon, whether you liked it or not, and even though you might be a more experienced pilot than him, you damn well cut your engine and started praying.

'Taken his last cut' – a euphemism for dead.

Even on the largest carriers and with the slowest aircraft, there would usually have been too short a landing run available if it hadn't been for the arrester wires. These ran thwartships across the aftermost third of the flight deck. When aircraft were landing, they were raised some six or eight inches above it. As he approached, with plenty of revs and in a tail-down attitude, the Stringbag pilot had no undercart to remember, no flaps. But he mustn't forget his hook. This, when he lowered it, dropped below the level of

* In plate 10 a batsman may be seen in action as I come in to land in mid-Atlantic.

the tail wheel. The hope was that on touchdown he would pick up a wire with it, which would arrest him very firmly.*

Each of the half-dozen wires was hydraulically controlled to come forward with the aircraft, exerting increasing pressure till it brought her to a standstill. Once a Stringbag had picked up a wire, she would be stationary in thirty or forty yards.

At sea when an aircraft was landing, if there were others on the flight deck, they'd be moved as far forward as possible. A cable-and-wire barrier was then raised thwartships astern of them So if you missed all the wires, including the Jesus wire, as the last of them was known, and (as would then be almost certain) couldn't pull up in time, you went crunch into this fairly resilient barrier, probably bending the prop and shock-loading the engine, but at least not damaging other aircraft. On the smaller carriers, this reduced the available landing run to under 300 feet – less than twice the *width* of today's runways at Heathrow and one-fiftieth as long.

Our 'dummy deck' at Arbroath came complete with batsman and arrester wires. No barrier was necessary. Here during our three weeks we each carried out nearly 100 Aerodrome Dummy Deck Landings, or addles as they were known. Our progress was slowed because the chosen runway faced into the prevailing wind, but the wind showed a perverse reluctance to blow in the prevailing direction. But by the end of the course, as we grew in skill and confidence, and learned to put ourselves unquestioningly in the batsman's hands throughout the tail-down approach, we could guarantee to pick up a wire every time.

Batsmen were in general excellent but at sea there were inevitably disasters and the pilot after a dicey landing might have some acid words for 'Bats'. Our perils were immortalized in one verse of a squadron song:

> *I thought I was coming in quite all right but*
> *I was fifty feet up when the batsman said 'Cut!'*

* See Plate 9

And loud in my ears the sweet angel voice sang:
Float float float float float float float float float – PRANG.

I once watched appalled as a Stringbag approached too high in mid-Atlantic, was signalled too late to go round again, missed all the wires and caught the top of the barrier with his wheels, ploughing headlong into the aircraft parked forward of it. The whole lot went up in flames and three men burned to death.

We should have ended with a taste of the real thing, but the real thing was in very short supply. There were now (June 1941) only six carriers in operational service. *Glorious* had been sunk in the evacuation of Norway. *Illustrious,* severely damaged in January by German Stukas in the Med, would be out of action for a year. The even newer *Formidable,* sent to replace her, had just suffered a similar fate. This left *Furious, Argus, Eagle, Hermes, Ark Royal* and the newly-commissioned *Victorious;* all but the last two were antiques, and the *Ark* would be sunk in November. *Indomitable,* though laid down in 1937, would not come on station till the very end of the year.

There were shore-based squadrons in Malta and North Africa but the losses of existing carriers and the unending delays in completing new ones already meant that the Navy, in total contrast to the RAF, were beginning to get more air-crew than they could use. Small wonder that not even the ancient *Argus* could be made available for the consummation of our training.

Whilst we had been at Crail, the TBR squadrons in *Victorious* and *Ark Royal* achieved what probably comes second to Taranto as the Stringbag's most famous victory, their vital part in the sinking of the *Bismarck.* This newest battleship in Hitler's navy, probably the most powerful warship in the world, had sallied forth into the Atlantic accompanied by *Prinz Eugen,* an equally modern cruiser. So long as she remained at large, *Bismarck* would be a leviathan among the minnows: whenever she sighted a convoy, every merchant-man and escort vessel would be at her mercy. The transatlantic lifeline was threatened with total severance. There was panic in Whitehall. The Navy could send in pursuit its own battleships and supporting warships, but both enemy vessels were exceedingly fast, very heavily armed and would certainly not have ventured forth from Norway if they hadn't felt confident of survival, that they could take on or evade the combined might of all that could be thrown against them.

And so they would almost certainly have done, had it not been for one unexpected factor they understandably failed to take into account. The humble Stringbag.

Bismarck and *Prinz Eugen* were known to have sailed from Bergen on the night of May 21st/22nd 1941. On the evening of May 23rd they were sighted by the cruiser *Suffolk*, skirting the Arctic pack-ice between Iceland and Greenland, making twenty-seven knots. So bad was visibility that *Suffolk* was only seven miles away, well within range, at the moment she came in sight. The cruiser promptly turned around and disappeared into the mist without a shot being fired. Her sister-ship, *Norfolk*, did the same an hour later. Note that whilst Stringbags were later ready to fly in and attack *Bismarck* from a range of less than a mile, two whopping great cruisers had no alternative but to keep out of range.

At least they could report the enemy's position. Next day, in better weather, the spanking new battleship *Prince of Wales* and the old battle-cruiser *Hood* approached the scene of action. Within a few minutes of coming within range of *Bismarck's* guns, at a range of over fourteen miles, *Hood* was sunk with almost all hands. Shortly afterwards the *Prince* was so heavily damaged that she found it prudent to turn tail behind a smokescreen and took no further part in the action. *Bismarck* had also been hit but her performance scarcely impaired.

The two cruisers shadowed her but never ventured within range. This was left to the Stringbags. The situation was grotesque. That evening (May 24th) nine Swordfish from *Victorious* were armed with torpedoes and ordered to attack. They were led by Lieutenant Commander Eugene Esmonde, the Irishman later awarded a posthumous VC for leading the attack on *Scharnhorst* and *Gneisenau*. Try to imagine the scene: these nine paper-and-string joke-planes flying unescorted in daylight to strike the world's most powerful warship. They approached at eighty-five knots, dived from cloud at 1500 feet and carried out a perfectly coordinated attack in the face of the most intense fire. One pilot had fallen two minutes behind the rest and went in on his own. Amazingly every Swordfish survived, and at least one hit was scored, reducing the enemy's speed by seven knots.

The two cruisers, whose sole job was to shadow *Bismarck* from beyond the range of her guns, managed to lose her during the night. All next day, though great men-of-war from as far away as Gibraltar had now converged on the area, the Navy couldn't find *Bismarck,* which was left to the RAF: a Catalina flying-boat located her next morning. She was alone. The undamaged *Prinz Eugen* had gone off on her own and was to make it safely to harbour, eluding the entire fleet.

Once again it was the Stringbags who were called upon. They now settled *Bismarck*'s hash. Six flights from *Ark Royal,* some eighteen aircraft, went in to attack that evening, dropping at under 100 knots from ranges as low as 1000 yards despite all she could hurl at them. It's not known how many hits were scored, but her maximum speed was cut to a bare seven knots. Even more important, one torpedo luckily struck her rudder and jammed it at an angle so that the giant wounded battleship could only turn in circles.

From this moment when she was helpless, the great ships of the Royal Navy were finally ready to close within range of her guns and attack with shells and torpedoes. A flotilla of destroyers went for her during the night; next morning the capital ships moved in. At 1040, pulverized by their combined firepower, Bismarck turned on her back and disappeared beneath the waves.

It was a famous victory. I suppose *Hood* was considered a good swap. There must have been forty warships ranged against *Bismarck.* Yet she would have escaped the Navy and found Brest's safety but for the Stringbags of *Victorious* and *Ark Royal.*

After an absurd fortnight at the Royal Naval College, Greenwich, to learn to behave like officers and gentlemen, we were fully trained at last, ready and eager for action. The only small problem was that action was hard to come by. The RAF were crying out for pilots but the Navy, with so few carriers, and its chronic shortage of aircraft, seemed to have a surplus. Many new-fledged officers went for the time being to such pedestrian tasks as drogue-towing or communications. Only the best (or so we liked to think) were appointed at once to operational squadrons. A handful replaced casualties and found themselves in action almost at once, the rest went to squadrons that were 'working up' ashore.

When at home at Killegar on two weeks' leave after Greenwich, I learned that I'd been appointed to 811 Squadron at RNAS Lee-on-Solent, headquarters of the FAA, known as HMS *Daedalus*. To report on July 15th. If the number of a squadron began with an eight, it meant it was operational. So this was it – or so I thought.

Arriving that summer evening at Lee. Up the road from *St Vincent* where I'd started twelve months earlier. The same train from London, the same ferry across Portsmouth Harbour, a rather longer bus ride. The small grassy airfield with no runways, right alongside the town, a pleasant seaside resort complete with pier. Salutes this time as I entered.

Envious to see, dispersed at intervals round the airfield perimeter, nine gleaming gull-winged monoplanes among the Stringbags and Albacores. We were supposed to be able to recognize every aircraft that flew. But these I had never seen before. What new secret weapon, what doing here? And Christ, next morning I find I'm to be flying them. Vought-Sikorski Chesapeakes, Pratt & Whitney Twin Wasp Junior engines, newly arrived from the States. Closed-cockpit divebombers, all mod cons, Jesus what a line! Having imagined myself almost certainly Stringbag bound, grown to love the old lady *faute-de-mieux*, the *mieux* suddenly materialized. As though a sex-starved male, newly married off to a comfortable if pie-faced lady of uncertain age, had been suddenly thrown into bed with a captivating and extremely willing bobby soxer.

There had been eight-elevens before. The last one had gone down with *Courageous* in 1939. This was a new squadron forming up from scratch and our task was to try out these aircraft, of which little seemed to be known, though they were hardly the most modern in the world. We had been allocated to *Archer*, one of half-a-dozen escort carriers ordered in May to be built in the States, and expected to be ready for us, with unbelievable optimism, before the end of the year. The question we had to answer was whether our glamorous Cheesecakes (as they soon became known) were suitable for the rough-and-tumble of hunting U-boats from a small carrier in mid-Atlantic, the work for which *Archer* was intended.

At the start we had only six pilots and no observers. Our Commanding Officer, Lieutenant 'Pig' Lucas, was an extremely experienced, very old pilot. Must have been pushing thirty. He seemed decent enough though rather staid, and hardly less remote than God to a junior sub; I don't know how he acquired his unfortunate sobriquet. The Senior Pilot, Alan McTurk, also had two straight stripes and long experience. Two of the three other pilots were fellow-rookies from 16 Course: Eric Cooper, a curly-haired north-countryman, and Robin Shirley-Smith, older than the rest of us, balding and actually married. Our numbers were made up by that law unto himself, Peter Bentley. Or such was the *nom-de-guerre* of this unpredictable Frenchman. Dark and Gallic, he had joined the Resistance after the fall of France before making it to England earlier that year. I never got to know his real name, which he could not use for fear of reprisals if he should fall into enemy hands, which is precisely what was to happen to him. Already a qualified pilot, he had at once offered his services to the Navy, been granted an almost immediate commission, joined us with 16 Course at Crail for operational training and was already a special friend. He had seen a Bentley outside the Admiralty when he went to volunteer: 'Bentlee ees English name? *Très bien*, I take.'

Peter's accent never seemed to get much better during the year until we lost him. He picked up bits of slang but usually managed to get them slightly wrong or to use them in the wrong company. On one exercise his voice came loud and clear over the radio – his aircraft identification letter by chance was P for Peter:

– Allo zees ees pee for Peetair. I 'ave feenish, I 'ave feenish. May I fock off now, please?

This was much appreciated by all the little Wrens in the wireless room.

I was the youngest and therefore most junior pilot in the squadron till our numbers grew to nine with the addition of a third RN two-striper, Murray Willcocks, and two pilots from 17 Course as they in turn completed their training, Jock Sayer and Denis Fuller. Jock in particular an old friend: six foot four, sable curly hair, rugged Scots face and gentle smile. With a lovely girl-friend, Molly, whom he married. Like me, he was under twenty-one and therefore an Acting Sub-Lieutenant, but I was all of two weeks his senior. And Denis, being only nineteen, was the merest of Midshipmen. So I rose to be the third most junior officer in 811.

Like girls of the same period she doesn't look much today when I examine her faded photograph,* but in 1941 the Cheesecake seemed a wonder and a joy. Unlike the String-bag she looked like a warplane and felt like one – more than twice as fast, fully aerobatic, flaps and VP prop, glasshouse, the lot. An unusual feature was that the under-carriage (retractable of course) was designed to be used as an airbrake: you lowered it before going into a dive and this kept your speed below 250, no matter what.

There was a further refinement. Have you considered the question of peeing? For a Stringbag pilot it was a very tricky matter. The routine was as follows. If, three hours into a patrol, it became inescapable, he first asked his observer for a suitable receptacle. The most popular because the biggest was a dust-marker tin, several of which we fortunately carried. After emptying over the side its contents of aluminium

_____
* See Plate 4.

dust, the observer passed it *complete with lid,* a vital matter to remember, forward over the bulkhead to the pilot. The pilot meantime flew one-handed while he undid his harness, unsnapped his parachute, unzipped his flying suit, unbuttoned his flies. Then he put the tin to use. It was of such a size that I always seemed to come within a tenth of an inch of filling it. No one knows what would have happened if a U-boat had been sighted at this instant.

That was but half the battle. The pilot put on the lid; now how to get rid of it? Experience soon taught me it was most unwise to try putting it over the side. Before you could drop it, half the contents would be blown back by the slipstream into your face. The approved technique was to hold the brimful container in the right hand between the legs at knee level, meantime flying left-handed; then boldly and firmly throw it vertically upwards as hard as you could. It was the done thing to warn your crew at this moment so that they could shelter behind a bulkhead but, if the operation were carried through with courage and resolution, the slipstream would whisk it astern at a great rate of knots – possibly striking the tail-fin but what matter? – with no more than the finest of sprays upon all concerned at worst.

What comfort in the all-American Cheesecake! There was a patented thingumajig, stowed under the pilot's seat, stainless steel, about the size and shape of a tin mug. When switched on, liquid was at once sucked back on entering it and conveyed under pressure by way of a flexible tube to an aperture in the belly. The belly of the aircraft, I mean. That's real luxury!

The Cheesecake was well suited for low-level attacks on U-boats, presumably the most usual employment foreseen for us, or for general reconnaissance, but was designed as a dive-bomber. As such it was remarkable. The technique was quite unusual: position yourself ten thousand feet or so immediately above your target and then descend vertically – and I do mean vertically – upon it. There wasn't any bomb-sight, you aimed the whole aircraft. Hold her thus to as low a height as you dare, press the tit and pull out. Well you could hardly miss. In a less steep dive you had to judge how far past your target to aim. As a bonus it is very hard, sometimes impossible, for a ground gunner to bring his weapon to bear on a target immediately overhead or for a fighter to keep after you.

It isn't too easy to dive vertically, not absolutely vertically, until you get the hang of it. If you just shove the stick forward and hold it there, you feel you're vertical before you reach sixty degrees. By the time you reach ninety degrees, which takes quite a steady nerve, you may well be past your target. And it feels like past the vertical. The trick was to do a half-roll so that you were momentarily upside-down, then simply pull *back* on the stick till your target was sitting on top of your engine cowling. You couldn't help being vertical, it's a geometric certainty. Hold her till you press the tit, then pull out, no problem.

On free weekends we could take our Chesapeakes with us. Wherever we wanted to go. Depart on Saturday morning, back on Sunday night. I twice nipped over to Oxford. This apparent extravagance – each round trip took over seventy gallons, the civilian ration for months – was not wholly unjustifiable, we had to learn map-reading. On both trips however I very nearly killed myself and that would not have been justified. My blood runs cold even now to think of the first time, not because I so nearly bought it but because I'd have done it before the eyes of my brother and sister, then in their teens, to whom I was showing off. On the Sunday morning we drove out to the airfield so that they could see just how clever I was. Left them on the perimeter. Took off, climbed, dived several times pulling out low in front of them. The last time, coming down vertically, left it that little bit too late and found myself running out of sky. Yanked back far too hard on the stick and went into a high-speed stall for the first and last time ever.

In a high-speed stall the aircraft sinks uncontrollably though in a nose-up attitude at about 150 knots. It happened over a forest and I sank so low before regaining control that I could see every twig, couldn't have been more than six feet clear. And it was just the purest luck I wasn't fifty feet lower.

Never told them. Made out it was all quite normal. Kay, Wynne, how nearly you saw your clever big brother plough headlong into those trees, the terrible explosion, then the enveloping flames.

Exactly two weeks later I took off to fly to Lee but hit weather near Swindon that I thought just bad enough to justify turning back for another night in Oxford, where Angel was. Having arrived over the airfield – it was little more than a landing strip, at Starvell Farm, near Kidlington – I dived into a low-level downwind pass, pulled up steeply, would have landed in three minutes. It wasn't to be. My engine stopped dead at about two hundred feet.

Fortunately I had plenty of speed but I'd reach mother earth in less than a minute and had to turn through almost 180° if I was to get her into wind. The countryside was wooded with only a single field of any size upwind. It happened to be a potato field. To reach it I'd have to lose height in the shallowest glide possible, at the same time continuing an extremely steep turn towards it. On glancing at my airspeed indicator for a fraction of a second, I saw to my horror that I was several knots below stalling speed. Why hadn't I already spun in?* It could now happen at any second – curtains. But the even more certainly fatal alternative, I knew in a flash, was to gain speed by steepening my glide-path or come out of my turn – either of which would have landed me in a dense forest. So there was nothing for it but to continue as I was until directly upwind. Somehow I just made it (flaps down, wheels up), ran twenty or thirty yards, hit an extra large potato-ridge and turned on my back. End of Chesapeake AL936 – but I could walk away from it.

You have to be careful after landing upside-down. It has happened to pilots that they release their lap-straps, drop three feet and break their necks. This I knew and avoided.

All right, the reason my engine stopped was fairly elementary, I'd run out of petrol. But it damn well wasn't my fault.

---

* You must spin off a rate-four turn at such a low airspeed; the only possible rational explanation is that my ASI was reading five or ten knots slow. And yet…

The fitter had certified before I took off that the tank was three-quarters full, relying on the petrol gauge, which turned out to be faulty, instead of using a dipstick. It was the universal practice to accept the mechanic's written certification on Form 700 that an aircraft was correctly serviced for the trip; and the gauge had been showing half-full when the tank was empty. My Lords of the Admiralty took a different view, however, and Pig informed me that I had 'incurred Their Lordships' displeasure', the next most serious expression of censure to ordering the endorsement of my logbook. Bloody unfair! They held that I shouldn't have accepted the fitter's word, which was the invariable practice, but checked personally with a dipstick. This we were now ordered to do for the first time. We conformed for about two weeks.

No more weekend flips, I fear. For anyone. Not exactly popular.

In September we were teamed with observers. Our Senior O. was Harry Hayes, the extremely experienced RN two-striper who would take over command of the squadron on Pig's departure. Next came Maxie Mays, an RN sub who also had operational experience. Smiling face, black curly hair. The seven others were all recently commissioned Wavy Navy subs, of whom the luck of the draw paired me with Bertie Ingham, quiet perhaps but solid and conscientious. Our somewhat contrasting temperaments dovetailed extremely well. Everyone called him Bertie but he is now Mr Arthur Thackeray Ingham, a retired magistrate and schoolmaster in Kidderminster.

We were to fly together for very nearly a year. Not long till our first little excitement. This was on October 17th, which happened to be my twenty-first birthday. A fine way to celebrate it! We were flying happily on a WT/X (Wireless Telegraphy Exercise) at 10,000 feet on a perfect cloudless morning. Bertie's very calm voice on the intercomm.

– I think something's on fire.

– For Jesus' sake. *What's* on fire?

At once getting the smell of it. Wisps of smoke in my cockpit. Instinctively cutting the throttle, propeller to fully coarse, steeply diving earthwards. How was the engine, Bertie wanted to know.

– Engine all right. Smoke from behind me. Stand by to bale out.

The safe thing to do was bale out at once. If the fire really caught, it would be all over in seconds. Cockpit now filling with smoke, glasshouse open, but I'd no intention of scrapping another Cheesecake if there was any way I could help it. Had to think of Their Lordships. Made the dive steeper and steeper, alternating port and starboard rudder, didn't lower wheels, doing over 300. Try to blow it out. Could be safely down in four minutes. After thirty seconds, Bertie's voice again.

– I think it's the wireless. I'm working on it.

– Well keep working. Not getting any worse. I'll try to make it to Worthy.

We'd been directly over Winchester. I headed my head-long dive for the Naval Air Station at Worthy Down, four or five miles to northward, began pulling out at 1500 feet, smoke at last abating. Now too low to jump, committed to getting her down. Bertie firing red Very lights, signal of aircraft in distress. Lowering flaps and wheels, prop to fully fine, plonking her down crosswind, the lovely bumpity-bump of the grassy surface beneath her.

– The fire appears to have extinguished itself, said Bertie (or something similar).

His diagnosis correct. It was indeed the wireless, as we still called the radio, that had managed to ignite. For reasons not remembered, if ever ascertained. A quick check of the airframe, the short hop back to Lee. Quite an unusual exercise in wireless telegraphy.

We all got pissed as hell that night. Happy birthday, dear Godders. Happy birthday everyone.

We had been given no inkling of it, but our *coup-de-foudre* with the sexy American teenager was coming to an end. The ample bosom of the Stringbag, our deserted wife-mother, complacently awaited us. We'd been putting in thirty hours a month, subjecting the Cheesecake to every trial and indignity. But Their Lordships from Pig's reports didn't like what they heard. A few days after my birthday Pig broke the news. We'd be leaving next week for Arbroath to re-equip with Swordfish. Our Chesapeakes would be demoted to non-operational duties.

Jesus what a comedown. Seemed a totally incredible decision. The verdict had been that our sweethearts were underpowered, would too often be unable to carry an adequate load from a small carrier. But the power of the Twin Wasp Junior, and all the performance data, had been well known before we started. Our exhaustive three-month trials had shown no defects, drawbacks, shortcomings. It seemed totally inexplicable, a perverse step backwards to what we'd thought was *temps perdu,* as though My Lords were determined at all costs that navy pilots should never have a halfway modern kite to fly.

The squadron duly left for Scotland. But my engine woud not start. Left behind with a fitter, Air Mechanic Irvine, to put it right, then follow on my own with him. Ready next morning, departure for what should have been a pleasant three hours' flying. No observer so no radio, and no navigational aids of any kind except magnetic and gyro compasses. And my two eyes and a map strapped to my knee. All quite normal.

Weather perfect leaving Lee, slowly clouding over, then sudden deterioration, ceiling getting lower, heavy rain then snow showers over Yorkshire. Decide to put down at Catterick, refuel, have a smoke, get a weather report. Weather report not good, very low ceiling, sleet and snow, mountains in fog, but how could I go wrong? Simply follow the coastline.

Not so easy however. Soon after take-off, find myself in cloud at low altitude, not totally sure where I am. Dangerous to descend, cloud might go all the way to the deck, better head east till without doubt over the sea, quite safe to descend there till breaking cloud. This occurs at under 300 feet, visibility less than a mile. But no problem, fly west till making landfall, follow the coast as planned.

The low-lying coast appearing. No recognizable land-mark. A railway line, then something like a colliery, then another railway line. Make a long sweeping turn to star-board, height 200 feet, just below the ten-tenths overcast. Approaching a large town, heavily built up, rain on black tiles shining. The town becomes a city, a great black river dividing it. The pinpoint I wanted. What else could it be but Newcastle.

Fly north-east across it – sorry for the noise, folks, I can't go any higher – into cloud for a few minutes by mistake, pick up a railway line that will lead me to the coast just south of Blyth, follow the shoreline northwards.

But it's getting beyond a joke. Ceiling now 150 feet, quite a heavy snow-storm, visibility half-a-mile. I see from the map an RAF airfield ahead – Acklington, only two or three miles inland. Simple to slip in. From the air it seems deserted. Just a couple of Spitfires, unattended at their dispersal points. But on landing I see groundcrew everywhere, mostly scan-ning the sky. What goes on? Taxi to the control tower, find it a hive of activity.

– Heading for Arbroath, had to put down, duff weather. Say what kind of a place is this? Why no aircraft?

– Two squadrons of aircraft, Spitfires. Scrambled twenty minutes ago. Bandit over Newcastle.

Bandit is the codeword for enemy aircraft. A terrible thought is forming in my mind.

– *One* bandit? What type?

– That's the funny part of it. A bloody 87. Didn't think they could get this far.

The Junkers 87, as I knew well from *Vincent* days, a single-engined, gull-winged divebomber. As was the Chesapeake.

– Well I'll be a son-of-a-bitch. Jesus let's hope they get the bugger.

One by one the Spits come home. I chat up a young pilot. No, never saw him. Ground control lost him, in cloud north of the city.

– And do you know what? The lucky bugger flew straight through the entire Newcastle balloon barrage at cherubs two [200 feet].

My knees weakening.

– You mean the balloons were *up?*

– Every bloody one of them. Red alert as soon as he crossed the coast. All in cloud, he couldn't have known they were there, thirty of them. And flew straight as a die, heading north-east, through the whole fucking lot.

– Well Jesus Christ Almighty the lucky bugger. The goddam lucky bugger.

Stayed the night there. I always liked fighter-boys. Real *esprit-de-corps,* we swopped squadron songs and all got pissed together.

Never a word to anyone.

IV

THE GOLDEN FARTHING

Like trying to fly a truck. That's how it seemed to us to be once more driving a Stringbag after Chesapeake delights. Can the controls always have been so ponderous, needing a ham-handed thrust on the stick, an almighty boot on the rudder-bar, to get any real response, when our silvery Cheesecakes had soared and gyrated to the smallest touch of a finger? No more the easy rolls and effortless loops, with perhaps a stylish half-roll off the top among the clouds, then the breathtaking vertical dive with the needle beyond 300. And no more the comfort and class of a closed cockpit, the ease of the peeing machine. It was effort enough to hoist the nose into the air till it approached vertical, shove the stick hard over, then feel her waver hesitantly into the gentlest of stall turns, just about the limit of her aerobatic capability.

And coming in to land was there really *nothing* to remember, no cockpit drill *at all?* Fixed-pitch prop again, fixed undercart, no flaps. So just go on ahead and put her down, son.

We were told we had maybe a month for a renewed working-up period, starting again from scratch, before *Archer* would be ready; then the Atlantic awaited us. That's what we were told and a month would be none too long. A pilot's not a pilot till he is totally at home in his aircraft, can fly it instinctively without looking at his instruments, to the last limit of its capability, and extract every ounce of its performance however meagre. That's what we'd learnt to do from tentative beginnings with our all-American Chesapeakes and had become sensitive, gentle-handed pilots in the process – ready for anything, none better. Now, to fly well, we had to learn to fly badly again: not to be afraid to ram the stick hard over near the stall, then pulling the ever-faithful Stringbag with a burst of throttle and plenty of top rudder into the steepest of turns with a wing-tip swishing the treetops, knowing by instinct with only a knot or two to spare just what liberties to take. Try that with a Cheesecake and RIP. And every day the Stringbag flew more as we remembered her and we slowly began to love her again.

At the same time as we waved farewell to our Chesapeakes in November 1941, our squadron strength was reduced to a mere six aircraft, though we would still have eight aircrews. This, it had been decided, would be half *Archer's* establishment; the other half would be fighters. Amazing to think now, seeing the serried ranks of high-powered bombers and fighters operated from the mammoth carriers of today, that a dozen aircraft would be the most the likes of *Archer* could send forth.

The Swordfish carried a regular crew of three, so Bertie and I were now joined by Leading Airman 'Tommy' Thomas, laughably known as a Telegraphist Air Gunner, or TAG for short. Laughably because we didn't have any guns. It had finally been conceded that there were virtually no conceivable circumstances in which a bumbling biplane, with less than half the speed of any likely hostile aircraft, could ever bring our machine-guns to bear. So out they came. We recognized the logic of this reasoning and later felt no resentment at going into action with no defensive armament at all. It reduced our load and it gave our air gunner (as the TAG was nonetheless still usually known) freedom to give his whole attention to the wireless.

Our observers, on the other hand, had a new toy to play with. We were one of the first squadrons in the Navy to be equipped with the latest ASV, as airborne radar was known.

A primitive version had been in use since May 1941. It was capable of detecting a large vessel on the surface at a maximum range of twenty-five miles, and could also be used to locate and identify a coast-line. The range varied widely with the size of the target and the skill of the operator: it was hard to pick up a submarine, even if fully surfaced, at more than four or five miles.

By Christmas we were fully worked up and ready for action. And action is certainly what we wanted, eagerly awaited, which meant killing and being killed. Just as we had from the first – from the time we put our names down, I suppose. And yet we were such unaggressive, happy-go-lucky fellows, nothing blood thirsty about us, no murderous tendencies whatever, no neuroses. And this impatience for action, for putting our lives at even greater risk, far greater, was shared by just about all of us – not only in 811. Today people can well understand that aircrew enjoy their flying passionately throughout training and working up, but perhaps think they must be dreading, seeking to postpone at all costs, the time when the killing starts, when they face the daily possibility, even the likelihood, of violent death, eternal extinction. It was the complete opposite. I don't know why or how, but every man jack among us wanted one thing above all – to see an end to working up, to non-operational flying, and begin the real thing. Death? What's death?

War make murder glorious. It was what society and convention expected of us and therefore became respectable and acceptable, to others as well as ourselves. So smooth-faced young men, who should have been working in offices or playing tennis or reading Greats, could set forth on murderous missions for glory rather than obloquy, undepraved by raining death. At the same time, by some process of self-deception not easy to explain, I know that I myself never stopped for a moment to consider, factually and objectively, that the sole purpose of the skills I was so assiduously acquiring was to kill human beings as efficiently as possible. Show me a submerging U-boat and I would joyously, without any thought beyond it, have dived into the split-second synchronized attack we had practised twenty times, in which the eighteen depth-charges from the three aircraft in each flight would hopefully blow it to pieces. And all the unseen Germans who had been diving for their lives – unseen, that was an important part of it – would be blown to pieces with it. Yet the killing bit, somehow or other, remained deep in my subconscious. A submerging U-boat – come on boys, this is it! This is what we've been waiting for!

And how about getting killed? Not necessarily in action, but through any of the hazards we faced unthinking every day? Narrow escapes were commonplace for all of us. Yet it is true to say, however absurd it may have been, that I was still totally convinced of my own immortality. By this I don't mean that I ever said to myself, in so many words, you are never going to be killed. It was simply that the thought of death never entered my head. This has nothing to do with bravery; indeed it makes bravery impossible. I completely took for granted that my life would continue, no matter how many might perish around me. So long as this absurd fallacy remained firmly fixed in my mind, I was a pretty damned good pilot.

Since we were all of us longing for action, it became increasingly hard to bear when no action came our way. It was a ludicrous situation. The early months of 1942, England in sorest straits, the Battle of the Atlantic being lost through shortage of air cover, with merchantmen sunk daily by the exultant packs of U-boats, and here was a squadron, its murderous aircrews trained to the last degree, fully equipped and armed, ready and eager to fly forth against any foe, left kicking our heels in Scotland – first at Arbroath, then at Machrihanish – flying dozens of navexes, homing exercises on Ailsa Craig, waiting in vain to be called upon. OK, something must have happened to *Archer,* but you would have thought their blessed Lordships, unless they had carelessly forgotten our existence, would have found *someone* for us to kill.

It was on February 11th, when we were kicking our heels at Arbroath, that the battle-cruisers *Scharnhorst* and *Gneisenau* left the French harbour of Brest for their dash up the English Channel to the safety of the Fatherland. It had long been foreseen that this golden opportunity of destroying them might arise, which would change the whole balance of naval power; since February 2nd their departure was thought to be imminent so there had been ample time to make all the preparations. Amongst these was the movement to Manston in Kent of the six Stringbags of 825 Squadron, then working up at Lee, to take part in the attack on these immensely powerful vessels, which would be very heavily escorted. We didn't know it till later but Their Lordships gave active consideration to sending 811 to join them. We could have reached Manston in four hours and we were far more experienced than 825, who were not even fully worked up. The CO was Eugene Esmonde, already mentioned as leading the attack on *Bismarck*, a pilot of the utmost gallantry with a long and distinguished record, but most of his aircrews were only recently out of flying school. Had the Admiralty taken the fateful decision to send us, we would have suffered the same disaster and very few of us would have survived.

Why they sent 825 is a question that has never been explained – and it would take some explanation. There is no attempt to do so in the report of the Board of Enquiry. Shore-based operations against enemy shipping in the Channel were not a normal function of naval aircraft. The RAF had many squadrons of fast modern bombers standing by for the operation to which Esmonde's little striking force would make an insignificant addition. Bomber Command had 242 aircraft ready to take part; there were also fifty Whitleys of which it would be reported, though they were far faster and less vulnerable than the Swordfish, that they were 'a type unsuitable for day bombing'. Coastal Command had three-dozen torpedo-dropping Beaufighters briefed and ready. To support these, thirty-four squadrons of fighters were standing by, comprising over 500 Spitfires and Hurricanes.

The entire débâcle, perhaps the sorriest of the war, went wrong from the beginning. One solitary aircraft – a Hudson of Coastal Command – had the job of watching the approaches to Brest from dusk till 2300 when another would replace it. It was a pitch dark night and the Hudson's ASV just happened to pack up at 1920. It was 2238 before the next took over. A careful watch was then kept up till morning and nobody realized that *Scharnhorst* and *Gneisenau*, accompanied by the heavy cruiser *Prinz Eugen* and a powerful escort of destroyers and E-boats, had slipped out at 2120 during those 198 minutes when Brest wasn't covered at all.

The RAF flew two other single-aircraft patrols during the night, and a dawn sweep by two Spitfires, but the enemy armada was not sighted until 1042, when two Spits who weren't even looking for it but chasing a couple of Messerschmitts just happened to fly over it by mistake. The fleet was then approaching the Straits of Dover, having covered 300 miles undetected. For unexplained reasons the pilots were in no circumstances permitted to use their wireless and had to return to base, where they landed at 1109, to report the sighting for which half the RAF was waiting.

The events that followed pass all comprehension. Alone of all the aircraft, Esmonde's squadron, as a naval unit, came under the command of Vice-Admiral (Dover), who received the news at 1130 and ordered the six Stringbags to take off for their attack one hour later. This was supposed to be coordinated with an attack by four Beaufighters, the first little wave of all the Air Force aircraft that were waiting in their hundreds. But the Beaufighters couldn't get airborne till 1340, seventy minutes after Esmonde's though they had been standing by for a week.

It was known that extremely heavy air opposition would be encountered and it was therefore arranged on the telephone between VA (Dover) and Fighter Command that five squadrons of Spitfires and Hurricanes would accompany 825. However only one of these reached Manston by 1230 and its ten Spitfires soon lost contact with the much slower Stringbags. So Esmonde's Swordfish, which took off precisely on time in very bad visibility, flew alone and virtually unprotected towards their immensely powerful enemy, now ten miles north of Calais, as it steamed with all guns manned, aided (and surely amazed) by the fact that no previous attack of any kind had been launched.

They approached in two flights of three. Before reaching the powerful destroyer screen they were engaged by the enemy's most modern fighters in strength. Esmonde's own aircraft was the first to be badly damaged. His port mainplanes were 'shot to shreds' (according to a survivor) but the Stringbag kept flying as Esmonde headed at low level over the destroyers towards the capital ships they encircled. Both the pilots with him, Kingsmill and Rose, were also hit but flew on, though Rose was badly wounded, his air gunner killed, his petrol tank shattered by cannon fire. Esmonde's aircraft crashed into the sea when hit again some 3000 yards from the battle-cruisers. Kingsmill and his observer, Samples, were wounded, the aircraft further damaged. But they closed within range of their target, *Scharnhorst,* and Kingsmill could aim and drop his torpedo before being forced to ditch. Rose did much the same: he pressed home his torpedo attack, also on *Scharnhorst,* and was able to turn back over the destroyers before his engine succumbed.

Of the second flight, led by Lieutenant Thompson, nothing can be reported. Flying astern of Esmonde's, they were never seen again by any of those who survived.

So ended the most incomprehensible, most badly planned, most gallantly led operation in the history of naval aviation. No hits were scored on the enemy fleet. Of the eighteen officers and men taking part, thirteen were killed and four seriously wounded. Lee, who was Rose's observer, alone emerged unscathed.

Esmonde was awarded a posthumous VC. The four surviving officers, all RNVR sub-lieutenants, received DSOs, the one surviving gunner a CGM, the next highest decorations for gallantry. They had been picked up by allied torpedo-boats after over an hour in their dinghies.

During the rest of the day, the enemy flotilla was attacked by the RAF as well as by torpedo-boats and a handful of ancient destroyers, but to no avail whatever. Of the 242 modern bombers sent out with full fighter escort, 188 'failed to locate the ships or were unable to attack them owing to low cloud'. So states the Board of Enquiry's report. No hits were scored by the twenty-eight fast torpedo-bombers (Beaufighters) sent out additionally, three of which were lost. The only redeeming feature was that both battle-cruisers were quite badly damaged by mines laid ahead of them by aircraft of Coastal Command.

The Board found that no blame could be attached to anyone for the whole shameful disaster.

At the end of February, Pig Lucas was transferred at very short notice to take over command of 832 Squadron in *Victorious,* whose Albacores less than a week later were led by him on a notably unsuccessful strike against *Tirpitz* in the Arctic. His place as CO of 811 was taken by his observer, Harry Hayes. Sharp featured with deep-set eyes and raven hair, he was rather short in stature but had the sinewy build of an athlete, never flagging energy and those qualities of inspiring leadership that cannot be described but are felt instantly. Harry had been on ops before any of the rest of us except Alan McTurk had soloed. He flew many missions in Skuas over Norway, where he was finally shot down and taken prisoner but not before winning a DSC. I don't know how he got back to Britain but he made it in time to join 811 as Senior Observer in Chesapeake days.

He was approachable but never *too* approachable. None of us would address him, now that he was boss, as any thing other than 'Sir', nor expect to be addressed by anything less formal than our surnames. But this didn't prevent us from having many excellent evenings with him. By nature he was gentle and quiet-voiced, but his eyes could flash with anger or contempt, his rebuke cut into the heart, when foolishness or incompetence had earned it. Despite his record he was still a mere two-striper, so must have been well under thirty.

As a result of Pig's departure I found myself elevated. With six aircraft we normally flew in two flights of three. McTurk, as Senior Pilot, became the CO's driver and they led the leading flight. And on me fell the CO's choice for leader of the second. Experienced pilots were beginning to get scarce. Barely twenty-one, I had flown not quite 100 hours in Stringbags out of a total of only 360, including dual, since joining the Navy. But Willcocks, Cooper and

Shirley-Smith had departed and this was more than had been flown by any rival for the honour. Of whom only Jock Sayer and two midshipmen were junior to me however.

It was on March 16th that we moved to RNAS Machrihanish, otherwise known as HMS *Landrail* (officially) and Machrijesus (unofficially), on the now-famous Mull of Kintyre not far from Campbeltown. An appointment to Machrijesus, one of the FAA's main bases for disembarked front-line squadrons, was always greeted with groans, for it was miles and miles from anywhere, there was no nearby city with neon-lit bars, no accommodating Palais de Danse full of yours-for-the-asking popsies. But I always loved it. Purple mountains, the sparkly sea with beach and grassy sanddunes. Where Bertie and I, or Jock and I, went for long walks along the shore looking for plovers' eggs or hoping to see an eagle. Or borrowing clubs to play a free round on the yellow-bunkered golf links. And about a million Wrens if you were looking for a girl, as everyone was, always.

It seems beyond belief nowadays, when the breathalyser rules supreme and drunk driving has become socially unacceptable, that we flew so often when half-seas over. Or, if you prefer, pissed out of our minds. In the evenings we were almost all heavy drinkers (unless due to night-fly) with rollicking choruses of flying songs or ribald doggerel around the off-key piano. No harm in that. But at lunchtime, with half the day's flying still ahead of us, we would assemble as often as not, unless some really tricky flying lay ahead of us, at the bar we had left twelve hours previously for the ritual know as ginning up. For gin was our usual lunchtime tipple: it was cheapest – a penny a tot at sea – especially pink gin, because then the mixer was free. Three doubles, often far more, before swerving in for a meal with much laughter and back-slapping.

On May 19th we were to spend the forenoon beating up the pongoes (in other words the army) near Dumfries, then land at the RAF base there for refreshment. After which we expected to fly straight back to Machri. Our plans, appropriately in Burns country, ganged agley. Ginning up had just ended when we were given the news that en route for Kintyre the squadron was to climb to angels eight (8000 feet) and carry out a synchronized dummy torpedo attack at sea level on the target-vessel *Cardiff.* No escape. We were all plastered. I do recall that I felt some slight qualms as we sailed together over the silvery Clyde with our target zigzagging far below us, hardly able, like everyone else, to focus on my instruments, my head buzzing in the thin air (of course no oxygen). Diving so steeply in unison. Starting to pull out at under 1000 feet, levelling off as ever on the wavetops. And by God my camera was to show, as recorded in my log-book (with the brief comment 'What a party!'), that I scored a hit amidships.

In the coming months we carried out many such attacks, dropped depth charges galore on dummy U-boats, beat up pongoes all over Scotland, became expert with ASV. By day or night they all came alike to us. We must have been the most worked-up squadron in the Navy. Not that we didn't from time to time have excitement, danger, tragedy. A merchantman, *St Briac,* torpedoed during the night: we flew off at dawn, armed with depth charges in case the U-boat was still around but mainly to search for survivors. A pitiful half-dozen found by the CO and McTurk in the only boat to get away. Discovering ourselves, when on a peaceful night exercise over the sea, unexpectedly mixing it with a squadron of JU-88s laying mines off the coast: even if we hadn't been totally unarmed, what could we do but signal their position and make ourselves scarce? Our first real deck landings, a day's visit to *Argus,* the same old *Argus* of 1917 vintage, to find no trouble at all in picking up a wire on her spacious, islandless flight deck after so many hundred addles.

When all the results had been tabulated and analysed, I again came out top of the class at the gentle art of torpedo dropping and was therefore chosen as the pilot for a series of test flights to try out a brilliant new invention intended to protect merchantmen from attack by torpedo. The top secret idea was to have booms protruding outboard at intervals along the merchantman; reinforced netting would be suspended from these booms, running well below sea level. The approaching torpedo was supposed to entangle itself innocuously in the underwater netting instead of running those few extra feet to hit and destroy its target. It was intended primarily for defence against U-boats but should be equally effective against aircraft and my task was to drop a series of dummy torpedoes aimed at a vessel, the *Empire Heywood*, equipped with this protection to see if it worked. She would be steaming in the Clyde at fifteen knots and, to make things easier for me, would take no avoiding action.

The trials could hardly have been less successful. Owing to a design problem, the netting did not cover the forwardmost twenty feet of the 500-foot vessel. I carried out six 'attacks' from a range of 800 yards or so, each time returning to Machrihanish to pick up another dummy torpedo. The first one, for reasons never ascertained, took it into its head to run in circles and therefore never reached its target. On the second, fourth and fifth runs, my torpedo malignantly sneaked ahead of the netting and struck the vessel a hearty whack on the bows – completely by chance, of course – in that one small unprotected area. Even without a warhead, the repeated impact of a fast-moving underwater missile weighing almost a ton caused some sizeable dents and dinges to *Empire Heywood* apart from damaging the torpedoes. On the sixth run, my aim was bang on: the tin-fish struck the netting amidships but sailed unimpeded through it, hit the target an almighty whack with scarcely diminished impetus, then broke in two and sank. Only on the third run did the netting carry out its intended function.

I thought it rather unfair, but I was awarded my first and last OIF as a result. The citation read that 'being required to aim a series of dummy torpedoes at 480 feet of netting allegedly protecting a certain vessel, to wit the *Empire Heywood*, steaming in perfect visibility on a steady course at predetermined speed, he kept his finger so firmly inserted that on three out of six occasions he missed the netting but struck said *Heywood* certain resounding blows in that exiguous forward portion of said vessel unprotected by said netting'. The OIF, short for the Most Highly Derogatory Order of the Irremovable Finger, was a decoration we had invented, awarded by the boss in an elaborate little ceremony to any pilot or observer guilty of an advanced degree of finger trouble. Its name derived, of course, from the injunction (in its original form) to 'get your finger out', which means for Christ's sake stop being so clueless and do the thing properly. Lengthy research has failed to reveal where and when the phrase originated, nor indeed have I ever been perfectly sure, to tell the truth, in which particular aperture the guilty party's finger was supposed to be inserted. But the expression in one or other of its countless variations – 'Out with the finger', 'Remove digit', 'Select out' or simply 'Dedigitate', to mention only these – quickly became a service favourite, soon spread to Civvy Street and has now passed into the language. (Its use in speeches by such eminent personages as the Prince of Wales and his father removes at least two of the apertures I'd thought possible – at least I suppose it does.)

A pilot or observer could win the order any number of times, though *digitalis,* as the disease was known, would eventually lead to the ignominy of a training squadron or even to permanent grounding. One of our pilots achieved the award so often that he became known simply as Fingers. He was very young, still a midshipman when he joined as a spare pilot, very dashing and good-looking, and could well have developed into a first-class operational pilot; but he kept making the most ridiculous mistakes and someone should have foreseen that one of these would eventually be fatal. But Fingers kept on flying. One fine morning, for example, our six aircraft were in their usual tight formation (two vics in line astern) on our way to attack a target vessel in the Clyde with dummy torpedoes. Fingers was the CO's port-side wingman, whilst I was leading the second flight, a few feet behind and below. When at some 8000 feet over Campbeltown, I was appalled to see Fingers' torpedo parting company from his Stringbag. The giant cylindrical missile, slung firmly till this moment beneath his aircraft's belly, began by sharing our forward momentum and therefore remained horizontal (at least for the time being); it seemed to lose height extremely slowly, though this must have been an illusion. My port-side wingman, Denis Fuller, neatly throttled back, thus allowing it to descend just a few feet ahead of him. So, for several breathless seconds, 811 Squadron comprised six Swordfish and one torpedo flying in tight formation over Campbeltown.

Easily explained. Dreaming his own dreams, digit firmly inserted, Fingers had unintentionally touched the release button on the throttle; no other way it could have happened. ('I suppose I must have pressed the jolly old tit,' he agreed on landing.) A torpedo is usually dropped at well under 100 feet and is useless if dropped much higher. Now we all watched with fascination as the extremely expensive tin-fish, released from a greater height than ever before in history, described a great arc below us, nose falling ever so slowly till it was descending vertically. By great good fortune its original forward speed, all of ninety knots, was just sufficient to carry it beyond Campbeltown into shallow water offshore, where it smashed itself to pieces. A second bar (at least) to the OIF for Fingers.

It was bound to end in tragedy. A week or two later we were taking part in combined ops with the Army over mountainous country in Dumfries. I led my flight in a series of dive-bombing attacks on their camouflaged positions. I was flying with Maxie Mays, now promoted to Lieutenant and Senior Observer, with faithful Tommy as TAG. Fingers my Number 3, with Georgie Morrison and PO Paxton in the back. Georgie a wee Scot from Aberdeenshire, not long in the squadron. Half-a-dozen dives, pulling out at fifty feet, give these pongoes something to think about! As on so many previous occasions. Time for one last dive, then home across the Clyde to Machrijesus for ginning up. But one little thing Fingers again forgot. He forgot to pull out. Flew straight on into the mountain. No way of discovering why. He and his crew scattered among the heather, our only deaths in all the months of working up although I don't know how we managed it.

Of *Archer*, in which we had almost ceased to believe, there was no sign whatever. Evenings round the out-of-tune piano, we sang our flying songs as we got pissed night after night. And I composed one to express our frustration, which was to be sung for years and years by succeeding aircrews of 811 long after it ceased to apply. To the air of 'The Road to the Isles':

There's a squadron going rotten
For it's waiting for the war
And the war is waiting for the Admiraltee:
Eight-eleven's simply heaven
If you want to stay ashore,
For we never, never, never go to sea.

To Lee-on-Solent and Arbroath
And Machrihanish we may pass,
We have searched the pubs and brothels far and wide.
Oh we've flown until we've grown
A pair of wings upon our arse,
But we'll never find the Archer *on the Clyde.*

It wasn't till long afterwards that we found out what had happened to *Archer.* And to the ten other escort carriers that should now or in the near future be protecting convoys from the growing onslaught of U-boats in the Atlantic. The story makes sorry reading.

The North Atlantic run was Britain's most vital lifeline. But losses on it were becoming insupportable. Even in the year to June 1941, over five million tons of allied shipping were sunk on it, three-fifths of which fell to U-boats. By the early months of 1942, U-boats alone were sending to the bottom half-a-million tons a month, which would rise to an all-time record of 700,000 tons in November – four or five ships a day – without counting victims of surface vessels, mines and aircraft.

Such losses could not have been sustained. Britain, had they continued, would have been starved into submission. They arose mainly because the convoy system was much less widely used than is generally realized: over two-thirds of the merchantmen sunk by U-boats in the whole course of the war were not in convoy at the time. It is hard to understand why so many unescorted sailings continued when in 1942, for example, 840 'independent' vessels fell to U-boats compared with 299 from convoys of which no fewer than sixty were stragglers. This was the worst year for convoys but losses from them had always been serious, about 200 ships a year. The main reason was that, though the available surface escort vessels did sterling service, air cover was shown early in the war to provide the most effective protection: during the first two years, not a single ship was sunk by U-boats when an air escort was present. But such cover, which was provided by Coastal Command from shore bases, was very far from being continuous, and there was a gap of some 500 miles in mid-ocean beyond their reach. It was here that most convoy losses were suffered.

The cover should have come from naval aircraft, operating from carriers that could move to the most threatened areas, or preferably sailing in company with convoys. Fully trained squadrons such as 811 were ready and waiting. We spent our days on practice attacks off Arran, our nights getting pissed around the piano, because there were just no flat-tops available for convoy escort duty in the Atlantic.

In fact there were practically no flat-tops. Their vulnerability, and the lack of foresight and urgency displayed by the Admiralty as part of Their Lordships' continuing unwillingness to give aviation the priority it deserved, are shown by the astonishing fact that by mid-August of this year (1942) a total of merely three would be operational, and one of these was the antediluvian *Furious*. Disaster had followed disaster. After the early sinkings, already recorded, of *Courageous, Glorious* and *Ark Royal,* Japanese dive-bombers had sent *Hermes* to the bottom in May and a U-boat saw the last of *Eagle* on August 11th. *Illustrious* had been severely damaged by JU-87s when with a Malta convoy in early 1941; she was still under repair. *Formidable* had suffered the same fate a few months later but returned to active service in March 1942. *Victorious,* commissioned in 1941, was still ticking over. *Audacity,* first of the escort carriers, had already come and gone, as recorded below. The spanking new *Indomitable,* held up after running aground during trials, had been badly damaged by Stukas the day after the loss of *Eagle,* and was not yet back on station. *Argus* had been retired, at least for the moment, for deck landing training.

The Admiralty were slow enough to appreciate the paramount importance of shipborne aircraft. And when the vessels so urgently needed were finally put on order in sufficient numbers, their readiness for operational use had to wait, in most cases, the overcoming of design faults that had never been foreseen and seemed to go on for ever.

The obvious requirement from the early days of the war had been a large number of small carriers, each of which needed to be able to operate no more than a clutch of Stringbags, to work solely on convoy protection. How to provide these quickly? The answer had been seen as early as 1940 by Captain M. S. Slattery,* the Director of Air Material, who proposed 'the fitting of the simplest possible flight decks to suitable merchant ships'. The suggestion was excellent but only one had been ordered. This was *Audacity,* a captured German banana-boat previously named *Hannover;* presumably for this reason, small escort carriers were known (among other things) as banana-boats ever after, whatever their previous function had been. Work was completed with admirable speed, she was ready for trials in June 1941, no snags came to light and she went speedily into action. But she operated fighters, the Martlets of 802 Squadron, against Condor bombers on the Gibraltar run, not Stringbags against U-boats in the Atlantic, during her short but active career. She went to the bottom in December.

Soon before her completion, Their Lordships at last fully accepted Slattery's proposal and ordered eleven escort carriers. Had conversion gone ahead on all of them and been as trouble free as *Audacity's*, the tide might have turned a full year earlier in the Atlantic and we wouldn't have been sitting on our arses in Machrihanish. But everything went wrong, as seemed always to be the case with any project involving naval aviation. Five of the orders went to British shipyards, six to the US. When it was decided that the former should be passenger liners, there was violent opposition

* Later Rear Admiral Sir Matthew Slattery

from the Ministry of War Transport, who had no intention of parting with so large a clutch of troopships. A bitter wrangle ensued, which the Ministry won hands down. Of the five vessels, only *Pretoria Castle* (already under naval control as an armed merchant cruiser) was released for conversion. And this would not be completed till mid-1943, owing to unforeseen design problems.

For the same reason the US conversions took far, far longer to come into service than planned. Most of these were merchantmen under construction rather than existing vessels such as *Audacity* had been. We had been led to expect that *Archer,* for which we were so impatiently waiting, would be ready for us late in 1941, the first (it was planned) of the batch. But, as we learned long afterwards, an unending series of disasters overtook her. During trials in January 1942 she collided with a merchantman. After two months under repair, she sailed from Charleston, Virginia, to Freetown; we should have joined her a few weeks later but extensive repairs were found to be necessary and it was June when she sailed for Greenock. A few days later, one of her own bombs exploded in the catwalk causing nineteen casualties and much damage. She was diverted to New York for this to be made good, but broke down in mid-Atlantic. It would be November before she was ready again and she was then dispatched with an American convoy to Morocco. On arrival in Liverpool she would again have to be taken in hand for machinery repairs, which kept her out of action till mid March 1943.

The second 'Woolworth' (as the US conversions were known) had been *Avenger:* she was at once sent on a Russian convoy in September and thence to take part in the North African landings, where she was sunk on November 15th, within days of arrival, by a single torpedo. Meantime two more, *Biter* and *Dasher,* became operational, but they too were sent to the Med. *Charger,* when finally completed, was coolly retained by the US Navy for deck landing training. This left only *Tracker:* her design had to be so completely revised in the light of unhappy experience that she did not enter the fray till late in 1943.

Another proposal of Slattery's, also made in 1940, had

been accepted much more quickly and whole-heartedly. It involved equipping merchantmen with catapults. These would enable a single aircraft to be launched but there was no question of it landing unless, by unlikely chance, within range of a friendly shore. After his one flight, the pilot would bale out over the convoy, to be picked up, he hoped, by an escort vessel. But the aircraft would be lost. Orders had been given as early as January 1941 for the equipment with catapults, in British shipyards, of no fewer than thirty-five merchantmen and in many cases the work was completed in three months. These vessels, known as Catapult Aircraft Merchant Ships, or CAM-ships for short, continued to sail under the Red Ensign with Merchant Navy crews and carried their normal cargoes.

They proved a success but had never been intended to protect convoys from U-boats, for which they were wholly unsuited. A U-boat never showed herself within sight of an escorted convoy, apart from the briefest glimpse of a periscope, and there'd have been few if any occasions when a Stringbag could have been launched with a good enough chance of success to justify its own predestined sacrifice. So it was invariably with a fighter, usually a Hurricane, that a CAM-ship was equipped. This was never launched till an enemy aircraft was visible and within range, so that the pilot would have at least an even chance of destroying a four-engined bomber in return for the sacrificed Hurricane.

And so it happened that all through 1942, that darkest of years in the Atlantic, not a single naval aircraft could play any part whatever in the defence of its bleeding convoys against the packs of exultant U-boats.

An alternative had to be found for us. It may be, I remember thinking at the time, that the boss had sent Their Lordships a transcript of our song to jog them into action. Perhaps they'd forgotten our existence. But they now at last decided, in the continued non-appearance of the long-awaited escort carriers, that they'd have to find some other way of getting us bumped off.

The first sign that something was afoot came on the

morning of July 24th (1942) when the CO strode purpose-fully into the crewroom. A broad grin on his face.

– All aircraft are to be flown at once to Donibristle.

A slight pause for effect.

– They will there be recamouflaged. They are to be painted black. Any questions?

Many questions. *Black* camouflage? What the Hell was the boss getting at? Night bombers of the RAF were painted black but no one could remember hearing of a sable String-bag.

Easy explanation. We were on the point of becoming RAF night bombers. Two of the squadrons allocated to the non-existent Woolworths, 811 and 812, were being lent to Coastal Command.

There was a touch of fantasy about it. We of 811 flew non-stop on August 6th in our newly-painted matt-black String-bags, a tight formation of six, to Bircham Newton in Norfolk – just on three hours for less than 300 miles. We were doing our best to look like aggressive operational bombers, but anyone who saw us bumble overhead and knew nothing of naval aircraft must have imagined we had escaped from a pre-war flying circus. Bircham Newton was a busy front-line RAF station, with two squadrons of Lockheed Hudsons, up-to-date twin-engined aircraft, newly acquired from the States. The dashing RAF types couldn't believe their eyes as our six biplanes fluttered into the circuit like six black crows, a tangle of struts and wires, to land with hardly any run at a ground speed of forty or fifty. What the hell were we doing there? When we somewhat diffidently mentioned that we'd come to assist them with their ops off France and Hol-land, astonishment turned to disbelief or pity. In *those* old crates? You poor unfortunate buggers! Many just fell about laughing. This was probably one of the many occasions when an Air Force pilot greeted his opposite number in the Navy with the jibe, to which we were well accustomed: 'Mr Orville Wright, I presume'.

The boys of 812, who also boasted six Stringbags, flew in later that day to a comparable welcome.

The question of our somewhat limited range presented

rather a problem. A Swordfish, if carrying a full war-load of 1800 pounds on the outward journey, could stay in the air for almost five hours. (As soon as the load was dropped, the aircraft put on a good ten knots in gratitude with a resultant fall in petrol consumption.) But this was enough for less than 400 miles owing to our extra-slow speed on the way out: the furthermost Friesians, for instance, would be beyond our range. We now learnt that Their Lordships had found the answer to this problem. What did we need with a telegraphist air-gunner? We hadn't any guns and the observer could do the telegraphy as well as the navigation. So Bertie Ingham was to move into the aftermost cockpit, hitherto occupied by Tommy Thomas, and his own would be filled with a second petrol tank, holding sixty-nine gallons. This would increase our range by some forty per cent.

Several problems arose from this clever arrangement, which however did not become fully apparent till we flew with a full load for the first time. And this, unbelievably, was not until we hopefully set forth on our first operational flight. The first fact to have escaped Their Lordships' notice was that sixty-nine gallons of petrol, complete with tank, weighed five times more than Tommy Thomas. Moreover they were sited some way aft of the centre of gravity, giving the Stringbag an unrectifiable and far from agreeable tail-down attitude till at least half the extra fuel had been used. Next little drawback: the ASV screen was irremovably located in the observer's cockpit and could therefore no longer be used. Out went our one modern piece of equipment; we were back to sharp eyesight and dead reckoning. A relatively minor worry was that the pilot would now at all times be totally surrounded by high-octane aviation fuel: 69 gallons immediately behind him and 167 gallons in the upper mainplane just above his head. Not healthy when the tracer's flying.

To fly our six Stringbags we now had nine aircrews – three 'gash'* instead of two. Peter Bentley, now a Lieutenant, was Number 2 in the CO's leading flight; Maxie Mays was his

* Navy slang for 'spare' or 'extra' – e.g. 'Duff show, no gash popsies' on leaving a dance hall where there were no unaccompanied girls.

observer. The CO's Number 3, Ian Whitelaw-Wilson, who had become a close friend of mine, had joined us at Arbroath and flew with one of our newcomers, Richard Townend. As leader of the second flight, with Bertie as ever behind me, I had Jock Sayer as my starboard wingman with Derek Price his looker; and Denis Fuller, promoted to Sub-Lieutenant, as Number 3 with Fred Eckersley to steer him.

Our three gash pilots, all Sub-Lieutenants, were Mike Wargent, Pat Weir and Brian Rose. Brian with his DSO ribbon was one of the few survivors of that suicidal attack by Eugene Esmonde's squadron on *Scharnhorst* and *Gneisenau* only a few months earlier. Elegant and suave, he still had eighteen bits of shrapnel in his back, which the doctors preferred to leave there, and a newly acquired stammer, but was already thought fit to return to action. Ironically, as happened to so many others, he was killed next year far from the scene of battle, having survived a second operational tour, when he descended through cloud into the crags of a Scottish mountainside.

Within three days of reaching Bircham, before our RAF pals had fully accepted that we were in earnest, that the Swordfish was in fact a warplane expected to go on shipping strikes with them, all their forebodings (of which we had none whatever) seemed to have been justified. Who could have foreseen it after all the long months of preparation? There was no night flying at Bircham Newton itself; our ops would be flown from the nearest available airfield to our target. The day after our arrival we flew to nearby Docking, where the long-range tanks were fitted. The next two nights, we stood by till 0200, Stringbags armed with torpedoes, ready to scramble at fifteen minutes' notice if RAF reconnaissance flights should locate a convoy off the enemy coast. Nothing doing. Such nights of waiting (of which there would be many) as yet involved no strain, which only builds up over the weeks and anyway we were much too self-confident and excited. By 2 am on those summer nights it was too late to take off and be sure of reaching the enemy coast, locating our target, carrying out our attack and getting clear of the area in darkness, which of course was essential; bitterly disappointed, we returned by road to Bircham and slept soundly till mid-morning.

On the third night everything was different.

No moon, no stars. The skies heavily overcast with ten-tenths cloud at under 1000 feet. Bertie and I, he encumbered with navigational equipment, walking to our Stringbag at its dispersal point. Its engine not yet running, our ground crew busy about it. The grass drenching from recent heavy rain but the met. forecast favourable: cloud slowly breaking, wind moderating and veering over the next three hours, a clear dawn and a sunny day tomorrow. So this is it at last, after all the months of flying together, our first-ever operational flight. For slung under the Stringbag's belly, in place of the torpedo of both the previous nights, waits a magnetic mine, our maximum warload, cylindrical and sinister. The squadron is to fly in formation to a precise pinpoint off the occupied Dutch coast, two or three miles south-west of Den Helder, and drop a pattern of six mines in the principal shipping lane. So we'll go anyway. This time no waiting for an RAF sighting report.

I climb in, clip on my parachute. Not much point when the whole op will be flown at under 500 feet, most of it at 100 feet, but part of the never-changing ritual. Feel for my harness, an X of webbing fastening over my breastbone; much better reason for this and I draw its straps together as tightly as they'll go. Page and Webb assist me, my faithful fitter and rigger, who for just over a year have maintained 'my' aircraft, Page the engine, Webb the airframe, first the Chesapeakes, now the Stringbags. Never a fault or error. Now Page slips a coin into my hand, grinning close to my face.

– Something to bring you luck, sir.

A golden farthing. I smile back, slip it in a pocket, think to myself: small difference that will make but thanks Pagey for the thought. And oh how careful I am to give every impression of nonchalance. Page and Webb now have the handle ready for the inertia starter on the port side of the engine. I glance at my watch: it's 2250. Take-off scheduled for 2300. I signal them to start winding.

Everything went wrong from the beginning. Alan McTurk would take off first, followed by Peter and Ian. Bertie and I would come next, then either Jock or Denis (I can't remember) and Brian Rose. We were to form up east of the airfield in our usual loose formation of two vics in line astern, dowse navigation lights on crossing the nearby Norfolk coast, head straight for the dropping area. My Number 2's Stringbag wouldn't start. I waited five minutes, he gave me the thumbs down signal (we were observing radio silence) and I taxied out to join the CO's flight on the perimeter, closely followed by Brian. We were to take off at 30-second intervals. No runways at Docking. An unpleasant surprise awaiting.

Ian's turn, then mine. Full boost override for maximum power, throttle wide open, release brakes and away. So slowly we moved forward I thought we'd just never come unstuck. Amazing and absurd that in all the months of working up, when we'd done just about everything else a hundred times, none of us even in daytime had ever flown with such a heavy load. Those damned new petrol tanks: we rolled and rolled and rolled. At long last, the windward perimeter hedge coming up ahead of me, I haul back hopefully on the stick, the only thing to do. Staggering off the grass, scraping over the hedge, the cold night air in my face, intent only on keeping airborne. I glance as the ASI – a fraction over sixty and *this* bloody lot under me. Controls as heavy as hell, almost no response to the ailerons. Flying grossly tail-heavy, though trimmed fully forward.

– Don't know if I can fly this kite.
– Jesus, what's the problem?
– Bloody overloaded, can't get the tail up, can't gain speed.
– What'll we do then?
– Try praying.

Without more speed I can neither climb nor turn. Keeping straight and low, I watch the ASI rise painfully, start a long slow turn to starboard just barely climbing. It seems to take for ever, the tail so low I'm half expecting to stall earthwards at any moment. But the Stringbag as ever keeps flying. Reach 100 feet, see Brian coming up painfully on my quarter to take his position.

A sudden heavy fall of rain, the last of the night. Visibility maybe 400 yards. I make a long slow orbit with Brian, looking for the others.

– Buggers must have gone on. What's my course for Helder?

– 084. Are we going on our own then?

– What else? The kite's flying if you can call it that. It can only get better as we use up the bloody gas.

– Can you make airspeed 75?

– For Jesus' sake, I can hardly make 60.

It's a fact that a Stringbag's performance is liable to variation, and the explanation was partly that mine was having rather an off night. I suppose the sensible thing would have been to turn back but I never thought of it. A few minutes later however Brian thought of it; he turned and headed for home just after we crossed the coast. We learned afterwards that his oil pressure was falling and he made an emergency landing at a small airfield nearby. So ours was now the only remaining aircraft in the flight and the squadron's fighting strength had been diminished to just four Stringbags.

Still hoping to link up with the others but how possible? I'm still on boost override, not normally needed at all and then only for take-off, so I can't go any faster. And *they* can't be going any slower. An aeronautical nightmare: top speed not more than 62, stalling speed not less than 60. We take maybe forty minutes from take-off to reach the coast, dowse navigation lights, descend to 100 feet, keep course at 084. (We'll fly the whole op at this low altitude in the hope of remaining undetected by radar.)

– Hey did you feel that slipstream?

– Yes they're somewhere dead ahead of us, maybe a mile: keep the same course.

If you are flying close enough behind another aircraft at the same altitude, you can feel the characteristic turbulence caused by its slipstream, so we know we're not far behind. At first from time to time I feel it ahead of us as we skim across the waves towards the enemy coast but each time a bit less noticeable. At least we know we're on course: navigation by slipstream a new invention. I soon give up hope of catching them, we'll make it a solo effort. As I use up gas, the tail imperceptibly rises and I can cut back slowly to cruising revs. The long-range tank three-quarters empty after not much more than an hour; the Stringbag nearly herself again.

I don't know how long we took to reach our dropping position, but I don't believe I exceeded seventy the whole way out and with a light head wind it must have been nearly three hours. The night still black as pitch. I fly as low as I dare and seem to have kept below the radar: no search-lights, no fighters, no gunfire, as Bertie fixes our position as accurately as possible without the help of ASV. When I press the tit and nearly a ton of deadweight falls from the String-bag, she jumps for joy like a newly-delivered mother. I have to jam the stick forward and re-trim her or she'd have leapt 300 feet. At once she is a bird again, controls normal, cruis-ing at nearly 100 knots.

Those mines were devilish inventions. They were set to go off when a certain number of magnetic fields, usually in the form of enemy merchantmen or mine-sweepers, had passed within their range – perhaps eleven, perhaps seventeen, per-haps two-dozen. With each individual mine, the number could be varied according to current tactics. So a sweeper could make multiple passes over the area and assume it to be clear. Five or ten ships later... whoomp. I suppose they became inoperative with the slow passage of time so that none is still lethally waiting – but who knows?

Lights on approaching the friendly coast, climb to 500 feet, sailing back to Docking. A brilliant dawn reddening the piled cumulus astern of us, maximum visibility. I land with seventy gallons, enough for two hours: the whole flight, just short of five hours, my longest ever. The boss has been back twenty minutes.

– Made it on your own, eh? What happened?

– Bloody duff engine, sir, couldn't catch up. Is Rose OK?

– Yes, landed at Langham. Losing oil pressure. We're wait-ing for Bentley and Whitelaw-Wilson. You didn't see them?

– Jesus, no. Saw no one.

– We lost contact off the Dutch coast. Must have got adrift

on the way home. Probably short of petrol and landed somewhere else. Well you boys had better get to bed. We're on standby again tonight.

No feelings of apprehension. Peter and Ian two of my closest friends in the squadron, Ian and I sharing a room at Bircham. Falling into bed already daylight. Waking five hours later, Ian's bed beside me still empty, its smooth white cover undisturbed. No, impossible. To the ops room, the CO grey-faced, up all night, no word of either aircraft. For Jesus' sake, what the hell can have happened? It slowly comes to us as another two hours go by: they've bought it. Somehow or other they've bought it. One third of the squadron wiped out on our first op. The CO's aircraft and mine the only two to have carried out the mission.

The golden farthing?

We learned months later that Peter and Maxie had come down in the sea not far from our dropping position, been picked up, taken prisoner. No other details. Never a word of Ian and Richard. After VE-day I met Peter at a Lee-on-Solent reunion. For three years, despite his still-strong accent, he had managed to keep his Free French status secret. I asked him what had happened.

– I never know. One meenit I am flying, the next I am sweeming.

That's all he could tell me.

V

A CRACK IN THE ARMOUR

Later the same day two new Stringbags were flown in to replace our losses. Soon afterwards two replacement aircrews joined us straight from flying school and we were back to full strength, nine crews and six aircraft.

We stood by at Docking till the small hours of the two nights after the debacle, armed with torpedoes, but the RAF found no targets for us. Meantime controversy surrounded our long-range tanks. They had been used successfully by at least one other Swordfish squadron, 815, which had been lent to Coastal Command for similar duties in 1940, but its pilots had all been highly experienced, with not less than 1000 hours each. Our new boys had hardly flown at all at night in Stringbags. (My own total when I joined 811 was exactly ninety-five minutes.) The boss held that our aircraft, when carrying a mine or torpedo in addition to 236 gallons of petrol, not to mention the crew and our unusable ASV, were grossly overladen, unstable and unsafe: certainly the margin for error, especially during the first hour, was practically nil. All the pilots agreed with him. The point was soon conceded: a week later the tanks were removed, we got back our TAGs and our ASV. But now our range was substantially reduced. The end of our road became the island of Terschelling, the third closest of the Friesians.

This cut down our number of possible targets. We flew

some twenty-five operations during our four months with Coastal Command. For every one we flew, however, we were two or three times on standby, waiting most of the night in vain, on windy comfortless airfields, for a suitable target to present itself, and personally I'd rather go on an op than be hanging around in flying gear till the small hours ready to scramble at fifteen minutes' notice. At first, in the general absence of enemy convoys, we were mainly engaged on minelaying, which went under the code name of 'gardening' – the mines were known as 'cucumbers' – either along the main enemy shipping lanes off the European coast, or at the approaches to such harbours as Le Havre or Ostend. Strange now to realize that a target such as Le Havre was beyond our range from Norfolk: we would fly at dusk to RAF bases in the south of England such as Manston or Thorney Island, deposit our mines as required, and return to Bircham next morning.

Our efforts were not invariably brilliant. On the night of September 15th, for instance, we were down to three serviceable aircraft, which we flew to Thorney Island for gardening off Le Havre. One of the pilots (let him be nameless) completed the sortie without hostile intervention, climbed out of the Stringbag on his return and walked with his crew across the airfield to make a precise report of his dropping position in the ops room, and none of them ever realized that the cucumber was still firmly slung under the belly of the aircraft. The pilot, who was senior enough to know better, had forgotten to make the switch that activated the release button on the throttle; hard to understand how he could have somehow failed to notice that he hadn't dropped his load. Needless to say, an immediate OIF.

The German gunners frequently pooped off at us, but it wasn't till September that I came under very close fire indeed and I must say I was lucky to get away with it. For a couple of weeks I'd been flying with a new crew. One of our new boys was an RN Lieutenant – his surname was Coy and he was therefore known as 'Bashful' – who had joined us direct from observer school. Although he was far less experienced than the RNVR subs who had been a year with 811, his

1. Commander Edwin Dunning, flying a Sopwith Pup, makes the first ever deck landing on board a British warship, HMS *Furious*, 5 August, 1917. See page 27.

2. The SS ('Submarine Searcher') 'Blimp', used in the First World War to protect convoys from submarine attack – much as Stringbags were in the Second World War. Note the semaphorist. See Appendix 1.

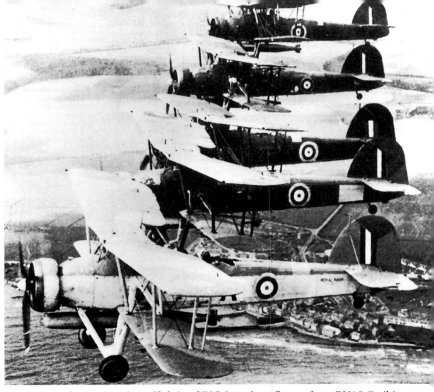

3. Torpedo-carrying Swordfish Is of 785 Squadron fly out from RNAS Crail in
   May, 1941, to 'attack' a target vessel in the Forth. See pages 33 et seq.

4. The author, then Sub-Lieutenant Godley, and his ground crew, Air Fitter
   Page (centre) and Air Mechanic Webb (right), with their Chesapeake dive
   bomber of 811 Squadron at Lee-on-Solent, August, 1941.
   See pages 48 et seq.

5. Swordfish about to land on HMS *Tracker* being directed by the batsman. Note the lowered hook and the rocket projectiles under the mainplanes.

6. Officers of 811 Squadron at RNAS Machrihanish, May, 1942. From left: Alistair Laury (killed June), Maxie Mays (PoW August), Derek Price, Bertie Ingham, Georgie Morrison (killed June), John Godley, Jock Sayer, Denis Fuller, Fred Eckersley, Harry Hayes (C.O.), Ian Whitelaw-Wilson (killed August), Alan McTuck (Senior Pilot). Absent: Peter Bentley (PoW August), Richard Townend (killed August).

7. Lieutenant-Commander Ransford Slater, OBE, DSC, RN, is greeted by Chief Officer Campbell, MN, on the flight deck of the MAC-ship *Empire MacAlpine* after the first ever landing on board a merchantman, May, 1943. See page 113.

8. The MAC-ship *Adula* newly converted. Note arrester wires and barrier with one Stringbag of 'P' flight parked forward. The ship is turning to windward to receive Godley's aircraft, from which the picture was taken by Jake Bennett, February, 1944.

two straight stripes were held to entitle him to the role of Senior Observer in place of Maxie, which the others found less than amusing. And the CO decided that I, as flight leader, should have the Senior O. for company. So I waved farewell with many regrets to Bertie, who teamed up with Pat Weir, and found myself flying with this out-and-out rooky who was however technically senior to me, though this counted for nothing in the sky. My new TAG had been flying long enough to hold the exalted rank of Petty Officer: his name was O'Nion so he was known inevitably as 'Onions'.

Before dusk on September 18th, the RAF reported a convoy of merchantmen, heavily escorted, heading westward towards the Friesian Islands but still beyond our range. We were standing by at Docking, armed with torpedoes, and at once flew the half-hour to Ludham, ten miles north-east of Norwich, where we would be fifty miles closer. (To think that fifty miles made such a difference!) By 2230 it was decided that we should be able to reach them, but we'd had no fix since night. So each crew was allocated an individual search zone. If one of us managed to find the enemy, he was to send out a sighting report; all would then hopefully rendezvous for a combined six-aircraft attack. My area was close inshore from Den Helder to Vlieland, which would take me within fifty miles of my maximum possible range. Jock Sayer had the area immediately ahead of me, off Vlieland and Terschelling, which left him no margin at all.

It took over two hours to reach Helder, and it was clear the Germans were waiting for us: I was surprised by searchlights as we made our landfall at about 200 feet and streams of gunfire at once came sailing out at me. It was tracer, probably from a battery or two of Bofors guns, and tracer of course can be seen; this helps the gunner, because he can tell where his fire is going, but it also helps the pilot, because he knows he is under fire and how best to evade it. I came under fire many times from tracer, and it's always the same: the shots when they leave the gun seem to be moving so slowly, so innocuously, so silently, like Roman candles at a firework display. But then they accelerate rapidly and lethally; you are suddenly in the thick of them. However you have had those seconds to take avoiding action. This gunfire was not accurate, and I had no trouble evading it, by making a steep diving turn to sea level. The tracer passed harmlessly above me and ahead of me; at the same time the searchlights lost contact.

We resumed our patrol and a few minutes later it happened. Without the smallest warning, eight streams of tracer, coming from dead astern, passed (as it seemed to me) a few inches above my starboard upper mainplane. I acted instantly and instinctively. Close the throttle, make the steepest possible diving turn to port. The tracer kept coming but now above me and to starboard. The immediate danger was over.

I had at once known a night fighter had picked us up. (We were able to identify it as an ME-109.) How he managed to miss us is something I have never been able to understand. It was a clear night and we were flying, fully laden, absolutely straight and level, at about eighty knots. If a Stringbag pilot gets an enemy fighter on his tail, and knows it is there – as he should – before the enemy opens fire, there shouldn't be any problem: the steepest, slowest possible turn *towards* him (to starboard if the fighter is on his starboard quarter, to port if on his port quarter) and the fighter's very much wider turning circle makes it impossible to bring his guns to bear. But on this occasion we had been well and truly jumped, a sitting duck, and by all the rules of air warfare should have been blown to smithereens.

The Messerschmitt picked us up again, but Bashful and Onions, who were responsible for keeping the lookout astern, now had their eyes skinned and saw him in good time. I took the appropriate avoiding action and he never got the chance to open fire.

We continued our patrol but Bashful soon calculated that we had gone as far as we could. We were off Vlieland; we had been flying for two-and-a-half hours and would have to bring back our torpedo, which would mean less saving of petrol going home. We landed at Ludham with ten gallons after over four hours – enough for fifteen or twenty minutes.

One of our aircraft was missing, my old friend Jock Sayer

and his observer Derek Price. But I couldn't believe it – not Jock! He'd have got away with it somehow! And sure enough he had. He had located the convoy just a few miles east of our furthermost position, and sent out a sighting report, which no one had picked up (presumably owing to his low altitude). So he had attacked on his own and thought he might have hit one of the merchantmen despite extensive flak. But he was at the very extreme limit of his range and, even without a tin-fish to bring home, ran out of petrol just as he crossed the Norfolk coast. Although it was still dark, he was somehow able to pancake in a meadow, bending his Stringbag quite badly, but he and his crew were able to walk away from it without so much as a scratch. And that's the kind of landing of which we used to say: 'If you can walk away from it, it's a good one.'

Just a few days later, the boss called me into his office and told me that Alan McTurk was leaving 811 to take up a new appointment. I felt a little thrill of anticipation. Everyone liked Mac and we'd be sorry to see him go, but after his departure I'd be the most experienced pilot in the squadron, even though my total flying time was still less than 600 hours, and the only officer left of those who joined it when it formed

– His replacement, Baldwin, is an RN two-striper. I'll have to give him the job of Senior Pilot, but he's straight from flying school. So I'm taking you on as my pilot; we'll be leading the squadron together.

– Jesus, sir. Thank you, sir.

Though I remained a sub-lieutenant, this was a very real promotion in terms of responsibility and, I suppose, prestige. The position was rather unusual since Harry was an observer; most bosses were pilots who as such led their squadrons from up-front in the driver's seat, with total leadership throughout every mission. Now I would be flying the leading aircraft; Harry, as before, would be in very definite command of the squadron from his back seat in the observer's cockpit behind me, but in many emergencies or when the flak started flying, or in the very heat of action, the immediate instinctive decisions, made within split seconds, have to be taken by the pilot – no time to wait for orders from the boss, who in any case, as an observer, would be in no position to lead the squadron fully, as a pilot can. So I moved from 'L for Love' to 'A for Apples' – a spanking new Stringbag, the replacement for one of those lost, which the boss and McTurk had pounced on as their own.

I felt just a bit chocker, I must admit, that I hadn't got the job of Senior Pilot. It was the same as happened when Bashful had been appointed as Senior O., as though Their Lordships considered that a Wavy Navy sub-loot was competent to take on the most demanding duties in the air – where the responsibilities now given me would be ten times greater than Baldwin's – but that an RN two-striper was needed for the administrative duties of Senior Pilot or Observer. Virtually all officers joining squadrons from flying school (with about 200 hours in their logbooks, fewer than fifty in first-line aircraft) were RNVR subs who had joined the service like the rest of us as bluejackets. But a few were career officers who after four or five years on general duties had specialized in aviation. They had precisely the same flying experience as the others on their training course, but stepped at once into senior positions in the squadrons. (One such officer on my own course had been below average as a pilot and it was only by great good fortune that my Stringbag and I were not scattered over a mountain as a direct result of his irresponsible leadership.)

Thus it happened that in 811, engaged on demanding and hazardous operations, we now had a makey-learn pilot as Senior P. as well as a makey-learn observer as Senior O., whilst most of their subordinates could fly rings round them and had to act as their wet nurses. This, in my own experience, was typical of the attitude of straight-ringed officers in general, and Their Lordships in particular, towards us of the Wavy Navy.

But the boss, Harry Hayes, was our undisputed leader, our much-respected Ahab, wiser and more experienced than any of us by years. To be his pilot, to share leading the squadron with him in action, would be a privilege I'd never dared to dream of.

Flying was suddenly different during the three months I flew with him. With Bertie or Bashful, if I flew carelessly or bent the rules a bit, I knew they would cover up for me just as I would do for them. With the boss in the back, I had to concentrate every minute on flying as damn well as I could, especially with the rest of the squadron astern of me. Nothing could have compelled me to become a far more accomplished and more responsible pilot more quickly.

It happened that the very first time we flew together was on the most eventful, exciting operation yet.

At 1553 on the afternoon of September 25th, an enemy convoy of fourteen merchantmen, heavily escorted, was sighted by an RAF reconnaissance aircraft. Like the previous week's, it was heading west-south-west off the outermost Friesian Islands. The nights were now much longer and it seemed certain that it would come within our range in the hours of darkness. Two Bircham Newton squadrons were ordered to stand by, ourselves and the Lockheed Hudsons of 320, an outfit of Dutch exiles who took special delight in plundering the shipping lanes of their homeland. We were down to five serviceable aircraft each – such was the relatively minuscule scale of Coastal Command ops in 1942. Our Stringbags were armed in readiness with torpedoes, except Denis Fuller's which was to act as flare-dropper, and the Dutch Hudsons with bombs – four 250-pounders each. (It was a remarkable fact that our single-engined biplanes could carry nearly twice the war-load of the sophisticated Lockheeds. At less than half the speed, it had to be admitted, but who's in a hurry?)

Before dark we flew those precious fifty miles to Ludham, unnecessary for the Dutchmen but for us perhaps decisive, and sat round playing poker, revived by tea and sandwiches, waiting for word from the ops room as on so many previous nights. At 2300 we received confirmation from a Hudson on recce that the convoy had passed Borkum, and would certainly come within our range not more than five hours later. So we'd get them.

The plan was that the Hudsons would carry out a medium level bombing attack between 0400 and 0410. One of them, known as the rooster, would fly on ahead, locate the target, and 'roost' at a safe height over it, so that the rest of the squadron could home on it, thus saving time and making navigation simple. The primitive radar in our Swordfish allowed of no such luxury. From 0410 to 0420, the Hudsons were to stooge around at 3000 feet, just out of range of gun-fire, hopefully drawing attention from our Stringbags, which had those same ten minutes in which to come doddering in at sea level and launch our tin-fish from a range of 800 yards or so.

Our departure was timed for 0215. The Hudsons would scramble nearly an hour later and get there well before us. Taking off first for the first time ever! The rest of the squadron forming up quickly on me as I made the long slow turn to the course the boss had given me: Denis, as flare-dropper, tucked in on my port quarter, the other three – Baldwin, Mike and Pat in extended echelon starboard. A tail wind to help us but a pitch black night. Course set for Vlieland. A hundred minutes' flying by the compass and then needing no radar to home on 320's rooster. At 0355, from a range of ten miles, seeing the long streams of multi-coloured tracer streaking up at him – we could home on it visually, no trouble.

The enemy convoy was now heading south-west, some five miles offshore. Our plan was to come from the east on its port quarter, that's to say from landward. So we detached Denis Fuller, who was to start dropping flares to the west of our target at 0410; it should thus be silhouetted between us and his flares. I then led the rest of the squadron (from now on the tactics of the attack were completely in my hands) at 1500 feet in a wide circle astern of the convoy, out of range of their gunfire. At 0400 the Dutch boys began their attack, and every gun was blazing at them. With any luck the din created would drown the modest rumble of our engines and enable some of us to sneak in undetected.

We reached our attacking position on time and made a wide orbit waiting for the flares. All this while, the brilliant streams of tracer, streaking vertically upwards at the Hud-sons as they attacked, showed me the convoy's exact position though as yet I could not see it. Then the first of the flares, descending on its parachute like an artificial moon, and the whole target plainly visible. Without any word or signal – for the whole manoeuvre had been rehearsed so often that we all knew what to do – I closed my throttle and peeled off in a diving turn towards it. The rest would follow behind me at intervals of five seconds; it was each man for himself.

Losing height steeply and silently towards the enemy vessels as the long line of brightly-glowing flares now lightened the whole night sky ahead of me beyond them. I could quickly pick out what seemed the largest of the merchantmen, make the best possible estimate of her course and speed and size. Alter course whilst diving to come in a bit ahead of her port beam. Get quickly to sea level, leave time enough to lose speed to under 100 knots before letting go the tin-fish. The CO's voice laconically over the intercomm.

– Good luck, boy.

– Thanks, sir. I'm going for the big one.

Reaching seventy feet, opening up the throttle, barely skirting the waves. Well within range of their guns now, but still no answering fire. Flying straight and level, speed ninety-five, height fifty feet, range perhaps half a mile. I take careful, deliberate aim and press the tit.

Three seconds later, as I go into my getaway with the steepest of turns to starboard, all hell breaks loose around me. It was precisely now, as my torpedo splashed into the water and headed towards its target, that the whole bloody convoy seemed to open up on me. Was it the splash they saw? Or, I wondered afterwards, had they already spotted me but thought such an antique biplane must be a training aircraft of their own that had somehow managed to wander on the scene? However that might be, I was now in the thick of tracer, seemed to be coming from everywhere.

– Starboard, turn to starboard, came the CO's terse command. (He was better placed in the back to see where the heaviest fire was coming.) I shoved the stick hard over.

– Now come hard a-port. Hold her there. Keep as low as you can. Now starboard.

I was using full boost override; with my load gone and the petrol tank half-empty, I soon reached 110. It seemed an hour but can't have been much more than a minute before the gunfire began to fall astern of us and much of it had now been redirected at the others as they followed me.

– Do you think we may have got her, sir?

– I don't know. You made a good attack but with all the flak coming at us I couldn't observe results.

Not surprising. It would have taken a good minute for my torpedo to reach its target and then we were in the thick of it. Impossible to watch one particular vessel when we ourselves were struggling for survival.

We were to make our ways home individually. I flew in a wide circle, back astern of the convoy, and we carefully surveyed the aircraft for any sign of damage. It seemed unbelievable but we could find none. Our faithful Pegasus was humming away happily, there'd been no loss of petrol, no fall in oil pressure, all controls normal. As we could confirm when safely back on the ground, not a single shell had struck us.

A strange event tantalized us as we wheeled and turned for home. The last of the flares had dowsed itself as it fell into the ocean but star-lit visibility was about a mile though we were still keeping low. And ahead of us, isolated, there now loomed a shape – a shape that became quickly the shadowy silhouette of a very large merchantman, beam on, unescorted and stationary. A sitting duck I couldn't possibly have missed and no way of attacking her.

The journey home was uneventful and we landed at 0600. The Hudsons of 320 had been back nearly an hour. All our Stringbags came home safely. The last to land were Pat and Bertie. It was Pat's first operation – he probably had no more than some four or five previous hours of night flying in Stringbags – and he'd managed to fly at under 100 feet over the whole damn convoy without launching his tin-fish. He was hit a dozen times, but turned back and made a second run in darkness after the last of the flares had gone. His was the only aircraft in either squadron to be damaged.

All our boys had pressed home their attacks but none

made any claims. Then came word that the last Hudson to leave the area had clearly seen, at 0425, the glow of a burning vessel. And an RAF recce at first light reported three damaged merchantmen. So some of us began to have second thoughts.

– I couldn't see my target clearly but maybe I was lucky.

– Like I said, I dropped a wee bit high but the tin-fish may have run OK.

– My dropping position was perfect but we couldn't observe results, I said. Too much flak, too busy taking avoiding action.

And so it may have been at 0413 that morning, or thereabouts, that I first killed a human being – unless one of my mines had already blown a few to pieces. Today that possibility, however remote, whatever the circumstances, would totally appal me. In 1942 I exulted in it. Didn't really think consciously that there were men going about their duties in that merchantman, no different from any others, with wives and mothers and children. It was all totally impersonal. I'd been taught to attack shipping, it was my job, what I was ordered to do, what was expected of me. Human life, hard though it is to accept it now, never entered into it. And, if it had, I would have felt no guilt and readily dismissed the thought. Weren't they only bloody Jerries? *

We stood by again that night but no suitable target presented itself. With nine crews and six aircraft there were always three crews off-duty and next evening we were one of those stood down. The boss had the use of a car and he suggested to the five of us a booze-up in King's Lynn, the nearest town of any size. There'd probably be a dance on and we'd pick up a bunch of popsies. You bet, sir! Chocks away!

* I have recently (1995) seen the official report made at the time by the enemy. The convoy was bound from the Elbe to the Hook. It comprised nine merchantmen, not fourteen as we'd been told, with eight flak-carrying escort vessels. They claimed one Hudson shot down (it wasn't) and one torpedo-bomber 'probably' shot down, which must have been Pat Weir's. They didn't know Pat! The report admits 'a number of near misses' but claims no major damage was caused. But they would say that, wouldn't they?

As we walked out to the car, the boss gave me a grin.

– I can't see this lasting much longer. May as well make the most of what time we have.

He said it in such an off-hand way that I didn't realize what he meant and probably just grinned back. Then I fell to thinking about it. *What* wouldn't last much longer? There hadn't been any buzz that we'd be leaving Coastal, maybe going to sea. We had all the time in the world left. Even when *Archer* was eventually ready – if we were still destined for *Archer* – there'd be many more evenings ashore. What ever did he mean?

It slowly came through to me as we drove past the sentries and bumped towards King's Lynn along the dusty country road. The boss was quite casually informing me that in the near future we were most likely to be bumped off, to buy it. ('Killed' was a word we never ever used.) This realization had a very deep effect on me, so that still after all these years I can clearly see the CO's face as he passed that sentence in those brief sentences. And of course he was perfectly right. In a couple of months we had now lost nearly half the squadron, and on a mathematical basis we should indeed have little time to 'make the most of it'. Yet right up to now I had this unshakeable conviction that I would always get away with it no matter how long the odds – an absurd fallacy I can't begin to explain, however clearly I remember it. Now, coming from the boss with all the respect I had for him, and in such an offhand manner as though he were speaking about the weather, those words made me consider the possibility – even now, no more than that – of death being just round the corner. They made the first small crack in the silver armour of wholly irrational confidence in personal immortality in which I had encased myself, the first of many that would strike that armoured suit, one blow after another during the next three years, till it lay scattered in pieces around me.

After several nights of standing by at Docking, our next op should have been a gardening run from Manston but my logbook records laconically: 'Engine caught fire on starting, so negative Ostend.' We all three sprung swiftly from the Stringbag as flames enveloped the circular cowling of the Pegasus; they extinguished themselves before the arrival of the fire tender and Peggy seemed none the worse for it but by the time she had been checked over and restarted the rest of the squadron were halfway to their target. Two nights later we were gardening off Den Helder – no problems – and then followed a series of fruitless nights standing by at Docking, waiting in vain for the RAF to find a target for us off Holland or Belgium.

Increasingly tiresome, these dark hours of tension. It was late October, the nights colder and longer, we had to be ready to scramble at any time between sunset and the small hours. And no facilities at the windy little airfield with its drafty tents and rickety tables beyond cups of cocoa and sandwiches. At the end of the month, word came from above that we were moving our main base from Bircham Newton to Thorney Island, a well equipped Coastal Command air station – it actually had runways – between Portsmouth and Chichester. From here the French coast from Cherbourg to Dunkirk would be within our tiny range and it was hoped this would prove more fruitful. And we could spend our nights on stand-by in the relative Ritz-like luxury of the Officers' Mess itself.

But first, heaven be praised, we were to get a full week's leave, already overdue. I was still engaged to Angel but she'd been a WAAF for over a year, our leaves seldom coincided and we'd slowly been drifting apart. I thought of going home to Killegar but found myself on the phone that evening to Betsy, a long-legged blonde I'd met and laid in Edinburgh, that ever-fruitful hunting-ground, a few months earlier on a weekend from Machrihanish. Yes of course she remembered me. Yes she could make it to London. Yes of course. Yes. We arranged to meet at the Cumberland Hotel.

Betsy was very old – she must have been nearly thirty – and had a husband in the rag trade (and the background). I passed an instructive week. When it was over, before I'd even left London, I was assailed by dire remorse and wrote a long letter to Angel telling her all about it. A week at the

Cumberland with a middle-aged married woman! And if I could do *that*, I asked, how could I truly love her? What kind of a husband would I make? And so on.

A pity perhaps. We broke it off but both returned to Oxford after the war, have kept in touch ever since and are still good friends. Who knows, it might have worked. In any case it could hardly have been less lasting than either of the marriages we contracted not much later.

Back once more on the well-remembered Portsmouth train. A busy six weeks ahead, with eleven squadron sorties (of which I took part in nine) despite the winter weather. A whole new enemy coast to explore: gardening off Cherbourg and Le Havre, reconnaissances from Havre to Boulogne or from Cap Barfleur to the Somme, patrols against E-boats in mid Channel, escorting allied convoys. We encountered frequent opposition but never lost an aircraft. Not all our ops were brilliant. On November 10th we were down as often happened to five serviceable aircraft. One pilot got bogged in the mud and had to be left behind. Another failed to locate Cherbourg, which must have taken some doing with its searchlights as busy as usual. Three cucumbers our only output. And the boss and I had a near escape.

Entirely due to my carelessness. Approaching the entrance to the harbour, flying close inshore at fifty feet, airspeed ninety knots, the searchlights sweeping low on the water ahead of us. But as each beam moves towards us I ease back on the stick to climb over it or forward to pass under. Shadowy silhouettes of the main harbour installations now visible, within range of even the lightest machine-guns but my matt-black Stringbag not yet seen. Plonk goes my cucumber in the narrow harbour entrance, then hard a-starboard for home.

A minute later the angry voice of the boss.

– For Christ's sake get back to fifty feet. What the hell are you doing?

Shoving the stick forward without even checking the altimeter. Realising I'd allowed her to climb to nearly 300 feet, as a Stringbag was wont to do after dropping her load if you let her. And then, not more than two seconds later, six bursts of heavy flak going *whoomph whoomph whoomph* some fifty feet above us and ahead of us. The Stringbag buffeted but unscathed as I screech to the safety of the wavetops.

I knew well what had happened. We'd been picked up by radar. I'd unintentionally climbed high enough for our blip to appear on their screen. If I'd stayed at sea level, they'd never have known we were there. We had survived, as could so often happen with Stringbags and would happen to me several times again, because they simply couldn't believe we were going so absurdly slowly as their sophisticated equipment must have indicated. Perhaps 120, possibly 100, but surely not ninety-five! And so they missed slightly ahead. They were those few feet above us because of the CO's terse order to dedigitate forthwith, which must have come just as they opened fire.

A buzz went the rounds soon afterwards that *Archer* was finally ready for us and heading for Scapa Flow. This seemed to be confirmed when the boss gave us the definite news that we'd be leaving shortly for Hatston in the Orkneys. I flew my last op under Coastal Command on December 16th. Two days later the squadron set forth on the long flight north: four hours to Donibristle, two days' break in Edinburgh (Betsy again) whilst they recamouflaged our Stringbags, then four more hours to Hatston. We were to get ten days' leave, then to sea at last. Or so I fondly imagined.

I very nearly didn't even get my leave. The day we reached the Orkneys I met my old friend Ivor Faulconer, who had been a fellow-rebel at Eton and on my pilots' course. He now held the scarcely elevated position of Shagbat pilot in the battleship *King George V,* which we'd seen lying at anchor in Scapa Flow as we flew in. The Shagbat, as the Supermarine Walrus was known without much affection, was a truly monstrous invention: a single-engined amphibious biplane with a pusher prop, the only aircraft in service that was slower – by a knot or two – than the Stringbag. Yet designed by the company responsible for the Spitfire. Most battle-

ships and many cruisers carried a Shagbat capable of reconnaissance or spotting but very little more: she would be
launched by catapult from her parent vessel and on return,
taking on the role of flying-boat, would come down in the
sea alongside to be hoisted inboard by crane. However the
senior officers in such warships were far from renowned for
their airmindedness and their Shagbats were seldom used,
unless to bring the Admiral to a conference or the Captain
to a cocktail party.

The *K.G.V* was sailing in a day or two on a three-week
sweep of the Arctic in the hope of finding *Tirpitz*. Ivor now
on the point of rejoining her.

– Like to come for a flip? We can have a bit of a session,
you can get a boat ashore tonight.

An hour later Ivor was putting her down in the placid
water of Scapa and taxiing alongside. We'd hardly been
hoisted inboard when we chanced to meet the Commander.
He gave me an icy glare.

– Hey, Faulconer! Who's this young feller-me-lad?

– A guest of mine, sir. Brought him aboard for a gin.

– It's more than a bloody gin he'll get. We're sailing in an
hour, no more boats ashore.

Just like that. Not another word. The full extent of my
plight came extremely quickly home to me. *K.G.V*'s departure had been put forward but no one had told Ivor. I was
now marooned aboard her and would be spending my
Christmas leave in almost continual darkness, tossing on
stormracked and icebound waters, with the off-chance of a
major engagement if the enemy should be sighted.

– Well we'd better have that gin.

We were on our second or third – duty-free gin in those
happy far-off days was one old penny a tot – when an urgent
message reached us from the Officer of the Watch. A boat
of a kind seemed to be heading our way.

Dashing to the ship's side. Through the gathering dusk, a
leaky looking bum-boat with a solitary occupant, its pop-
poppop engine now surely directing her towards us. A ladder thrown over the side, down which I scramble. A cargo of
fresh vegetables is hoisted aboard the flagship. I leap into

the bows. Ten minutes later, well on our way to Kirkwall, and *K.G.V* has slipped quietly from her moorings and is heading for open sea.

I went to Oxford for Christmas, where my mother had a temporary abode – all her abodes were temporary – then on to Killegar for a few days of Irish peace. No way. My smiling stepmother greeted me with the green-enveloped telegram brought by bicycle from Killeshandra at lunch-time: RETURN HATSTON FORTHWITH. Forbidden to discuss past or planned activities even with family, I was left with silent speculation. I assumed *Archer* had arrived ahead of her oft-postponed schedule and we'd be joining her at once. Next day hitched a ride in a Sparrow from Belfast to Turnhouse where the weather closed in, but the day after by DH-86 to Hatston. No one else there from 811. It was Hogmanay and everyone getting pissed. Badly hung over, summoned by Commander (Flying) next morning.

– Happy New Year. Sorry to have recalled you. You've been appointed to HMS *Excellent*.

Excellent? What the hell was going on? This was no ship despite the HMS but a naval barracks on Whale Island near Portsmouth, universally known and detested as the most spit-and-polish, bullshitty, disciplinarian establishment in the entire Royal Navy. So far as I knew, it had never had any association with flying.

– But how about the squadron, sir? We're on the point of embarkation.

– I'm afraid it looks as though you won't be sailing with them. You're due for a rest, you know. Eighteen months in a front line squadron.

I was appalled. There was nothing whatever Commander (F) could do about it, I was to leave for Portsmouth immediately. He could only suggest that I submit a request to be sent back again when I arrived there. Well for the love of Jesus. Perhaps I might be due for the so-called 'rest period' that was supposed to come eventually to all aircrew who survived an unspecified length of time in the front line, but it was too much to depart on the very eve of sailing.

'You'll never see the *Archer* in the Clyde...' Was it to be true then?

At *Excellent*, where everyone wore gaiters and tore about at the double on an unending expanse of asphalt saluting anything that moved, I found the news even worse than I'd feared. A dozen pilots, hand-picked for this distinction, were to be trained as Air Gunnery Officers, a newly-created post dreamed up over Whitehall tea-cups. A two- or three-month course. Each would then be appointed to a carrier where he'd be in sole charge of all aircraft ordnance – bombs, guns, ammo, depth charges, torpedoes. We were summoned before the Captain. This was an honour, he told us, a recognition of our power of command, sense of responsibility, qualities of leadership. We would receive accelerated promotion to the exalted rank of Lieutenant.

– But how about flying, sir, I dared to enquire.

Oh we wouldn't be flying any more. Perhaps an occasional air test. But no appointment to a squadron.

Despair descended. Flying still my delight and joy, my life. Bugger the recognition, they just couldn't do this to me. I at once submitted a passionate letter to the Captain having the honour to request, etc., that I be returned forthwith to my squadron, etc., and stating my reasons in no uncertain terms. Meantime I set out to show conclusively, beyond the smallest doubt, that I was totally unsuitable in every possible way for the distinction chosen for me. It had all been a frightful mistake! No officer has ever before shown such abysmal ignorance of how machine-guns and tin-fish worked, nor such total inability to learn. I would return from evenings 'ashore', half seas over, singing flying songs fortissimo. I was always late on parade. I wore battledress in the wardroom: this comfortable rig was beginning to be favoured by aircrews though not officially approved and was unknown outside the Branch. I could pull a Browning to pieces with some difficulty but couldn't put it together again. I lost my gas mask.

My request to rejoin 811 was turned down, but in seventeen days I convinced everyone at *Excellent* that I would never, never make it as an Air Gunnery Officer. And for my 'rest' I was appointed to the Admiral's staff at nearby Lee-on-Solent, where I'd first joined the squadron in far-off Chesapeake days.

The Admiral, known by the acronym of RANAS, for Rear Admiral Naval Air Stations, was responsible for the administration of all naval aviation ashore in the UK. My first act on reaching his headquarters, which adjoined the little airfield I already knew so well, was to submit a similar request but this too was unsuccessful, though addressed to RANAS in person – Rear-Admiral Clement Moody. He was sympathetic but firm. I set about my unwonted duties as a staff officer, of which I knew far less than of air gunnery, in fact nothing, only a little bit consoled by the knowledge that this was now no more than a temporary sentence, that I'd eventually return to front-line flying duties.

Soon afterwards, in March, 'my' squadron, as I continued to think of 811, became the first to enter the Battle of the Atlantic, at long last, over a year later than planned. As I was soon to learn, they were reallocated at the last moment to *Biter*, which along with *Dasher* became available to fight the U-boats on returning from the Med, a few weeks before *Archer*. The jinx on the Woolworths continued. *Dasher* blew up and sank on the Clyde after turning back with engine trouble on her first convoy. *Archer's* sorry story was to end in October, after only two sorties, when she was 'reduced to care and maintenance', in other words retired, with new defects beyond economical repair.

But the appearance on the North Atlantic scene of *Biter* and *Archer* made a vital contribution to the long-awaited turning of the tide that was about to take place in the hard-fought Battle of the Atlantic. By chance it coincided with the regaining by the Enigma code-breakers at the Government Code and Cipher School (GCCS) at Bletchley Park of the ability to decode – and to decode ever more quickly – the signals passing so recklessly between U-boats and their bases, often giving their positions and future movements. Right up to the end of the war, the enemy never tumbled to Bletchley's skills. Amazing! This coincided with ever-improv-

ing techniques by the growing number of escorting warships. On May 22nd, which would happen to be my wedding
day, it is now known that all U-boats were ordered to sus-
pend attacks on North Atlantic convoys and they were not
resumed till September. In a month, forty-one had been
destroyed, a quarter of all those at sea, and the date is recognized as a vital landmark in the fight to defeat the U-boat
menace. To these victories my former comrades made a
handsome contribution, whilst I myself was bravely pushing
a pen.

A desk in a grey office. Shared with Alec Fraser-Harris, a
young two-and-a-halfer who was Staff Officer (Operations).
We were known as SOO and SOO-2. I had an in tray and an
out tray. A varied assortment of documents appeared at
intervals in the former. On each of which I was expected to
propose action, then transfer it to the latter. This I did to
the best of my ability, somehow never imagining that any
notice would be taken of the minutes of a Wavy Navy sub,
no matter how well I drafted them as I gained confidence,
and being greatly surprised to come across many of them
approved verbatim, turning up as Admiralty Fleet Orders, or
headed sheets reproving officers much senior to myself, or
letters to the Admiralty (which had to begin with the for-
mula 'Be pleased to represent to Their Lordships').

Missed the squadron like hell and was green with envy
when I read of their exploits. But once I had finally
accepted that such a rest period was an inescapable feature
of an operational pilot's life, I began in a way to enjoy it,
especially for example when I could propose a letter to the
Captain of an Air Station ordering him to endorse his own
logbook for negligent flying, which he duly had to do.

My rest period wasn't always so damned restful. I managed to wangle a flight from time to time and on one of
these would quite certainly have perished if I hadn't dis-
obeyed one of the cardinal rules of flying. In the workshops
of the adjoining airfield, a badly pranged Stringbag had
been in for extensive repairs and now required a flight test.
This was just the kind of flip for which I happily volun-

teered, and was to take with me the fitter, Renshaw by name, who had done the work on the engine. The day had already been memorable because Ralph Richardson had turned up flying a Shagbat, which he'd parked near the control tower on the southern perimeter of the airfield. He and Laurence Olivier were both serving in the Fleet Air Arm on non-operational duties. The wind was southerly, from the sea, and I taxied the Stringbag halfway to the northern perimeter, all I'd need for take-off, ran up the engine, turned into wind and opened up.

Everything seemed normal but at just over 100 feet as we approached the control tower, climbing steeply at seventy knots, my Pegasus stopped dead. No warning, just silence. The elastic, as we used to say, had broken My third total engine failure.

Now the cardinal rule, never supposed to be broken if your engine fails on take-off, is *never turn back*. There's too great a danger of spinning. Carry on straight ahead and plonk down where you can. That was all very well but at this instant as I approached the perimeter the sizeable town of Lee-on-Solent, sandwiched between sea and airfield, was spreading out ahead of me. Carry on straight ahead and I'd have pancaked in the shopping centre. Curtains. Curtains for me, curtains for Renshaw, curtains for God knows how many others. So I made the split second decision that rules were made for breaking: forward with the stick, then the steepest possible turn to starboard to try to keep her within the airfield. I was semi-stalled as we twisted earthward at something over fifty but the dear old Stringbag never dreamed of spinning. We 'landed' with a terrible crump, writing off the undercart, shock-loading the engine as the prop ploughed into the ground, and neatly removing the tail of Ralph Richardson's Shagbat with my port mainplanes. But we could both walk away from it.

I was absolved of all blame and indeed commended for 'prompt if unorthodox action' to avoid causing 'possibly heavy loss of civilian lives'. Not to mention my own and Renshaw's.

The nights had been promiscuous since Angel and I broke up. In reaction, which was somehow associated with my temporary respite from the uncertainties of operational flying, I found myself going steady with a pretty little Wren who worked in nearby *St Vincent*. Penny's father, Rear-Admiral Cecil Reyne, was one of those gallant senior officers who came out of retirement as soon as war broke out for the arduous duties at sea of Commodore (Convoy) and was not deterred from returning to them when, the previous Christmas, he had his ship sunk under him at the age of sixty-one. He'd be knighted next year. Penny lived with her family in nearby Alverstoke and it was delightful to spend evenings in the home atmosphere of Brookfield instead of the pubs-and-hops life to which I'd grown accustomed. Apart from other things she mended my socks, pressed my tie, even repaired my shirts.

Despite her ministrations I fell ill at the end of April: exhaustion, high temperature, loss of appetite. It took some days in the sick-bay for glandular fever to be diagnosed and I was carted off to hospital. This happened to be a former mental home near Basingstoke, which the Navy had taken over for treating infectious diseases. But it still had its previous trappings, or lack of them: no handles on the inside of the doors or on the bath taps, and a couple of padded cells (unoccupied), adjacent to one of which my private room was located.

The infection subsided after a week or two and I began to feel something like myself again. Penny said she'd try to visit me and I remember being touched by her kindness in coming all that way to see me for three hours. During those three hours I asked her to marry me. I'd been told that convalescence was often long and I'd be getting a month's leave: this seemed a chance that might never recur for more than a week-long honeymoon. So we fixed the day for soon after my expected discharge.

Thus I became engaged, my lymph nodes still infected with *mononucleosis,* in the Basingstoke madhouse next door to a padded cell.

On our return from Ireland we set up house in a furnished room in Lee. Penny biked daily to *Vincent* and I to FONAS (for Flag Officer Naval Air Stations), as RANAS in the meantime had mysteriously become. I was apparently quite recovered but my blood count, said the doctors, was not yet right (too many leukocytes) and I couldn't rejoin an operational squadron till the red cells had restored the *status quo*. Meantime I managed to get an increasing amount of flying. There was a derogatory phrase we used – 'He flies like a married man' – and I wanted to be sure it would never apply to *me*. (It didn't for two more years.) So I kept my hand in whenever I could get hold of a Stringbag or a Proctor.

As my red cells proliferated, my return to action came closer. Alex Fraser-Harris asked me if I had any preference and he could probably fix it for me. Barracudas and Avengers were now in service, the former a gremlin-ridden Fairey product no one liked, the latter an American bomber supplied by Grumman under lease-lend, both actual monoplanes, more resembling World War II aircraft though far behind the RAF's. Or I could have opted for Albacores, but these no one had *ever* liked. The Stringbag was the lady I knew and loved; I determined to be faithful to her. In early September I was appointed to 836. The aircraft it flew were Swordfish and it was based at Maydown in County Derry. It had been my first choice.

At the same time I was recommended for the accelerated promotion that I'd forgone when I got *Excellent* to sack me. But I was still flying. It had been worth the wait.

VI

COBRAS AND CROCODILES

Penny was due for some leave. We planned to travel to Derry by way of Belfast and Killegar. If we left Lee-on-Solent after work on the Wednesday, my last day as SOO-2, we'd be home the following evening. I was to report to Maydown on the Sunday but there weren't any Sunday trains so we'd be less than two days at Killegar. The packed-full train to Heysham for the night crossing, I with all my worldly goods in one large kitbag and one green pusser's suitcase. Then disaster. A highly officious Security Control Officer, always remembered as Captain Low, DSO (an army Captain, a mere pongo), notices that although in uniform we are going to the Free State. We explain we intend to change clothes in Belfast, post our uniforms to Derry. He won't wear it. So we dash to our respective heads, the boat on the point of sailing, change into civvies, present ourselves again with uniforms packed away. The eagle eye of Captain Low, DSO, still awaiting us. You can't take your uniforms to the Free State.

– We're *not* taking them. We're posting them on to Derry, where I have to report on Sunday.

All to no avail. Too late to phone FONAS and the boat sails without us. I in fury, Penny in tears.

We head for nearby Morecambe, where Captain Low, DSO, has his headquarters, to be on the spot to resume hostilities next morning. All hotels are full or too expensive. We

end up on palliasses in an RAF guard room. A restless night.
Next morning to Security and I get through to Fraser-Harris.
– Let me speak to the bugger.
The girl on the switchboard, a tight-skirted AT, allowed
me to listen in. Alec (who had been my best man and was
now proving his worth) managed to make it sound as
though FONAS himself was speaking. Captain Low, DSO,
grovelled. Yes sir. I deeply regret sir. I quite understand sir.
So we were first on board that night. We would now be at
Killegar less than twenty-four hours but a telegram from
Alec extended my leave by a day in compensation, so we
didn't have to depart till the Monday morning. And therefore had half a day more at home than we'd originally
expected, thanks to the gallant Captain.

By train on Monday from Cavan across the border to
Omagh, by bus from Omagh to Derry, where we put up at
the City Hotel. And later that evening to Maydown. A windy
little airfield not far from Lough Foyle, across which the
mountains of Donegal were frequently visible. 'If you can
see the mountains, it means it's going to rain; if you can't
see them it means it's raining' – such was the local dictum.
The conditions were primitive, a collection of Nissen huts, a
toy-like control tower, often a sea of mud, yet this was the
headquarters of the squadron that would grow to be by far
the largest in the Navy.
As I knew already, it had been formed six months earlier,
in March 1943, to provide the personnel and aircraft for the
succession of MAC-ships, as Merchant Aircraft Carriers were
universally known, that would become operational in the
course of the next twelve months. MAC-ships, not to be confused with CAM-ships of which I've written already, were the
result of going all out, at last, on Captain Slattery's proposal
in 1940 for the protection of Allied convoys: the fitting of
'the simplest possible flight decks' to existing merchantmen. The jinx-ridden escort carriers were far more elaborate conversions than he'd intended and with the exception
of *Audacity* took much too long to complete. The MAC-ships
really had the simplest possible flight decks – and the small-

est – so their conversion was sometimes completed in as little as five months. And they would continue to sail with Merchant Navy crews, and to carry their normal cargoes, as Slattery had suggested.

They were either grainships or tankers. These, unlike almost all other merchantmen, can easily be adapted to load and unload their cargoes despite a flight deck running the full breadth and almost the full length of the ship. (Grain is handled through trunkways as though it were a liquid.) Their flight decks were minuscule, with a uniform width of just sixty-two feet. Those of the grainships were somewhat shorter, varying from 413 to 424 feet, than those of the tankers (460 feet). But the grainers had a hangar below-decks aft, complete with lift, giving room for four Stringbags with wings folded. The tankers – alone among carriers – had no hangar, so their aircraft, when not airborne or ashore, were permanently on the flight deck. And because the first pilot airborne therefore had aircraft astern of him, which reduced the take-off run available, it meant that three Stringbags were the most they could operate. The absence of a hangar meant they were always exposed to the elements, which did them no good at all, and often made maintenance work difficult and unpleasant, if not impossible.

The decision to go ahead with MAC-ships had been taken the previous June (1942) when work was started on the first two grainships, *Empire MacAlpine* and *Empire MacAndrew*. By October it had been decided to convert ten more, four tankers and six grainers. Their Lordships were now so sold on the concept that an eventual total of thirty-two was considered. This was to be cut to nineteen; the last seven were tankers. *Empire MacAlpine* was ready the following April and operational in May. She was followed in July by *Rapana*, the first tanker conversion, which involved less extensive work and therefore took less time than the grainships'. *Empire MacAndrew* was completed soon afterwards. The remainder came into service in the course of the months ahead at irregular intervals.*

---

* For details of all MAC-ships, see Appendix 3.

The MAC-ship's design was brilliant. It was easy to see the splendid simplicity of the conversion. Just about everything below the level of the flight deck was unchanged, apart from adding some extra accommodation for the 'air party' as we were known, so that the outline of the original merchant-man was still clearly detectable. Above that level, everything chopped off, in particular the smokestack (for which a hori-zontal funnel was substituted) and the bridge. The all-welded flight deck with half-a-dozen arrester wires was built with telescopic joints to allow for contraction and expan-sion. The usual 'island', constructed like any other carrier's on the starboard side some way forward of amidships, housed the bridge, wheelhouse, and control platform, with the chart room below – this the MAC-ship's nerve centre.

She would be joined as she neared completion by her Air Staff Officer (ASO), an RNVR two-and-a-halfer immediately responsible for all Navy personnel aboard, not only the air party but also the doctor, the batsman, the ten ship's gun-ners, four signalmen and three or four ABs. Like all of these he came under the Master's overall command though in practice this was never exercised. The ASO's primary task was to organize the flying details, first during working-up, then as might be ordered during the passage of each convoy by the Senior Officer in the escorting warships (SOE). The Master had the same crew of officers and men as in an unconverted vessel, with perhaps an extra mate and an extra 'sparks'.

As each MAC-ship neared completion, a new flight would be formed for her at Maydown: three or four Stringbags as appropriate with their aircrews and maintenance unit. With half-a-dozen spare flights, there was eventually a total of 92 aircraft in the squadron, which made it not only at least four times larger than any other in the Navy but in a special way unique. Instead of being a single cohesive unit that flew and fought together, its component flights became autonomous when at sea, under their own flight commanders, though still very much part of 836.

The routine was always the same. Each new flight, identi-fied by a letter in alphabetical order as it was formed, from

'A' Flight onwards, would have four or five weeks at May-down to get together before flying to join its newly converted parent vessel as she steamed down the Firth of Clyde from her anchorage at Gourock. A month of trials in the Clyde. The MAC-ship would then join the next available North Atlantic convoy, her clutch of Stringbags providing air cover when needed. On approaching the coast of Canada, these convoys would split in two: some vessels would be destined for New York or other US ports, the others for Halifax, Nova Scotia. The MAC-ships' western terminal was almost always Halifax. Her aircraft, or such as were still serviceable, would fly ashore to the RCAF airfield at nearby Dartmouth as soon as the safety of coastal waters had been reached. Five or ten days ashore whilst the MAC-ship took on her cargo and awaited the departure of the next homeward-bound convoy; this was known as 'turning round'. The process was then repeated: on nearing the coast of Ireland we would fly our serviceable aircraft ashore to Maydown, wait while the MAC-ship turned round at Gourock, and so on *ad infinitum*.

So it would soon happen, about two years later than it should have done, that no North Atlantic convoy would lack air cover against U-boats at any stage. It was very seldom indeed that a U-boat could work effectively in weather that grounded Stringbags, and before long there was at least one MAC-ship, sometimes two or three, accompanying each convoy. Their presence made a handsome contribution to the effective final victory in the long-fought Battle of the Atlantic.

The U-boats, after licking their wounds since May, resumed their assault in September, the month I joined the squadron. They now worked in packs and about 150 of them were soon operational. But the continuous availability of air cover and greatly improved techniques by surface escorts would force them, for the most part, to abandon pack tactics by November and rely mainly on individual attacks. They achieved little success. Between September 1943 and May 1944, only sixteen merchantmen in North Atlantic convoys would be sunk by U-boats (compared with a peak of fifty in the worst month of all, August 1942) and only five between then and VE-day, though the number of boats at sea rose to 185 in mid-1944 and at the end of the year was still about 140. Only two of those twenty-one losses were sustained in convoys escorted by MACs.

Although at any given moment over half the aircraft of 836, latterly much more than half, were scattered in different ships across the Atlantic or at Dartmouth, an astonishing cohesion held the squadron together as a single fighting unit with an unsurpassed *esprit-de-corps*. This it owed to its ever-revered Commanding Officer, Ransford Slater, under whose charismatic spell I forthwith tumbled. An RN two-and-a-halfer with a grinning, weathered face, inspiring powers of leadership and great personal charm, he had himself led 'A' Flight when they joined *Empire MacAlpine* for her trials and maiden voyage. When his wheels touched her flight deck, it was the first time an aircraft had ever landed on a merchantman. He was now permanently at Maydown, ruling his scattered empire from a cramped office in a Nissen hut, sending forth the new flights and welcoming back the old.

Ransford had seen from the start that full success depended, more than anything else, on building and maintaining the best possible relations and the greatest mutual respect between the civilian MN crews who would sail the MAC-ships and the RNVR aircrews who'd fly their Stringbags. It easily might not have worked. In peacetime, even in wartime, an attitude exists between RN and MN officers like that between boys from public schools and grammar schools. The former in both cases, with no justification at all, assume they possess an innate superiority. The latter, who are often far more competent professionally, regard their RN counterparts as over-privileged snobs. There is seldom if ever any real contact between them. This traditional antipathy had to be broken down. Slater, too human a man to have felt such antipathy himself, inspired in his officers a deep personal pride in their Merchant Navy involvement, which was made easier because all of us apart from the boss himself (unless there were one or two now-forgotten exceptions) belonged to the Wavy Navy, serving 'for hostilities only' from a very wide range of social backgrounds with no class-consciousness at all, rather than straight-ringed career officers with their Dartmouth-or-similar schooling and traditions.

All of us, for a start, were enrolled in the Merchant Navy on joining our first MAC-ship. We signed the ship's articles as deck hands, and were supposed to receive a shilling a month, and a bottle of beer a day, to bring us under the Master's jurisdiction. (The shilling, like a peppercorn rent, was never actually paid, but seven bottles of beer for each of us were left by the chief steward in our cabins every Sunday.) Ransford Slater had realized that this would entitle us to wear the small silver MN badge in the lapel of our naval jacket, which had never been done before. It was presented to us by the Master when we signed the articles and unfailingly worn thereafter. Any apoplectic RN officer ashore who had asked what the devil we were doing, wearing that damned badge when in naval uniform, would have been told firmly and with impunity that we had every right to do so.

I wasn't long earning that envied right. By the time I joined the squadron, five MAC-ships were operational. Reporting to the boss. And at once allotted to 'F' Flight, on the point of being formed for the tanker *Acavus,* the next conversion expected, due in the Clyde within a month.

– Come and have a gin with Phil Blakey, your flight commander.

My face must have fallen, I had more than enough experience to command a flight myself, so Ransford was careful to let me know his rule, that flight commanders had to have made at least one MAC-ship crossing. (Phil was an *Empire MacAndrew* veteran.) On completing my first trip, he promised, I'd be given a flight of my own.

Meeting all the boys. Phil and his observer, Gordon Robertson. In particular my crew, with whom I was to fly for an unbroken thirteen months on operations. My 'looker' was John Bennett, always known as Jake, a beaming round-faced Londoner of about my own age (I was now nearly twenty-three). He already had carrier experience, was totally unflappable and a magnificent navigator. Charlie Simpson was our 'gunner', as by force of habit our wireless operators were still ludicrously known – of course we had no guns. He was twenty, this was his first front-line squadron, but he was the best damned telegraphist I've known. A bluejacket with the rank of Leading Airman (equivalent to Corporal), he was lean and lithe with clean-cut smiling features.*

Our third crew were New Zealanders, Johnnie Gilbert and Peter Temm, devil-may-care airmen and splendid drinkers. Temm was known to everyone as 'Pro', a really brilliant example of nicknaming. But I once heard him tell a girl by way of introduction: 'My name is Temm, I'm a New Zealander. They all call me Pro, I don't know why.' The liquor had flowed, the hour was late, but I did my best to explain to him.

Each flight had its own batsman, and its own team of mechanics to maintain and service its aircraft. In tankers, with three Stringbags, we had a petty officer in charge, four fitters and four riggers to care for engines and airframes respectively, three electricians of whom one was a radar specialist, and two AMOs (air mechanics ordnance) to look after all our weaponry. A grand total of fourteen to keep all Stringbags flying, or as many of them as possible.

Our aircraft were pure white, the most effective camouflage for day-flying over the sea, but were otherwise standard Swordfish IIs. Except that in many flights, so great was our MN loyalty, we would paint out ROYAL NAVY on their sides and substitute MERCHANT NAVY. Which caused quite a bit of eye-rubbing if we landed anywhere other than Maydown or Dartmouth.

A month to get together as a team. For me the most vital part of this brief preparation was to learn the art of pooping

---

* I regained contact with Jake after this book was first published and had several joyful meetings with him and Charlie before his recent death. I had never lost touch with Charles; we still meet once or twice a year. At 72 he has just remarried after almost fifty years with a brewery – entirely appropriately!

off rocket projectiles, either on my own or in coordinated practice attacks with the two other aircraft of the flight. These armour-piercing RPs were our new top-secret weapon and greatly increased our offensive capacity against U-boats compared with the six depth charges always carried previously. Four were slung in racks under each lower mainplane and could be fired in pairs, or all eight together, as the pilot chose. They were so powerful that a single hit in the right place, let alone eight, could sink a U-boat. The technique was to approach the target in a dive of twenty degrees and aim just below the U-boat's waterline from an optimum altitude of 800 feet implying a range of half a mile. A pair of well-aimed rockets would pass clean through a U-boat, making bloody great holes below water level where they exited. That should be enough. There was only one drawback, we needed a ceiling of at least 1000 feet. In conditions of low cloud, we had to fall back on depth charges.

Our RPs were so accurate that I soon found it possible to hit a four-foot-square target almost every time.

Penny returned to *Vincent* after her leave. She had applied to be drafted on compassionate grounds as they were known officially, or passionate grounds as they were more usually called, to the naval base at Derry, since it appeared likely that I would be in and out of Maydown every six or eight weeks indefinitely. The Wrens were always considerate in such matters and she was back in Derry twelve days later. Another three weeks and we were ready to embark. Our ground crews went on ahead by train and boat to Gourock. And we stood by to fly aboard on October 23rd.

Airborne on that grey and gusty morning, ten seconds behind Phil Blakey. Quickly into formation with him, four feet between our mainplanes. Johnnie Gilbert joining us. Turning short of Derry for the usual show-off fly-past of the toy-town Maydown control tower at zero feet, all the boys waving. Following the Irish coast, skirting the Mull of Kintyre, climbing over Arran for our Firth of Clyde rendez-vous. And there, at once unmistakable, on a straight southerly course with her white wake streaming astern, our seemingly brand new parent vessel, our mothercraft *Acavus*, ready to receive us.

Jesus, she's like a postcard! A signal from Phil and we plunge down in a dive, discreetly steep towards her, maintaining close formation. Another little ceremonial fly-past, not too close, at flight-deck level. A signal from Phil and we break up into extended line astern as *Acavus* begins her turn into wind to starboard. The batsman on his port-side platform near the aftermost end of the flight deck. Phil begins his approach.

We could normally land three aircraft in less than a minute. But this is not the time for split-arse flying – the first-ever aircraft to land on, the arrester wires never used before, the ground crews for the most part unaccustomed to handling aircraft on shipboard, an inexperienced 'bats'. I am to leave at least three minutes between Phil's landing and my own. I see him touch down safely and taxi forward, the barrier raised behind him. Not more than ten seconds later, I'd normally be down. Instead I am still two or three miles astern.

'Come on ahead,' signals the batsman. My airspeed is sixty-five, I close the throttle slightly, ease back on the stick to lose five knots. 'Bats' changes his signal: 'A wee bit lower.' Slightly close the throttle, forward with the stick, till he's again telling me to come on as I am. A last-moment 'Come lower.' I throttle back; then, at fifteen feet or so as I cross the stern, the mandatory crossed-bats signal commanding 'Cut your engine'. I do so and sink gently to a three-pointer, catching the first wire.

Ground crews race towards me from the safety nets to disengage my hook. I taxi smartly ahead of the barrier and switch off. Half-a-dozen crewmen race towards me to manhandle my Stringbag alongside Phil's. The barrier already raised behind me, Johnnie's aircraft approaching. We clamber from our cockpits and head for the bridge as it lands.

Of the thirteen tankers converted, *Acavus* was one of nine belonging to the Anglo-Saxon Petroleum Company, all more or less sister-ships. She displaced 8000 tons, a midget by today's standards, and her one-shaft diesel motor of 3500 BHP gave her a maximum speed of only thirteen knots. Her flight deck, to be perfectly exact, was 461 feet long and sixty-two feet wide – less than a cricket pitch. She carried six Oerlikons, two Bofors guns and a four-incher.

We now had three weeks of intensive flying trials in the Clyde, returning each evening to Tail-o'-the-Bank, the MN anchorage off Gourock, for riotous sessions in the tough pubs ashore. Getting to know our new shipmates, getting to know our MAC-ship. The Master, Captain Peters, our undisputed deity. His three mates, addressed as 'Chief', 'Second' and 'Third', share his duties on the bridge, working the usual four-hour watches. Four engineers, a couple of wireless operators, the chief steward and his assistant – these our fellow-officers. And the new Merchant Navy language. No such thing as wardroom or mess. We have our meals in the saloon, our social life in the lounge, our briefings in the chartroom. And merchantmen often called boats, a terrible *faux pas* in the Navy. Cabins for the ASO, the pilots and observers, the doctor and the batsman, have been added amidships, two of us in each, with Jake and me sharing. Our air gunners and ground crews with their own accommodation further aft. The original catwalks still running forward and aft across the well decks, which in foul weather would be awash with swirling turbulent sea-water, to provide precarious access from the centre-castle to focsle and poop respectively.

Everything informal. We wear what we like, open-neck sports shirts, multi-coloured sweaters, suede shoes or flying boots. But usually a battle-dress top, with wings and gold stripes (and always, later, when flying on patrol, or we could be shot as armed civilians if downed and taken prisoner). And everyone keen as mustard, everyone on the job. The pride we take in our flying – seldom finger-trouble in MAC-ships. And our MN comrades determined to show, and succeeding, that they are the equals of their counterparts in escort carriers.

Sailing every morning from Tail-o'-the-Bank for exercises off Arran, deck landings to become accustomed to our

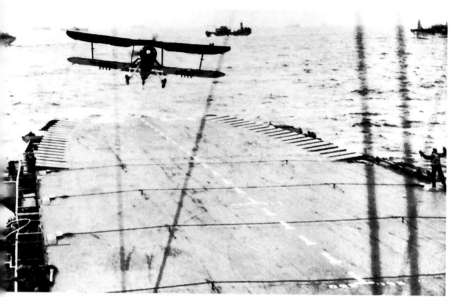

9. Lieutenant Godley and crew on the point of landing on board *Adula* in mid-Atlantic, May, 1944, with ships of the convoy in background. Note arrester wires and batsman (right).

10. Wrecked Stringbags on a MAC-ship flight deck after a storm.

11. A party gets going in Godley's cabin aboard *Adula* at sea. From left; Ian ('Flash') Parkin, Jack Harman (killed 1945), John ('Jake') Bennett, Doctor (now Professor) David Moffat, John ('Godders') Godley.

12. Stringbags of 816 Squadron, operating from RAF Perranporth, in their stripey D-Day livery, June 1944. See pages 146 et seq.

13. The 'pregnant' Stringbag: a Swordfish III of 835 Squadron, January, 1945.
The bulge in the belly housed ASV Mk X equipment. Note Rocket
Assisted Take Off Gear (RATOG) under each lower mainplane stub.

14. Grumman Wildcat VI fighters in line astern prepare to take off from an
escort carrier.

15. This picture of *Nairana*, taken from the flight deck of *Campania* in the course of the passage to Murmansk, gives a vivid impression of conditions under which even Stringbags could not operate except in dire emergency.

16. Lieutenant-Commander Godley when CO of 835 Squadron. Picture taken on board HMS *Nairana*, at anchor in Kola inlet, 14 February, 1945.

17. 'The bloody Barra'. A Fairey Barracuda in fair typical position after landing on board an es carrier.

exiguous flight deck, practice attacks with RPs or bombs, ASV homing exercises, radio drill. The Master and the mates becoming skilled at turning swiftly and precisely into wind, the pilots to taking off and landing with as little delay as possible, so that in convoys we will be out of station for not five seconds longer than necessary. All equipment has soon been tested and no snags have come to light – how different from the gremlin-ridden Woolworths! And we're ready for action on schedule.

Never told in advance our date of sailing. But on November 15th all shore leave is cancelled so we know it will be soon, probably before next morning. And sometime in the small hours I hear the anchor being raised, the gentle throb of the engine. Up with Jake to the flight deck and we are already under way, the unlit banks of the Clyde moving slowly on either side of us. A westerly wind from ahead of us, twenty or twenty-five knots, and soon just the least bit of motion on the ship, bringing her to life. Looking back to our three white Stringbags, wings folded, chocked and double-lashed for safety in their accustomed positions aft. The shadowy shapes of other merchantmen moving with us. A cold inhospitable night. Back to the warmth of our cabin to see what morning brings.

Ships on the Atlantic run were allocated to convoys according to the maximum speed they could guarantee to make good in normal weather. There were twelve-knot convoys, ten-knot convoys, eight-knot convoys. (And I once sailed with a four-knot convoy, a collection of antique tubs, none of which could make more than walking speed. We took three weeks to cross the Pond and in one period of twenty-four hours, with very strong headwinds to northward of the Azores, covered just over fifty miles.) This one, which we found assembling off Ireland when we surfaced for breakfast, turned out to be a ten-knotter, meaning a passage of two to three weeks. Some fifty or sixty ships, of all possible shapes, sizes and nationalities, some from the Clyde and some from Liverpool, taking up their preordained positions in nine parallel lines, six or seven ships in each. Our naval escorts shepherding us: a destroyer and ten smaller warships – frigates, sloops and corvettes. (This was the only time on all my Atlantic crossings that we had anything as powerful as a destroyer to accompany us.) They settle down in their stations: three or four ahead of the convoy, three or four on either flank.

All convoys had these two separate but coordinating components, the merchantmen flying the Red Ensign sailed by the civilian crews of the MN, their escorts under the White Ensign manned by the Royal Navy. A well-understood dichotomy. The former were under the direct and sole command of the Commodore (Convoy), a senior officer in the RN or RNR, the job for which my father-in-law had so happily volunteered. The Commodore's ship, a merchantman like any other, had always the same position in the convoy, the leading vessel in the central column, from which he could order changes in course or speed to be obeyed by all merchantmen. The escorts on the other hand, each under her own Captain, came under the overall command of the senior amongst them, known as the Senior Officer (Escort) or SOE, who allocated their positions in the protective screen around the merchantmen or dispatched them on special missions, such as seeking out a suspected U-boat or picking up survivors.

There was continual close liaison between SOE and the Commodore, who could converse by Aldis lamp or VHF radio (which could not be picked up by the enemy at a range of more than a few miles).

The MAC-ship, with her hybrid status as tanker or grainship and also as aircraft carrier, was unique in coming under the direct command of both these officers as appropriate. She was under the Commodore in her role as merchantman. But her flying operations were decided by SOE, in direct communication with the Air Staff Officer in the MAC-ship. And the Master would then manoeuvre his ship so that we could operate aircraft as required. To give us the safest berth compatible with maximum freedom to do so, we always had the same position in the convoy, the last vessel in the same centre column as the Commodore.

A good strong wind was blowing on this grey November morning. This would shorten our take-off run, so our Stringbags were parked with wings spread and RPs loaded one behind the other, ready to scramble at ten-second intervals within a few minutes, if necessary, of receiving orders from SOE. Always heading westerly and soon the mountains of Donegal had fallen below the horizon.

During their two years of service, from May 1943 till VE-Day, MAC-ships made 323 crossings of the Atlantic on convoy escort duty and only one of the 217 convoys they accompanied was successfully attacked. This was just off the coast of Northern Ireland and the Swordfish had already flown off to Maydown. Two ships were lost. Their aircraft flew 4177 patrols and searches, an average of nineteen sorties to a crossing or just about two a day. Patrols were routine flights, usually round and round the convoy at the limit of visibility (these were known as Vipers) or back and forth a specified distance ahead (which were codenamed Adders). There were also Cobras and Crocodiles. A search, which could be a Lizard, Python or Mamba, was more serious: it meant flying to a position up to 100 miles from the convoy and searching a wide area round it, in which one or more U-boats were known or believed to be operating.

SOE could obtain such information in three quite separate ways. If a U-boat were on the surface and within about ten miles (which would happen very infrequently), she could be detected by shipborne radar but not identified as a submarine. Much more important, the enemy throughout the war never came to realize the extent to which their cavalier use of radio was assisting us. Signals were passed back and forth between U-boats and their far-off bases often several times a day. Amazing! If one of these were picked up by an escort, it was quickly possible to establish the U-boat's bearing or, if picked up by two separate vessels, her position, by High Frequency Direction Finding (HF/DF or Huff-Duff). The signals were in cipher and not immediately intelligible. But they were gratefully received by the organization at Bletchley that went under the name of the Government

Code and Cipher School (GCCS), where since early 1943 it had again become possible to decipher them quickly. Many of these helpfully cooperative signals, if from the U-boats, gave their exact positions and intentions; or, if from their bases, such vital facts as their future operational areas and patrol lines. This information was of immense value in routeing convoys away from U-boats as well as in directing attacks on them. And the enemy never got wise.

During this first crossing of mine, we flew fewer than the average number of sorties because we ran into a gale, which grew into a storm with winds of sixty knots and over. You can't fly when the windspeed is greater than your stalling speed – you'd be taking off backwards – and *Acavus* was pitching so heavily that the forward end of the flight deck often dipped under water. But these same conditions, which continued off and on for half the trip, also immobilized the U-boats. All our three Stringbags were damaged in the battering they took and work on repairing them was extremely difficult, often impossible, without protection from the elements. Through bad weather and unserviceable aircraft, we made only ten sorties in seventeen days at sea.

No U-boats were sighted. But this certainly did not mean that our flights achieved nothing. The presence of supporting aircraft lifted the morale of all in the convoy. Very much more important, if there had been U-boats preparing to attack, we would have forced them without knowing it to stay out of range. A U-boat in mid-Atlantic spent much of her time on the surface, where her speed was much greater, twenty knots or more, and she wasn't using her batteries. She would submerge to attack a convoy – or increasingly, as U-boat captains became less daring and their radar more efficient, if they feared the approach of aircraft. Should a U-boat dive on detecting us, her top speed was cut to six or seven knots, which should prevent her from closing the convoy. And this was becoming perhaps our most important function, though we would almost always be unaware that we had performed it; a U-boat could normally detect aircraft before herself being detected. So no patrol need ever have been fruitless.

U-boats by 1943 were better armed than before to defend themselves against aircraft. Some would stay on the surface to fight it out. So, on sighting a surfaced U-boat, our orders were to report her position, then close her as quickly as possible, making use of such cloud cover as might be available to have the best chance of surprising her. If she crash-dived, the pilot would attack at once, hoping to fire his rockets or drop his depth charges when she was not yet fully submerged, or was still visible as a shadowy fish-like shape a few feet down. If she stayed surfaced it was left to the pilot's discretion: he could press home his attack (which he would certainly do if he had achieved surprise and could see the guns were unmanned but might otherwise think twice about) or keep safely out of range and whistle up support. All available aircraft would then be sent to join him for a combined attack. When the U-boats strengthened their anti-aircraft defences even further, the latter course was made mandatory.

The great majority of MAC-ship sorties were totally uneventful. We were doing vital work in keeping unseen U-boats submerged, but there's no use denying it rapidly became monotonous once the novelty wore thin, which happened rather quickly. My first two flights were typical of so many that were to follow. During daylight hours we were at perpetual readiness to scramble within not more than ten minutes if SOE should call on us. He didn't for three days, when we were 700 miles out, beyond the effective reach of Coastal Command aircraft, which had anyway been very little in evidence – the occasional Catalina. Believing there might be U-boats in the vicinity preparing for a dusk attack, he ordered continual air cover for the last four hours of daylight. Two single-aircraft Vipers, Phil to take the first and I the second. Each flight two-and-a-quarter hours to allow for overlaps. The wind from our port beam, so the skipper must fall barely astern of the convoy to make a turn of almost ninety degrees to fly off aircraft.

In the chart room below the bridge, the ASO gives us such brief briefing as is necessary – we already know exactly what to do. Take-off times 1420 and 1620, landings at 1635 and 1835. We reduce speed to three or four knots some fifteen minutes before Phil's take-off to bring us far enough astern of the ships closest to us, but not the least bit further, for our turn to windward. Captain Peters orders hard aport at 1417. The ship is pitching steadily on the long Atlantic swell but this should be no problem. The anemometer shows thirty-five knots over the deck. Phil starts his take-off run at 1420 precisely, is airborne before reaching the island. At once the Master orders hard a-starboard, full speed ahead, to regain station as soon as possible.

For two hours, the rest of us are standing by in full flying gear, our Stringbags in take-off position, rockets loaded and engines warm, ready to scramble if Phil should need support. No word from him. The procedure is then repeated. By 1610 my crew and I have clambered aboard the Stringbag, checked equipment, started and tested the engine. At 1620, headed directly into wind, a green light from the bridge and I signal 'Chocks away'. Throttle fully open, no need for boost override, release the brakes and we spring forward. Just keep her straight and wait for it. A climbing turn to starboard and away, the long lines of disciplined merchantmen below me. Seven minutes later the convoy is just barely visible: time to start my patrol. I do not see Phil who is ending his at this same moment at some other point in the ever-circling Viper.

Height 2000 feet, speed ninety knots. All trained to keep constant look-out. My gaze moving steadily ahead from port beam to starboard beam, not needing to check my instruments for more than a few seconds every ten or fifteen minutes. Jake devoting most of his time to his ASV, Charlie systematically covering the white-capped waves astern of us. All hoping for an enemy to pounce on, that pencil-thin grey shape in the rolling green-blue ocean, a telltale white wake, perhaps just a conning tower. On a Viper, no need for Jake to give me courses to steer: I fly clockwise round and round the convoy, keeping it just barely visible some fifteen miles to starboard. But our hours go by, we sight no enemy and at 1828 we turn for home. Back in the gathering dusk across our escort and the merchantmen as *Acavus* turns to receive us. The wind has freshened, the flight-deck pitching but no problems. We land precisely on time, make our negative report to the ASO in the chartroom, soon below decks to the lounge for mugs of cocoa and sandwiches.

All through the night the wind grows stronger and is blowing fifty knots by morning. The storm hits us next evening and for five days no flying possible. Our Stringbags take a battering, impossible to work on them. But on the sixth day the wind moderates to gale force and a request comes from SOE: the presence of a U-boat has been positively established by HF/DF some sixty miles to southward of the convoy on a bearing of 163. He asks for 'all available aircraft', provided we can operate in prevailing weather conditions, to fly at once to the area. We decide we can fly all right but only one Stringbag is serviceable and it happens to be my turn.

Ten-tenths cloud at under 1000 feet so six depth charges are loaded under my mainplanes in place of the customary RPs. The convoy already dead into wind, so no need to leave our station for me to scramble. *Acavus* pitching quite badly but this doesn't affect takeoff: with almost forty knots over the deck, my groundspeed is little more than twenty as we shudder skywards. Jake gives me a course to steer and I hold to it just below the clouds. Visibility five miles. The convoy soon disappears astern of us.

It was the first time, though it became a frequent experience, that I had flown out of sight of any vessel and far out of range of land. This brings a special sense of loneliness, especially when in a relatively small, single-engined aircraft with radio silence in force except in emergency or on sighting the enemy. On such flights, the monotony and vastness of that unending expanse beneath us becomes so intense that any break is always welcome – a slick of oil, a flight of sea-birds, a large patch of seaweed, a whale or an iceberg – and we would swoop down to examine it. Well over an hour to reach the U-boat's reported position. All eyes skinned but nothing to be seen. And we start our square search, which will take another hour, of the area surrounding it.

The inherent dangers of flying in these conditions, amazing as this now seems, really worried us not at all. We carried four inflatable dinghies – a big one in the upper mainplane,

large enough for all of us, equipped with all necessary
equipment, and a small one for each of us, which formed
part and parcel of our parachutes – and had total confidence (as we had to have) that our May-Day signal would be
heard if our engine stopped turning, that our well-equipped
dinghies would operate efficiently and that an escort vessel
would be sent for us and find us. Just how ill-placed this confidence turned out to be when put to the test, we were to
discover some months later.

We completed our search and headed homewards. *Acavus*
still pitching nastily, her stern rising and falling some fifteen
or twenty feet as she rode the long Atlantic swell. But my
groundspeed would again be so low that instead of landing
the Stringbag on the deck I should practically be able to
wait for the deck to rise up and catch the Stringbag. I
approached with a fair bit of motor and was given the signal
to cut, whereupon the deck rose so violently that the impact
neatly snapped off my tail wheel. I had no problem catching
a wire and damage was minimal – it was repaired within the
hour – but I must say it was a pity. It marred what would otherwise have been a record to take some beating: I was to
carry out an eventual total of 142 deck landings, by day and
night in all weathers, and on no other occasion did I damage my aircraft in any way, not even the smallest scratch.
This was my thirty-seventh, so I just managed to qualify for
the highly exclusive Centurions Club, for which the elusive
qualification was 100 consecutive prangless deck landings.

Others were less lucky. Prangs were fairly commonplace.
And one more disadvantage of having no hangar soon
showed itself. If, as a result of a quite minor accident such as
the undercarriage collapsing, a Stringbag became difficult
or impossible to manhandle forward and aft as necessary to
allow aircraft to operate, it would often be pitched overboard without delay or ceremony. But if a hangar had been
available where it wouldn't be cluttering up the flight deck
in the meantime, it could have been repaired in half a day.
After one such prang in *Acavus*, SOE was able to give us an
hour, instead of the usual ten minutes, in which to get the
deck cleared, because no immediate flying was required. We

removed such useful parts as could be quickly and easily extracted – the wireless, the clock, the bomb carriers, the radar set – and then announced on the loudspeakers that the Stringbag's corpse would be ditched in half-an-hour; meantime all could help themselves. The whole ship's company descended on it like ants. When the allotted thirty minutes had elapsed, there was nothing left to throw overboard. The entire aircraft had been sawn and ripped apart for souvenirs and was now distributed in small bits and pieces all over the ship.

We approached the Canadian coast on December 3rd without further incident. Only one Stringbag was flyable. We had hoped we might possibly make it home to Maydown by Christmas but the convoy took ten days to turn round. Ten days working on our aircraft, a little gentle flying, bashing round Halifax in the evenings. *Acavus,* in ballast outward bound, now fully laden with 7200 tons of crude oil – ninety per cent of her previous maximum load. In our new Stringbags to join her as she headed for open sea. Another stormy passage but now the wind, still westerly, helping to speed us home. We flew thirteen fruitless patrols: there were few U-boats around and none of them showed their noses. On Christmas Day, full of turkey and plum pudding, I flew a three-hour Viper in a gale. The weather remained inhospitable but all our Stringbags serviceable when we sighted the steep coast of Ireland and flew ashore to Maydown in winter sunshine on December 28th, Stringbags laden with duty-free drinks and cigarettes to take the place of rocket projectiles, goodies from unrationed Canada in preference to depth charges.

Penny, alerted by telephone, awaiting me at the airfield. Five days' leave ahead of us. Soon in unwonted civvies chugging south across the border, villages brightly lit, to the drumlins and streams of Leitrim, far removed from Crocodiles and Lizards in the unchanging peace of the green country, the old house looking silently down across two glass-flat lakes to the woods and the purple mountain, whilst *Acavus* sailed on eastward to discharge her crude-oil cargo in the blacked-out grime of Gourock.

VII

THE LUNENBURG SCHOONER

On returning refreshed to Maydown I was given command at once of 'P' Flight, taking Jake and Charlie with me. We were destined for *Adula*, the latest Anglo-Saxon tanker conversion, nearing completion in Falmouth. P is the sixteenth letter, so she was the sixteenth of the eventual nineteen MAC-ships. A month to get together with the two young crews allotted to me, 'Flash' Parkin and Stan Holness, Jack Harman and Dave Allen, all Wavy Navy subs straight out of flying school, who'd never landed on a carrier and had few hours in Stringbags. They learned quickly. They'd no alternative. A brief, intensive work-up, including a visit to *Argus*, that venerable antique, for six deck landings each, which were all my two young pilots would have behind them before facing the so-much-smaller MAC-ship and the rigours of the Atlantic. And on February 18th (1944) we flew to join *Adula* in the Clyde.

She was identical to *Acavus*. And a happy ship if ever there was one. Off and on I spent nearly a year with her and life aboard was so pleasant and easy-going that there was really no time for monotony, as there could well have been with the unchanging MAC-ship routine. The Master, Captain Rumbellow, an officer of the old school, always perfectly turned out, spick and span in full uniform, with eagle face, gold-peaked cap, and some of a Captain's exclusiveness. Our ASO, Brian Walsh Atkins, painstaking and meticulous, with his own very special sense of humour, crouched over maps and signals in the chartroom as he plotted our patrols – or deep in a game of chess with one of the mates, belowdecks in the lounge, as we pitched through the night on the long Atlantic rollers. Above all Bob Allen, the three-striped Chief Officer, life and soul of his own never-ending party, enveloping us in his laughter and high spirits, welding in friendship our whole ship's company with its Merchant Navy and Wavy Navy contingents.

Our doctor, David Moffat, had joined the service recently, after qualifying at Barts. It was a luxury for a merchantman to have a doctor. The mates' training included some rough and ready medicine, which normally had to suffice. We were a healthy crowd and there was not much in the medical line to keep Doc Moffat busy, though his enthusiasm and interest seemed always to find its way right to the heart of all our activity. And he took on sundry duties of which Barts had taught him nothing. For instance to take the windspeed over the flight-deck as we turned to operate aircraft. The last figure I'd see ahead of me, as I prepared to open up, was therefore always the doctor, muffled in scarves and dufflecoat, anemometer held above him, struggling to keep his footing in the exposed centre of the deck as we pitched all over the sea, shouting up the windspeed to Brian on the bridge, then dashing for the safety nets as I let go the brakes and surged forward.

Another non-medical duty Doc Moffat undertook, much appreciated by all of us, was that of auxiliary cook. The need for this arose from what seemed to us the extraordinary fact, but was really quite reasonable, that MN personnel worked strict trade union hours. For watchkeepers on the bridge or in the engine room, this meant four hours on and eight hours off round the clock throughout the trip. Most of the others worked from eight to six on weekdays, till noon on Saturdays and had a free day on Sundays. The stewards started work at seven-thirty, when we could get a cup of tea but nothing more. The magnificent three-course MN breakfast, which usually included curry, was at eight o'clock, not a moment sooner. The last meal of the day was at 1800. It often happened in the summer that we would take off for a dawn patrol at four or five in the morning. Unless we cooked something ourselves beforehand, we would be flying on an extremely empty stomach (which any doctor will agree is not to be recommended) and on return might have over an hour to wait before getting so much as a hot drink.

We therefore took care to bring good supplies on board with us and a primus stove. It was Doc who volunteered to have mugs of steaming cocoa, plates of fried eggs, fruit juice and other delights, awaiting us in the chartroom as we stumbled sleepily from our cabins on our way to the waiting Stringbags. The undeviating adherence to union hours sometimes had curious consequences. We had wooden ready-use stowage positions for RPs and depth charges, handily located for loading on the Stringbags as required. Once after a three-day gale I found them smashed by heavy seas. This would make arming our aircraft a longer, more hazardous operation and we could well be called for a dawn patrol next morning. So I sought out the ship's carpenter, whose job it would be, and asked him if he would kindly repair the damage with the least possible delay. But I'd lost track of the days in the hardship and sleeplessness.

– I'd be glad to do it first thing Monday, Chippy replied.

– Monday? What's today then? Isn't there any hope...

– No I'm afraid no hope, said Chippy. It's Saturday afternoon.

Our work-up went smoothly and we were on the eve of our maiden voyage when a grotesque accident put me ashore for a month and at the same time gave the Doc an unexpected chance to put his surgical skills to use. It was March 6th and we had left our anchorage early to spend the morning somewhere off Arran for a final bout of deck-landing practice. A stiff breeze was blowing, there was some movement on the ship, but no problems had arisen. Now in the afternoon we had the usual chore before sailing of hoisting rockets and depth charges from the magazine in the bows. I was in charge of the operation: two men on the focsle to operate the winch, a dozen on the flight deck, immediately above it, where a block and tackle had been set up, to unload each lethal cargo and take it aft to the ready-use stowage positions. The rockets were easy to handle but the much heavier depth charges, each weighing over two hundredweight, presented some little difficulty, swaying back and forth as the winch brought them individually a few inches clear of the flight deck where they were fully exposed to the wind. So I'd take a firm grasp with both hands of the heavy cable to steady it as soon as the winch stopped turning. The fourth or fifth time, at just this precise moment, the winch took an unkind extra turn. My right hand, which was uppermost, was carried with the cable into the steel trap of the hoisting gear.

– Reverse the winch! For Christ's sake reverse the winch!

Excruciating seconds before the faulty winch turns back. My hand emerges from the block with two fingers almost amputated. The first two. Below decks to the Doc, who gives me a shot of morphia before examining the mess. With no facilities for a delicate operation, he offers me a choice.

– Would you like me to snip them off? Wouldn't take a second. Or we could put you ashore to hospital. You'd have an even chance of saving them but no flying for a month or so.

Well, I opted for the latter, even though it meant missing *Adula's* maiden voyage. Talk about bloody finger trouble! Doc patched things up as best he could, a launch was whistled alongside. Swathed in bandages and dazed by shock and morphia I was soon tossing across the firth to the handiest operating theatre, in the naval hospital at Largs. A replacement to take my place for the trip was flown out that evening from Maydown.

The sequel was exceedingly macabre. Arriving after dark by ambulance at the hospital. To the theatre without delay. A general anaesthetic and perhaps midnight before they finish with me. I come round in the small hours, a ward of snoring sailors. What the hell – then quickly remembering. Jesus, how did the op go? I feel for my right hand to find the whole arm in plaster from elbow to finger-tips. Yes but *how*

many fingertips? Nobody about but I have to find out somehow. Wandering unknown corridors in overcoat and pyja-
mas, finding a sick berth attendant.

– Now then, sir, what are you doing out of your bed at this
hour of night?

– I want to know how many fingers I've got.

The SBA listens attentively as I tell my unhappy tale. So
sympathetic and helpful.

– I'll tell you what we'll do, sir. Go straight back to bed
and I'll see if I can find them.

– Find them? Find who?

– Your fingers, sir.

Of course, of course, my fingers. The obvious, only way. I
retrace my footsteps, the agonizing minutes pass, then the
SBA long-faced to my bedside.

– Sorry, sir, they had to take them off.

So the even money chance had gone against me. I admit
that I was downcast. No trouble about flying but the rest of
my life defingered. Uneasy slumber, no appetite for breakfast, unsmiling when the smiling surgeon comes on his
rounds in mid-morning.

– Take them off? Not a bit of it, certainly not. One of
them may be a bit crooked but I think we'll manage to save
it.

So what of the SBA? The explanation is simple. He'd
found someone else's fingers.

I was twelve days in hospital. Each finger fractured in two
places. When the plaster came off, I was appalled to see
them puffed to twice their normal size, a spongy purple
mess of broken skin, half-dried blood and pus. Something
must have gone wrong, I thought. They'd have to come off
after all.

– Jesus that looks terrible.

– No, no, said the surgeon, it's beautiful, simply beautiful.
Just what I was hoping for.

Day by day they came closer to usual size – and very nearly
to usual shape. Except that the terminal joint of my index
finger had been ground to pieces and now no longer
existed. The terminal phalanx surviving but welded

immoveably to its neighbour, twisted downwards and inwards. This was awkward (and still is), it made fiddly jobs difficult. Picking up small objects has been a problem ever since and it became hard to pull a trigger. It was one of my two typing fingers and I found myself hitting the next-door letter; a pianist would have been driven to distraction. But it's useful if anyone asks me the way and I want to indicate: 'Go straight ahead and take the first turning to the right.'

I couldn't fly for a month, but was ready to take over again when 'P' Flight returned after *Adula's* maiden voyage. Just my luck, it was the only time she ever went to New York so I missed out on Manhattan. There was one consolation: it had been decided to use her on the homeward run to ferry over a consignment of fighter-planes and her flight deck had been crammed full with thirty or forty Wildcats. So with no flying possible I'd have been idle anyway. Another consolation, on leave I wasn't idle. By the time we sailed again, Penny was three weeks late.

A joyous reunion with Jake and Charlie. How could we have known that our closest brush with death was just around the corner, from which we would emerge alive by a coincidental combination of circumstances so unlikely as to approach the miraculous?

We re-embarked in *Adula* on May Day, an ill omen in itself. (Mayday, alias *m'aidez,* is the international distress call.) Sailed for Halifax four days later with a large fast convoy in company with another MAC-ship, the grainer *Empire Macrae.* On May 9th (as I never knew till over fifty years later) signals from two U-boats reporting their position were intercepted and decoded by the GCCS cryptographers. One was *U548* (Oberleutnant Zimmerman), about 100 miles south of Cape Race, the other from *U1222* (Oberleutnant Bielfeld), some 200 miles east of Newfoundland. At the time these were the only two enemy boats in the western North Atlantic. Both were ordered to head for the Halifax approaches. This vital information, so carelessly divulged, was at once passed by Bletchley to SOE. He gave the Commodore a new course for the convoy away from them and ordered the first of over twenty sorties flown in the next three days by the seven aircraft available.

One or two of these were Serpents, to locate stragglers and guide them back to the convoy, but over half were Lizards. We sighted nothing but knew we had almost certainly performed our vital function by forcing the U-boats to dive on detecting our approach by radar before we were close enough to detect them in the same way, thus preventing them from reaching a position to attack.

The weather was deteriorating. For three days conditions were so hazardous, with an eerie combination of heavy swell and dense patches of fog, that we were not called upon to fly. The convoy forged steadily westward. In the small hours of May 15th, I was wakened by the Air Staff Officer. An urgent signal had just reached him from SOE. There was a U-boat on the surface some sixty miles to south-westward. The convoy's course had been altered some thirty degrees to northward and, if we could operate aircraft, he wanted all of us airborne at first light: two to fly Lizards to the area indicated, the third a Viper in case the enemy was already closing us.

Up with Brian to the flight deck. The night was bright with stars. The wind by now had moderated to less than fifty knots but a heavy swell was still running.

– Sure we can operate, I said.

– Well you and Flash had better take the Lizards, Jack will take the Viper. Eight RPs each. Scramble at 0740. I'll work out the search areas. You'd better go below, get a couple more hours of sleep.

None of us ever knew – not even Brian – how such vital information was obtained. It was one of the war's most closely guarded secrets. In this case we assumed that a Huff-Duff fix was responsible since the given position was beyond the range of radar and we'd never heard of GCCS. But it was of course Bletchley who had informed SOE that Herr Zimmerman would soon be preparing his *Frühstuck* some 280 miles south-south-east of Halifax. (Herr Bielfeld was 320 miles south-south-east of Cape Race, far enough astern of us to be no longer a threat.)

Wakened again at 0630. With all the boys to the chart-room below the bridge. Brian has plotted two adjacent rectangles for Flash and me to search. We are to fly divergent courses to them, thus covering more ocean on the journey out and back. Mugs of steaming Moffat cocoa. Then at 0715 clambering to the pitch-dark swinging flight deck. Our Stringbags already armed, the ground crews busy around them. The Master, beginning to drop astern of the convoy for his turn to starboard into wind, waves to us from the bridge. We lumber, joking, towards our aircraft, my own in front facing directly fore-and-aft amidships, the two others angled inwards to port and starboard astern of me at the aftermost end of the deck. A takeoff like any other. The first glimmer of light on the eastern horizon as the ship begins her turn. Glancing over my shoulder to Jake's pink face with Charlie grinning behind him. Pull down goggles, signal chocks away. A quick green flash from Brian on the bridge. Opening her all the way as the dimmed lights glimmer the length of the flight deck for the thirty or forty seconds it will take all of us to get airborne.

With almost half the available run to spare, my Stringbag lifts herself into the night with hardly a touch from me. I gently keep her nose down, gain speed to sixty-five, start a slow climbing turn to bring me round and over the convoy. The ranks of darkened merchantmen no more than black smudges, three or four in view at a time. I settle on the course already given me by Jake, adjust the gyro to zero, continue the climb at seventy. My exhaust pipe glowing red, an occasional shower of sparks from it.

We are something over a day's steaming from Halifax, about 300 miles, but haven't yet reached the warmer waters of the Gulf Stream. The convoy has held a northwesterly course at twelve knots, its maximum speed, since the U-boat's new position was established, so this should now be some eighty miles to our south. Jake has already plotted our course using an estimated windspeed and direction, which we will check when it gets light enough. With a following wind, it will take about forty minutes to reach our rectangle, which we are to spend an hour searching, covering some

1200 square miles. As we fly southward the sky slowly brightens, white then steely blue without a cloud. One by one the stars outshone, the sea its unending expanse of emptiness. We see no sign of Flash, already out of sight to eastward.

We start our search at 0820, as the sun bursts from the ocean. Our flight plan calls for a series of parallel tracks thirteen miles apart. We cannot be sure of sighting a U-boat, even in such perfect visibility, at a range greater than seven miles, and this allows a one-mile overlap. As always hoping for that slim grey shape low on the water ahead of us. But we sight no enemy and at 0920 turn for home. With the head wind it will take us more than twice as long as the outward leg but by 1045 we should be safely back on board.

And then, within ten minutes, three amazing events. First, near the limit of visibility, I see what appears to be, unless an apparition, a solitary vessel, which a moment later I make out to be a sailing ship. Way out in the Atlantic! With U-boats around!

– Jesus, boys, there's a sailing ship ahead of us!

– You're crazy, you're bloody seeing things.

– Must be the *Marie Celeste*, sir.

I tell them to take a look then, pointing a gloved hand fine on the port bow, my left arm out of the cockpit into the slipstream. Jake lifts his binoculars. Moments of disbelief.

– By Jesus you're right, John. A three-masted schooner, bare poles, seems to be stationary. What the hell's she doing?

– Shall we have a look, sir?

– You bet we'll have a look.

In all my Atlantic patrols, this was the only time I sighted the smallest sign of human life from the time I left the convoy till my return. Always the empty ocean. Now this chance vessel, located almost precisely where her presence would so soon be indispensable to save our lives, a dozen miles ahead of us. I alter course to bring us directly over her. Five minutes later, Charlie's voice on the intercomm.

– Hey, it's getting crowded. Isn't that a Swordfish, sir? Away on the starboard beam?

Again Jake swings his glasses (the only pair between us).

– It's a Stringbag all right. Must be Flash and Stan. Now there's dead reckoning for you.

A remarkable coincidence or else damned fine flying. After nearly two hours of DR navigation over an empty sea with no navigational aids, Flash and I are returning abeam of each other on convergent courses, now some twelve miles distant at the extreme limit of visibility, exactly as ordered by the flight plan. Either we are both within a mile or two of our correct positions, or else we have both run up precisely the same aggregate error. And this fortuitous chance sighting, in addition to the other, would be needed to save our lives.

The third event in this sequence three minutes later. My beloved Peggy, my beautiful Pegasus III, the most trusted engine in the service, decides at this moment she's taken us far enough. A brief splutter, then perfect and terrible silence.

To throttle back a Stringbag at safe height so that the engine is only idling; to revel in the sudden silence, hear the airstream whistling in the struts; to push down the nose till she is diving earthwards at 140 or more, then ease back on the stick till you are sedately soaring not far from the stall at sixty, losing height hardly perceptibly; to soar and bank like a glider among the clouds – these were among the darling pleasures of flying. It isn't so darling when sudden absence of power has been totally involuntary and there is now only the Atlantic 1500 feet below.

Not that we were yet for a single moment seriously apprehensive, not in fear of death. There was a hope I'd be able to coax my Peggy to life again. If I couldn't, a Stringbag was the easiest and safest aircraft to put down in the drink and would float for several minutes. Our Mae Wests in themselves wouldn't be much use, the water would be too cold, but we had our four dinghies and would at once break radio silence to send a Mayday. And there anyway by such a fantastic stroke of luck was this sailing boat, now much closer, just waiting to pick us up. Nothing to be alarmed about. But one by one these doors to safety closed on us.

Holding her directly towards the schooner in the shallowest possible glide, I jiggled the throttle, played with the mixture control, tried every trick I knew to get a spark from her. To no avail. Now came Charlie's laconic voice on the intercomm.

– Fucking radio, sir. Packed up.

Couldn't believe it! Engine and radio packing up together! Never before had Charlie failed to establish instant contact at such close range. Well thank God for the schooner. I dived through 300 precious feet, throttle wide open, then closed, then open again, hoping increased revs would do it. Silence.

– OK, I'm going to fire all eight rockets. Charlie, keep trying.

I wanted to lighten the aircraft; and the rocket projectiles made such a series of screeches that the schooner couldn't help but hear them if by some impossible chance she hadn't sighted us. I dipped our nose and fired them off in pairs, aiming slightly ahead of her – they dropped well short as I knew they would. Then having reached 150 feet I gave up trying with the engine and concentrated on ditching.

We were already headed upwind so I could continue straight ahead. At the last moment I hauled back all the way on the stick so that the tail dropped and was first to strike the sea. My forward speed over the water must have been no more than a mere thirty knots on impact. Settle down nice and gently.

Strange as it now seems we were all in the highest spirits. My only little minor worry apart from losing a valuable aircraft was that the big dinghy didn't eject and inflate automatically as it was supposed to do on ditching. However there was a fail-safe manual release in the upper mainplane above me. Unclipping my parachute and leaving it with my one-man dinghy in the cockpit, I clambered up to work it, not even getting my feet wet. I pulled the cable release and nothing whatever happened. First twinge of anxiety. I stayed on the wing pulling and tugging that goddam cable till the Stringbag sank under me – in 18,000 feet of water.

Only at this instant did we begin to realize things weren't

too good and five minutes later we were sure of it. Jake and Charlie were already in the ocean, shouting come on in, it's lovely. It was lovely for thirty seconds. Till we were in it we didn't realise what a heavy swell was running, how terribly cold the water. We hadn't reached the Gulf Stream and it wasn't far from freezing. Much worse, Jake's one-man dinghy had been forced forward on impact and he hadn't been able to reach it, whilst mine had sunk with the plane. We just had Charlie's; and three into one won't go.

So we all three clung on, hoisting ourselves as best we could from the water but immersed from the belly down. No more joking. The coldness with terrible speed took hold of us. And Jake and Charlie were soon being violently seasick. Yes, you can sure as hell get seasick clinging to a dinghy in that swell, even though you've never been bothered by it in the heaviest weather on shipboard. But at least we knew it was for only a few minutes. The schooner had finally been only two or three miles distant, though to us she was now out of sight with the heavy swell running.

Just one little thing we didn't know, she hadn't seen us. Was quite unaware of our existence, our growingly precarious existence.

As we discovered later, she was a fishing vessel, *Kasagra*, out of Lunenburg, Nova Scotia, a port not far from Halifax. She had her boats and nets out to northward, taking in the night's catch, and we had thoughtlessly approached from the south. Everyone hard at work, no look-out set, no idling crewman to see or hear us, not even those screaming rockets. So now our lives depended on the crew of the other Stringbag, trained to keep a continual systematic sweeping of the ocean. But they were young and inexperienced. Had they seen us go in, had they seen us at all? We knew within minutes as Flash Parkin roared low over us.

We owe our lives to him. He at once summed up the situation. If we had been ensconced in the large dinghy with full supplies, as he must have expected to find, no flap whatsoever. But we were half immersed in the water – we had about an hour to live unless picked up – and this crazy boat fishing. No way he could drop a dinghy to us but he could signal *Kasagra* to come on over and quickly. His observer, Stan Holness, got working with the Aldis lamp.

But how it now transpired that none of the crew was versed in the Morse code. Thinking Stan wished to establish their nationality, they found an outsize Red Ensign, stretched it out on the deck. No, no, no. Flash now began a series of dives on our position, returned to *Kasagra*, waggled his wings, returned again to our position, dropped smoke-markers, waggling his wings, firing red Very lights.

Meantime the three of us in increasingly serious trouble. The sea was quickly claiming us. Every ounce of energy, all our concentration, devoted to that dinghy, four-foot by two-foot, to keeping hold of it; and we were losing inch by inch. Soon it was only with our hands; we were immersed from the armpits down, then from the shoulders.

A few minutes later I felt myself at the limit of endurance. I remember telling the others I couldn't hold on any longer, that it didn't seem worth the effort. And they both looked back in silence. I guess they were feeling something of the same but I was the only one who said it. The physical exertion needed was just becoming too great. Death was so near that it was easy, the easy way out, almost welcome, certainly acceptable. And in a couple of minutes, had nothing intervened, I'd have let go, drifted a few yards, then slipped quietly and not ungratefully into and under the swell.

But at just this minute: 'Look, look, oh Jesus!' And there, seen through the fine spray blowing from the swell's crests, now for the first time were the tops of the three bare masts, rising and falling from view as *Kasagra* rose and fell with the waves. Soon the whole vessel. She drew near and put down a boat for us.

Afterwards we could all remember this rowing-boat heading for us. Coming alongside. Strong arms reaching down for us. Beyond that point, for all of us, oblivion. We had all held on, because we had to, far beyond our natural strength, kept going those last ten minutes (in my case anyway) only by the sudden knowledge that rescue was at hand. The instant it was no longer necessary, no longer vital, we all three lost consciousness, those arms around us, before even

being lifted into the rowing boat. We had been fifty-one
minutes in the water by Stan's stopwatch.

A yellow lamp swinging above me. Slowly moving with the
long regular pitching of a vessel. My head held back, a
rough hand slapping my cheek, the yellow lamp swinging,
my mouth held open. Now my tongue brought forward, a
few drops of burning liquor, I choke but manage to swallow,
half raise my head, I look around. Great bearded faces looking down at me, scraps of a gutteral language, a voice in
accented English tells me to lie still. Where in God's name
am I? I lie and listen, murmur of voices around me. The
appalling truth comes to me: they're Germans. I know
enough of the language to be certain. Confused memories
returning, a U-boat pack in the area, coming down in open
sea. They were watching it all at periscope depth nearby,
waited till Flash and Stan left, came aboard and lifted us off
the schooner! Prisoner now in a U-boat, heading for Kiel or
Hamburg! And where the hell are the others?
  – Hey, Jake, Charlie, where are you, what happened?
  – John, John, are you all right?
  – Jake! For Christ's sake!
Raising myself, turning towards the familiar voice, seeing
Jake and Charlie on bunks like mine side by side, half-naked,
just part-wrapped in blankets, sailors splashing cold sea-water
from buckets on their legs. Looking down, seeing I too am
getting this treatment, can feel nothing. Everyone smiling,
happy. For God's sake, that's a paraffin lamp, U-boats don't
have paraffin lamps! And the heavily timbered bulkheads.
  – You must rest now. Ja, take more cognac. For you it was
the closest, says the bearded face beside me.
  I'd been out for over an hour, was the last to come
around. Not very proud of that. But everything was all right,
we were safely aboard Kasagra. There was a German-speak-
ing community in Lunenburg, they explained, all loyal
Canadians though some could barely speak English. They'd
been told on their ship-shore radio that a corvette was coming from the convoy to collect us, would be there in four or
five hours, meantime they'd look after us.

141

Back in *Adula*, Doc Moffat tearing his hair out. Would the fishermen know how to treat exposure? Gangrene could result, leading to amputation, if our legs were warmed too quickly. Not yet knowing *Kasagra* had a radio link with the shore, he believed there was no way of getting the message to her. But Doc needn't have worried. The fishermen had been dealing with such cases all their lives, had more practical experience of treating exposure than he did. They cared for us splendidly, did all the right things.

I have few recollections of those hours aboard the schooner. The corvette, a vessel of the Royal Canadian Navy, managed to lose her way and arrived in mid-afternoon. Lashed to stretchers, we were somehow transferred to her across the still heaving ocean. Someone on board nicked the wings off my battledress as a souvenir; he was welcome to them. It was after dark when we made it back to the convoy.

We had hoped to be put straight back aboard *Adula*, but it was decided to transfer us to the hospital ship. In every convoy one of the merchantmen was so equipped, with naval doctors and SBAs, full medical and surgical equipment. When vessels were sunk the hospital ship would be desperately overcrowded but now we were the only patients. Everyone was most kind but we didn't get quite the coddling we'd expected.

The danger was still that we would thaw too quickly, with amputation from gangrene still a possibility. The treatment, now no longer used, was to pack us from the thighs down in hot-water bottles filled with ice-cubes. For the first eighteen hours we were kept on ice continuously, for the next (during which we reached Halifax) for alternate hours, then for one in three. From time to time the doctor stuck a needle into our legs to see if sensation was returning. For three days there was none but then recovery was quite rapid. *Adula* was to sail again with a homeward-bound convoy six days after our ditching, having spent only four days turning round. We couldn't be any use but we wanted to sail with her. I remember we were allowed ashore in Halifax, hobbling on crutches, the night before sailing, for a bash around the town.

We couldn't be any use but I badly wanted to get in the air again just to prove to myself I could do it. On May 22nd, my first wedding anniversary, the day after sailing, SOE called for a two-aircraft patrol. We had picked up a replacement Stringbag though we had no one to fly it and I persuaded Brian to let me take off first, make a rapid circuit whilst the two others were getting airborne and land right back on again. The weather was perfect, there wasn't any flap and he agreed.

D-Day was approaching (though of course we didn't know it), men and supplies were pouring into Britain, and this was one of the largest convoys ever to cross the Atlantic with well over 100 ships. Their entire escort comprised a frigate and four corvettes, together with two MAC-ships boasting six effective Stringbags between them. And we were to sail the whole way in a flat calm without sight or sound of the enemy. The moment *Adula* was headed into wind that lovely morning, I opened up my new Stringbag fully, was airborne (having neither crew nor warload) within 300 feet, pulled her round in a steep turn to port and was approaching to land soon after our third aircraft scrambled, a flight of less than a minute. My feet couldn't feel the rudder bar but it seemed to make little difference, I could do it in my sleep, I caught the first wire. I'd been back in the air again, back in my element. It was going to be all right.

But if the schooner had been there and not Flash Parkin's Stringbag, or the Stringbag but not the schooner, or – as was infinitely more likely – only the empty sea and sky, we'd still be there today, our white bones in the darkness of those 3000 fathoms. But how to calculate odds? The engine mightn't have failed, the big dinghy might have worked. We'd survived, that was all that mattered.

This was to be the crossing when a certain well-known card game took its most pernicious hold on us. We'd many other ways of passing off-duty hours. In fine weather when there was no flying, the flight deck became a kind of village green where everybody congregated. A fine open expanse for every kind of recreation, even walking: six times up and down its full length was a fraction over a mile. Ball games were hardly possible but five-a-side deck hockey was a favourite, with the arrester wires making it more interesting. It didn't matter how many pucks went overboard: Chippy kept us going with an unlimited supply. In the evenings chess and draughts, housey-housey, pontoon, whist, monopoly. Some of us were known to read books.

But poker, from the time we first joined *Adula,* had always been the most popular. A small school would get going most evenings in the lounge, which grew steadily as more officers, both Merchant Navy and Wavy Navy, were sucked into the whirlpool. Many of these had never played before and it's well known that learning poker by playing it can be exceedingly expensive. By now there was a perpetual school, sometimes two or three, from sunset till the small hours. Even at times in the dog watches.

Now it's another well-known fact that poker stakes have an ineluctable tendency to rise, even during an evening, let alone an Atlantic crossing. This is all the greater if no chips have to be bought, greater still if no money changes hands till the completion of each trip, which was the way we always ordered it. After each hand, we'd keep a written record of what had been lost and won. When the game folded, these figures would be totted and transferred to a master scoresheet. A player is much less likely to stake so vast a sum as a fiver if it means putting it on the table, actually seeing it there in cash, instead of merely having 'minus 5' entered against his name for payment at some ill-defined future date, especially if his worldly wealth at that moment amounts to three-pounds-ten.

We always played dealer's choice, whether draw poker, stud poker, or one of the many varieties. Anaconda became steadily more often chosen by the dealer, till in the end we played it nearly all the time. I won't go into its intricacies except to mention that it involves dividing the pot equally between those holding the highest *and lowest* hands after the fifth card has been revealed. You can take my word for it that with anaconda it is all the more probable that stakes will grow and grow.

We'd started in February, when first we joined the ship. Playing for pennies. It was shillings, with occasional 'raises' of ten bob, by the time I rejoined after my little bit of fingertrouble. On this present trip, it somehow got out of hand. In many schools the ante was all of five shillings, the opening bet the same, raises of a fiver by no means unknown. And in those days a fiver was a fiver.

As the Irish coast approached, so did the day of reckoning. When the last school folded, Jake and I took the score-sheet to our cabin. I won't say we were the best players in the world but at least we knew the game. And luck had stayed on our side. We were the only net winners out of twenty or thirty players, to the tune of over £400 – about ten grand today. We decided this was ridiculous. Some of the heaviest losers – a young Fourth Mate, perhaps, or a junior sub – could have no hope whatever of paying, at least for several months, what had given the illusion, right up to this dire moment, of being imaginary money. So we threw the score-sheet overboard.

From then on we played for matches.

Flash and Jack flew our two serviceable Stringbags ashore. Jake and Charlie and I, officially still grounded, went on with *Adula* to Gourock, thence by boat and train to Maydown. To find Penny already on indefinite sick leave pending discharge from the Wrens. In those days no early infallible tests were available. But though barely two months pregnant she had convinced a friendly naval doctor of her approaching motherhood mainly on the grounds, she told me, that she had developed a craving for fried onions. Besides having missed two periods. She on sick leave, my crew and I on two weeks' survivors' leave. Home across the border to Killegar, where D-Day came and went. My feet devoid of feeling, they were to be numb for several months, but soon I could walk without a stick.

Another green-enveloped telegram. I was to return forthwith to collect my belongings before taking up a new appointment. Now what would that be? Not long discovering.

VIII

BIRD-SEED BOYS AND
OTHER TALES

Happily Jake and Charlie had received the same instructions. We were being lent to 816 Squadron, operating under Coastal Command from Perranporth in Cornwall. A major U-boat offensive against convoys in the Channel had been expected after D-Day. And 816 were needed to help the RAF protect them. Flying Stringbags. Well it seemed unbelievable. We'd felt foolish enough in our antique biplanes when on loan to the RAF in 1942. Now, two years later, with a vast force of modern aircraft at their disposal, they still wanted a Swordfish squadron to help them perform their duties.

The airfield was on the north Cornish coast, perched on the edge of cliffs. Flying by day and night. But the expected offensive never materialized. We flew our patrols in the English Channel, in St George's Channel, in the Bristol Channel. Sighted nothing whatever. Penny joined me and we took a cottage in the village, in a steep street called Stippy Stappy with usual Cornish whimsy. I had the use of a service motor-bike (with sidecar) on which I roared between the airfield and Stippy Stappy, sometimes at four in the morning after flying a patrol. It was like a summer holiday.

But the weather at times not summery and the mad wisdom of sending Stringbags for this work was not infrequently evident. With our absurdly low speed and incomparable manoeuvrability, we could fly when the entire RAF was grounded.

In this we were assisted by two refinements now available: greatly improved ASV, accurate to within 100 yards, and radio altimeters. These gave our true height within ten feet. (Previous altimeters, which worked by measuring changes in barometric pressure, showed the height above the point of take-off. And even this depended on the pressure remaining constant. The radio altimeter told us our height above the sea or land below us at that moment.)

And yet... yet I found I was flying differently. After such a close call, which was my fourth total engine failure, coming on top of so many adventures and misadventures that I had taken in my stride, flying was never quite the same. No longer the invincible optimism, the joyous certainty that I would always come sailing home. I began thinking, if you keep dealing long enough from a pack, sooner or later the ace of spades comes up.

When such doubts develop in a pilot, it's the first sign that he's beginning to 'get the twitch', as we called it. Not a serious case, but the beginning though not yet recognized. The second chink in my armour. If the disease reaches its terminal stage, the 'twitched up' pilot is incapable of flying, or a serious danger to others if he continues. Sooner or later, unless he first gets himself bumped off, it is spotted and he is grounded.

The telltale signs are evident from three entries in my logbook during our month of flying with Coastal. June 26th: 'Returned early, weather.' July 8th: 'Returned, low oil pressure.' July 18th: 'Returned, oil temperature gauge unserviceable.' Excuses, excuses. Always before I'd have flown out the patrol.

We were wholly under RAF control and their efforts were not invariably brilliant. In the early hours of July 9th, returning from a three-hour patrol, the weather closing in on us unexpectedly as we skirted the north Cornish coast, navigating by radar. Soon the clouds ten-tenths at 250 feet and the airfield on its cliff-top must itself have been 200 feet above sea level. So I asked Charlie for a weather report and he accordingly enquired: 'HOW ARE YOUR ORANGES?'

The reply was immediate: 'ORANGES SWEET.' But soon I was forced lower. With the ceiling at under 200 feet, I had to be below the level of the cliff-tops.

– CONFIRM ORANGES asked Charlie.

– ORANGES STILL SWEET came the reply.

We were now due north of the airfield, ready to make our approach. Still ten miles offshore. Using ASV, Jake gave me the course for home. Perhaps this very low cloud extended only over the sea, clearing magically before the cliffs though it seemed unlikely. It was pitch dark with just a glimpse of the wavetops. I kept maximum height without entering cloud but soon this was eighty feet. Jake giving me the distance ahead of the cliffs, which he could tell from his radar (in which we had perfect confidence) with great accuracy.

– Two miles... A mile... Half a mile...

At 400 yards (ten seconds flying-time) I turned away. There was no way landing could be possible. The met. office must be basing their replies on what they'd forecast, without checking on 'actuals'.

– Tell them, put your heads out of the fucking window.

Charlie did just that. We orbited offshore. Several minutes later came their reply.

– SORRY, ORANGES EXTREMELY SOUR. YOU ARE DIVERTED TO PRESTWICK.

Well, we all burst out laughing. How could we help it, despite what was clearly a dangerous situation? Not only had they got their oranges wrong. They were so accustomed to controlling Liberators and Catalinas that a tiny detail had escaped them. We had less than an hour's petrol. And Prestwick, in Scotland, was about four hours distant. An awkward silence when we told them this. We were then instructed to try to get in at St Eval, a nearby airfield closer to sea level.

Somehow I just made it though nearly removing a church steeple in the process. The ceiling was ten-tenths at seventy feet and no other aircraft had landed for three hours. Within fifteen minutes, fog had descended to the deck. The oranges were lemons but we were down.

We were only wasting time. Our frustration was expressed, as so often, in a song. Written by the squadron's versifier, Bob Lepage, and bawled to the tune of 'John Brown's Body':

> Let's get back to sea again and catch up on our sleep,
> Let's get back upon the bosom of the rolling deep,
> Let's get back to sea again and get our piss-ups cheap,
> We're chocker with patrols from Perranporth.

Our hopes were soon fulfilled. Barracudas and Avengers had by now taken over to such an extent that there was nowhere left for 816 to go as an independent unit. On August 2nd, the squadron flew to Maydown to be embodied, in my case re-embodied, in 836 and MAC-ships.

To find that Ransford Slater was dead. Such a tragic, unnecessary loss. After all his hours of heroism without a scratch, he'd been killed when low-flying over the green hills of Derry, came those few feet too low. The way so many went.

He died when the squadron was at its peak, with over ninety aircraft. For several months, nineteen MAC-ships had been operational. And it can fairly be said that the Battle of the Atlantic had been won. The Germans by June had equipped all their U-boats with Schnorkels, enabling them to remain submerged indefinitely, and since the previous September (1943) had had the acoustic torpedo, which homed automatically on the noise of a ship's engine. But only if the U-boat could come within range. And the new U-boat commanders were a lesser breed than the dead who had preceded them. Faced by air cover that could now be continuous when required, except in fog or a whole gale, and escort vessels with increasingly sophisticated equipment and techniques, they were showing a marked reluctance to press home an attack. Losses from Atlantic convoys had fallen to an average of less than one ship a month. With many escort carriers now also in service, the Fleet Air Arm for the first time ever had more small flat-tops than were needed. It was soon to be decided that four MAC-ships should 'return to normal trading'.

Whilst we were in Cornwall, *Adula* had completed two round trips. Her aircrews were due for leave and a new 'P' Flight was formed, again under my command, made up of transferees from 816, to sail with her next convoy. They were all hardened, skilful fliers and no work-up was necessary. James ('Jazzmazz') Mason and his observer, 'Tug' Street, had won DSCs for sinking a U-boat single-handed. Our third pilot was a tough little Kiwi, Ralph Cocklin; his observer blue-eyed Dicky Mably.

We spent from now till Christmas ploughing back and forth between Gourock and Halifax. Equipped as in 816 with much improved ASV (but no radio altimeter). It could detect a surfaced U-boat at up to ten miles, maybe more in calm conditions with a skilled operator. But the Germans, too, had improved their radar and it should still always be possible for a U-boat to detect an aircraft at normal patrol height, about 1500 feet, before the aircraft could detect the U-boat. The new generation of U-boat commanders had taken to submerging more and more often if an aircraft appeared on their radar screen. So we had to keep in mind that we were performing (as we were) the vital function of forcing them to dive, and thus preventing an attack, or we'd have died of boredom.

By now there were usually two MAC-ships with every convoy. On our next trip outward bound, our 'chummy ship' was *Macoma*. It was a fast convoy, we were only twelve days at sea, but 'P' Flight put in twenty-one sorties and *Macoma's* much the same. Half of these were concentrated in two mid-Atlantic days, when there were frequent indications that U-boats were about and SOE called for continuous patrols during daylight hours, and offensive searches as necessary.

Action seemed most imminent at the end of those two days. I was flying a dusk Adder. This, it may be remembered, was a defensive patrol back and forth ahead of the convoy. Each leg about twenty miles. Keeping eight to ten miles from the leading escorts, which were not to be seen in the gathering gloom and deteriorating weather. It was a stormy, ominous evening with a wind of over thirty knots, which gave me a very low groundspeed when flying into its teeth on my northward legs. On what should have been the last of these, a dramatic signal from Brian in *Adula:* PROBABLE U-BOAT DETECTED BY RADAR IN POSITION 279ZZ10.* INVESTIGATE FORTHWITH. FLYING OFF BOTH AIRCRAFT TO SUPPORT YOU.

– Jesus, said Jake, that's within two miles. Steer 354. Bugger should be nearly in sight. Nothing on my screen though.

Altering course those few degrees to port. Opening up full throttle. Checking on my rockets. In less than two minutes we reach the given position. Only the empty sea.

– Bugger must have dived.

But then, as I begin to orbit the pinpoint, another signal from Brian: POSITION NOW ESTIMATED 287ZZ12. BOTH AIRCRAFT SCRAMBLED.

Another two miles to westward. So why can't we see her already? Even if not a U-boat but by some strange chance a U-boat-sized surface vessel, which would appear the same on SOE's radar screen. Yet no sign of a blip on ours. Dusk falling rapidly as I reach the new position. Nothing.

– Keep a look-out for the others.

I again start to orbit. Soon we sight the two other aircraft approaching us from eastward. They'd been airborne within nine minutes of SOE's first message. I swoop towards them to take over leadership. As we join up, a further signal reaches us. SOE would have been watching the blip of the two Stringbags as it neared the blip of the vessel.

– YOUR BLIPS HAVE NOW MERGED WITH U-BOAT'S. SHE SHOULD BE DIRECTLY UNDER YOU. HAVE YOU SIGHTED ANYTHING?

– NEGATIVE was Charlie's laconic reply.

We split up to search as wide an area as possible in the few remaining minutes before nightfall. Then no point in continuing. We re-form and head for home. Landing all three Stringbags in ninety seconds, though dark as hell and forty knots over the deck.

Not till long afterwards did I unravel the mystery of this

---

* Meaning ten miles from the Commodore's ship (ZZ) on a bearing of 279°.

invisible U-boat, still boldly on the surface with three String-bags overhead. There'd been a tiny error on the part of SOE. It was *my* blip that he'd mistaken for a U-boat's. He had homed me to myself. As I moved north, the blip of course moved north. And as I joined the others, the two blips inevitably merged. A classic case, in the words of Winnie the Pooh, of where the woozle wasn't.

We didn't even suspect this at the time. Understandably, SOE never admitted it to us. But he knew well what had happened – as I discovered thirty-four years later when coming on his report, safely filed in the Public Record Office.

I flew with Jake for the last time on October 18th. We'd just completed a return trip from Halifax on which a lack of U-boats and the presence of two other MAC-ships, giving us a maximum striking force of no fewer than ten aircraft, had combined with the weather to restrict our flying: a pre-dawn Adder on the 1st, a pre-dawn Lizard on the 6th, a dawn Serpent on the 13th (when we located and shepherded home a straggler), a Viper on the 14th, another on the 16th. Next day we were on stand-by, as was one MAC-ship every day by turn, so that we could celebrate my twenty-fourth birthday appropriately. We flew off despite hangovers to Maydown the following morning.

Here Jake found word that his rest period awaited him: he was to go on leave pending appointment to a training squadron. We'd been flying together on ops for thirteen months and it was hard to say good-bye.

A young observer named Wright, new to the squadron from flying school, was appointed to replace him (though to all of us Jake was irreplaceable). Although as flight commander I would normally fly with the most experienced observer, I didn't like to break up an existing team, so I took him on myself. My confidence in him was not exactly helped when we flew together for the first time, on a navex (navigational exercise) which involved taking off from Maydown, flying a pattern of courses well out to seaward, then homing to *Adula* off Ailsa Craig for his first deck landing ever. But for this final leg he committed the cardinal error of giving me a reciprocal: in other words, the course he asked me to fly was the diametric opposite of the correct one. On being given 284 to steer, I could hardly help knowing at once what had happened, but complied without comment to see if he himself would notice his error. But after flying westward for five minutes, I thought I'd better prompt him.

– Are your perfectly sure we're flying the right course?

– Yes, I think so. Donegal should be coming up on our starboard bow. Nothing on my screen though.

– On a course of 284? That's a wee bit north of *west*.

– That's what I make it.

I gave him two more minutes. Then:

– Will you kindly retract your digit without any further delay. We are *not* supposed to be heading for New York.

– New York? Of course not.

Then as the penny dropped: 'Oh, Jesus.'

For a while afterwards he was known as 'Wrong-way' Wright, shortened to 'Wrong' Wright, but the unkind nickname soon wore off. He turned out to be a first-rate navigator and never made any comparable mistake so long as we flew together.

The opportunities for smuggling on the MAC-ship run had always been, let us say, difficult to resist. Duty free liquor and smokes were available on board in modest quantities, while a varied host of luxuries, strictly rationed and in keen demand at home, were cheap and plentiful in Canada. Moreover our flights after each passage, whether to Dartmouth or Maydown, were always swathed in secrecy: for reasons of security, no one ashore knew we were on our way till we actually joined the circuit and requested permission to land. The customs would then be informed and several hours later a couple of sheepish officers would put in an appearance. We would then go through the formality of declaring a bottle of Scotch and a carton of cigarettes, but our booty would already be stashed away.

The temptation was all the greater because Nova Scotia was 'semi-dry': there were no pubs, you couldn't drink in public, liquor was strictly rationed. A Nova Scotian purchased his week's supply, it was wrapped up in the store, he couldn't open the package in public. So there was a flourishing black market, especially in Scotch, which was thus at a double premium. We could buy it on board for next to nothing – less than five bob a bottle – and flog it to thirsty Canadians for ten or twelve times that figure. The profit on a dozen bottles was thus something like £30, in those days a very handsome sum.

The question had always been what to buy in Canada that would show a similar profit when homeward bound. We amateurs were always content to bring back the latest cosmetics, or a dozen pairs of nylons, for lucky wives or girlfriends. On rejoining the squadron after Cornwall, I found that some of the boys had gone into the matter seriously. Lengthy research had shown that the most profitable commodity was nothing you might have expected. It was birdseed. And bird-seed in unprecedented quantities was now suddenly becoming available to little old ladies in Derry and maiden aunts in Antrim, whose budgies and canaries had been in imminent danger of extinction.

Remarkable but true. The hardhearted Ministry of Food had swept bird-seed off the market. And bird-seed, genuine bird-seed, is the one thing any self-respecting budgie expects to get. He will not be fobbed off with your breadcrumbs or your bacon rinds. So there was nothing the little old ladies wouldn't pay for the real thing. Even a few ounces. It was like dealing in heroin. Bird-seed was cheap in Canada and could be sold at a profit of several hundred per cent if conveyed, or do I mean convoyed, to Northern Ireland.

One little trouble, it's bulky. We were fairly good boys in 'P' Flight and never engaged in this humanitarian trade, so I do not know the logistics in detail. But the professionals were certainly bringing it home by the hundredweight, up to a quarter of a ton *each*, on every homeward run. The sacks would be stowed in the observers' and air-gunners' cockpits before take-off from Dartmouth, which left little room for their occupants. Our cabins were very small, so that four or five sacks of bird-seed would take almost all the available free space. But the pros were quite happy to put up with such trifling discomfort in return for the profit awaiting them.

When the time came to take off for Maydown, the precious cargo would be loaded once again in the after cockpits. A snag might here arise. More often than not, one or two of the Stringbags would be unflyable. It might then be a question of offering a suitable 'cut' to the crew of a serviceable aircraft, who in return would allow it to be used whilst they themselves went on with the ship to Gourock, returning by boat and train to Maydown. No one knows what would have happened if all three Stringbags had been *hors-de-combat*.

At Maydown a well-rehearsed strategy was put into operation to get the booty as quickly as possible from the airfield to Derry before the arrival of the Customs. So the pros between Scotch and bird-seed were each clearing not less than £100 on each round trip. And the little old ladies were delighted, not to mention their canaries.

I had trouble myself with customs, or rather I *didn't* have trouble, when on my way with Penny to Killegar for a weekend after one of these autumn crossings. I was the only member of the squadron whose home was close enough to Maydown to make such visits possible. The others might venture as far as Portrush, or across the border to Buncrana in Donegal, where steak and girls were plentiful, or just take it easy in Maydown. But I could be home in four hours. Penny, now six or seven months pregnant, would soon depart for Brookfield rather than waiting husbandless in Derry for the sake of a day or two together after each trip. We headed by train in civvies for Clones in County Monaghan, where my father would meet us.

With free first-class tickets we had a compartment to ourselves as far as Omagh, where we found we had to change. The train from Omagh, which would rattle through Newtownbutler and on across the border, was more crowded, and we shared our compartment with one other passenger, heavily built and square-faced, in civvies as we were, with thin lips and thick Northern accent. We fell into conversation and I mentioned that I was heading home on leave after several weeks at sea. He offered no details of his own occupation beyond mentioning that he was a civil service official.

As the border drew nearer, I enquired if the customs were as perfunctory as ever, mentioning with a grin that I'd some duty-free goods with me. Cases were never opened. A rude surprise awaited me.

– God they've got terrible strict, he told me.

I expressed amazement. The border was always wide open.

– That's all changed now. Didn't they tell you? There's a new chief inspector, they go through everything. If you've more than a nip of liquor you'll be in trouble.

– But this is terrible, I exclaimed. I've five bottles of spirits and 600 cigarettes.

And I proceeded to enumerate in detail the various goodies I'd brought from Canada or bought free of duty on board.

– They'll take all, he said.

We were soon approaching Newtownbutler, the Northern border station and our companion's destination. I could hardly believe what he'd told me and felt sure I'd get away with it, somehow or other, despite his total pessimism. But as the train drew to a standstill, I saw to my horror that he was looking along the platform for a customs officer, spotted one, was waving him to our compartment.

– Well Jesus Christ Almighty! He's going to rat on me!

The fresh-faced young officer came respectfully to our door.

– There's no need to inspect this man's baggage, he told him. He's a naval officer on leave.

Then turning to me with the smallest hint of a smile.

– *I'm* the new chief inspector.

My last round trip in a MAC-ship. Brian Walsh Atkins on well-earned leave. He'd never missed a day in over a year with *Adula*. His place as ASO taken for this voyage by Peter

Elias, a young two-and-a-halfer, swarthy and dark-eyed, with a distinguished record behind him. We again sailed in company with *Macoma* and there were reports of U-boats aplenty, especially during the first five days, when *Adula* alone flew fifteen sorties, six of which were Lizards, and *Macoma* as many again. Nothing. The U-boats were diving, we were compelling them to keep their distance.

The weather then deteriorated and we in *Adula* flew only nine sorties in the remaining ten days of the passage. One of these I cannot help remembering. I'd had a dose of the shits. A dawn Lizard to the pinpoint provided by HF/DF. Searching the given area round it. As I turn for home, the dose reasserting its presence. No good asking for a tin. Nothing whatever to be done about it except wriggle uncomfortably and open up the throttle. My predicament gets worse but at last we sight the convoy. Only to get a red light from *Adula* indicating do not attempt to land.

For Jesus' sake. What the hell's the matter? At this time of all times. I'm literally bursting, or beginning to burst, as we orbit for ten interminable minutes. Then a signal by Aldis lamp: OUR ARRESTER WIRES UNSERVICEABLE AAA YOU ARE TO LAND ON MACOMA. And *Macoma,* only now, beginning to drop astern before turning to windward to receive us, moving all her three Stringbags forward, it seemed so slowly, lifting the barrier behind them.

It happened that the flight embarked in *Macoma* was one of several in the squadron composed of officers and men of the Royal Netherlands Navy. After landing on a carrier other than your own, there are normally one or two little niceties to perform. A friendly word to the aircraft handling party on clambering down from the Stringbag. Strolling aft to the island to pay your respects to the Master, then below to the chartroom for debriefing with the ASO. To hell with the niceties. I leap headlong from the Swordfish before the prop stops turning.

– Where are the bleeding heads?

As bad luck would have it, the Dutch air mechanic to whom I addressed this simple question failed to understand it.

– The heads, for Christ's sake. The shit-house. The jacks, man. *La toilette.*

Blank incomprehension. Then happily realizing that *Macoma* and *Adula* were in all probability almost identical twins. Finding the same companionway, thence to the haven I was seeking. Ah then, what blessed relief!

Ten minutes later I report to the bridge. Hearty laughter all round. Repairs to the arrester wires took only a couple of hours. After an excellent meal with the Dutchmen, preceded by several Bols, the two carriers turned into wind together so that in less than a minute I could fly from one to the other. We flew Vipers all next day and kept the U-boats down. Two days later, we flew ashore to Dartmouth.

Homeward bound we were routed far to the south, almost to the Azores, to avoid the worst of the weather or as a result of intelligence reports. But flying was possible on only three or four days in mid-Atlantic, when SOE sent us on a series of fruitless Lizards to investigate fixes. Then idleness till we came within sight of land: for once our first glimpse of it was the Cork and Kerry mountains rather than those of Donegal. No further operational flying expected. But as dusk was falling an urgent signal from SOE: an HF/DF fix from within half-a-mile of Irish territorial waters, off the Old Head of Kinsale, not far from the entrance to Cobh, some fifteen miles to our north-east.

We very seldom flew night sorties, but the sea was calm, visibility perfect, the first stars bright in the sky, the first lights glimmering from coastal villages. The presence of this surfaced U-boat posed a serious threat to the convoy: if she detected us by radar and was allowed to stay on the surface, she could easily reach an attacking position two hours later, even less. So our Stringbags were called to scramble, two to fly Lizards to search the area round the pinpoint, the third a Crocodile Port. Meaning a patrol back and forth along the port flank of the convoy, in this case between the convoy and the coast. Each sortie almost three hours, hoping to ensure that the U-boat would be astern of us and submerged by the time we landed on.

We drew straws and I got the Crocodile. A few minutes of twilight after take-off. Such a clear December night that I could clearly see the coast from start to finish of the patrol. The lights of Skibbereen, of Clonakilty, of Kinsale, as the convoy steamed north-east. No black-out in my neutral homeland. Then after two hours the glow over Cork city. Knowing that a U-boat, surfaced or now submerged, lay somewhere in those seemingly placid waters. Mistakes can be made with radar, but a position found by Huff-Duff meant an enemy vessel was certainly present.

And we nearly had an incident. An international incident. Which would have been extremely unfortunate. The observer on one of the Lizards saw a clear blip on his screen. A couple of miles offshore, approaching the entrance to Cobh, within territorial waters. This by no means deterred the pilot from investigating. At a range of less than a mile, the blurred outline of what he took to be the U-boat. He at once dived to attack. But happily came to realize in time that his U-boat was a fishing smack. Sighs of relief all round when he told his story afterwards.

By the time we'd landed we knew our enemy was safely astern of us. It was my last operational flight with 836. Next day, from somewhere off Holyhead, we flew ashore to Maydown.

A sequel long afterwards. After each trip, the Air Staff Officer made a report of it to Their Lordships, with copies to the Commander-in-Chief (Western Approaches), the Flag Officer Carrier Training, the Captain at Maydown and sundry others. Peter Elias saw fit to mention that in the three months since we'd rejoined *Adula* on September 11th we'd completed 156 hours of operational flying. And in over a hundred deck landings in all weathers, not even a minor accident, not a scratch. (About forty of these were after non-operational flights, so our average sortie was about two-and-a-half hours.) He also gave an account of an event that had seemed quite unremarkable at the time: we had oiled one of our escorts in mid-Atlantic. I believe this was the first time it had been done by a MAC-ship and it was of some significance that it was possible, but it presented no problems at all. Even when, by chance, two Stringbags were called upon to scramble while the oiling was in progress. In no way was taking-off affected, since the oiling hose ran down the starboard edge of the flight deck without diminishing the width of deck available. It might as well not have been there.

I unearthed this report long afterwards in the Public Record Office, with the comments and recommendations of the officers on the staff of both C-in-CWA and FOCT. At C-in-CWA there had been rancorous disagreement, with real and growing acrimony evident, on the question of whether we deserved a 'bun', as a letter of congratulation was apparently known, for flying off when oiling. If these senior officers could argue so bitterly on such a trivial matter, what were they like on issues of real importance? Some thought it little more than routine (as we did) and considered that buns would be cheapened if awarded so easily. Others thought a bun to be in order, though unable to make any real case for their opinion in the long series of increasingly angry minutes that followed the proposal. Had they nothing better to do? In the end the pro-bun faction prevailed: an appropriate letter was drafted and approved.

Over at FOCT it was our long prangless record that was held to be bunworthy. Accordingly (I now discovered) a signal was sent to Maydown on December 16th: 'The personnel of "P" Flight are to be congratulated on flying 156 hours of operations, involving 103 deck landings, without accident, while embarked in my *Adula*.' This was followed soon afterwards by C-in-CWA's missive: 'It is considered that the flying off of two search aircraft whilst oiling an escort reflects credit on the Master, J. M. Rumbellow, shows initiative on the part of the Air Staff Officer, Lieutenant-Commander Elias, and skill by the pilots of "P" Flight.'

I don't know what happened to these two buns. Perhaps they got lost in the post. But I never got to know about them till I came upon them, thirty-three years later, filed away in Kew. Although they were somewhat stale, I gobbled them with relish.

Adula, after ten months continuously at sea, was due for a brief spell in dry dock, so we were all given nearly three weeks' leave from December 10th. For me this was doubly fortunate. Not only would it include Christmas, but more important I would be with Penny when our baby was expected on December 17th. But the 17th came and went, Christmas came and went, no baby. I had to be back at Maydown on the 28th, which meant leaving the previous evening. The time came for departure and still I wasn't a father.

The long journey to Derry. Arriving to find *Adula* not expected to be ready for at least another week. And then, on New Year's Day, a phone call from Penny's brother: it's a boy.

Persuading my new boss, John Callendar, to allow me four more days. Taking my Stringbag with me. Floating next morning in a south-easterly direction. To find Penny happy as a lark. With day-old Christopher, pink and wrinkled, safe in his cot beside her.

IX

ELEVATION

I returned to Maydown on January 6th, 1945. Expecting to rejoin *Adula* within a week, then back to the familiar MAC-ship routine. But I was in for a surprise, one hell of a surprise. Summoned on the 13th by the Captain.

– I'm pleased to tell you that you have been appointed to take over command of 835 Squadron. You are promoted to Lieutenant-Commander. Congratulations.

Completely speechless apart from a muttered thank-you sir. In peacetime it normally takes eight years as a two-striper to reach this dizzy height. In my case sixteen months. Promotion to equivalent rank when barely twenty-four was not unusual in the Army, still less in the RAF. But it would make me one of the youngest two-and-a-halfers in the Wavy Navy.

– The squadron operates from HMS *Nairana*. It is at present at Machrihanish, due to re-embark next week. You will take over command the day after tomorrow.

So soon. Oh Jesus. Jesus, would I be able for it?

– Aye, aye, sir. Is it Stringbags, sir?

– A mixed squadron. Let's see, fourteen Swordfish IIIs and six Wildcat VIs. They've been having a rough time, it seems. Convoys to Murmansk and a shipping strike off Norway. Morale, I gather, is not particularly high.

My apprehension and exultation growing simultaneously. Two-and-a-half stripes. Commanding twenty aircraft. Forty officers and nearly 200 men. But would I be able, would I be able? This, after so long, my very first appointment to one of His Majesty's ships. No problem, I thought, in the air leading the Stringbags. (The Wildcats, which were fighters, would fly and fight independently.) But knowing nothing at all, after the total informality of Coastal Command and MAC-ships, of all the RN mysteries. Such a weight of responsibility. And morale 'not particularly high'.

– Has the previous CO bought it sir, I enquire.

– No, he's due for his rest period. Overdue, I think. Along with a few others. They really seem to have earned it. His name is Jones, he's an observer. Lieutenant-Commander Valentine Jones, RNVR. You know him? All the better.

Dazed to my cabin. Many thoughts confused. The power and the glory, yet such feelings of inadequacy. For the first time in my life. But now I'd be the boss. Somehow or other I've just got to pull it off. On Russian convoys, Christopher twelve days old. To say farewell to Charlie after fifteen months of flying with him. Put on a bold face, for Christ's sake. But all the White Ensign rigmarole: requestmen, defaulters, up spirits, darken ship. What the procedures? The paper work, the flying programmes?

Was I even fit for the flying? Leading thirteen Stringbags. And today the thirteenth. But thirteen lucky for some. Telegram to Penny. My new address HMS *Nairana*, c/o GPO, London. Though floating in Arctic waters. Get my uniforms altered, find a tailor in Derry. A half stripe, you understand? By tomorrow. Leaving the next day for an unknown destination and destiny.

How had I come to be chosen? There were many two-stripers senior to me. But Val's successor was needed at once, so had to be a pilot or observer serving in home waters, or ashore in the UK, preferably in a Swordfish squadron. And by now, at last, these were rare: apart from 835 and 836, there was I think only 813 in *Campania. So* the field was greatly narrowed. I wasn't the most senior of the two-stripers available but must have been thought the best qualified. I'd never have commanded a squadron and reached this lofty rank if Val's rest period hadn't come due at this moment. In another three months, both 835 and 813 had been disbanded. So this my last and only chance.

Two days of relentless ribbing by my 'P' Flight shipmates. Yes sir, no sir, three bags full sir. Drinks with Charlie in Derry. And meeting Douglas Graham, my classical tutor at Eton, the only master I'd respected, now a Navy padre. 'You seem to have caught up with me.' Appearing sheepish with my halfstripe in the Mess, not really believing it.

Taking off next morning in abominable weather for whatever fate awaited me. Without an observer, just another pilot as passenger. But I could find my way blindfold. Ceiling less than a hundred feet, visibility half a mile. Picking up the Mull of Kintyre, following its steep crags northwards to the low-lying golf links, well remembered. Sneaking in, over its recognized fairways and bunkers, as a driving rainstorm swept me. The only aircraft to take off or land that day.

To find things far worse than I'd expected. I'm hardly out of the Stringbag when an unknown young officer approaches.

– Are you the type who's taking over from Val? Well there's one or two things you'd fucking well better know. To begin with, the fucking Captain's crazy...

What to do? Pull my rank? Demand he call me 'Sir'? No question of it.

– Pipe down about the Captain. If I'm to hear anything, I'll hear it from the C.O.

– I'll take you to him. He'll tell you the fucking same. Thank Jesus I'm leaving with him tomorrow.

That's something anyway. Finding Val in his office. Extreme fatigue in his eyes. He does his best to fill me in. The squadron seems near breaking point. Incessant flying in foulest Arctic weather. He's afraid my job not easy. Several of the boys had been far too long in ops, and seven of these, six pilots and an observer, would depart with him next day, when replacement aircrews arriving. The main trouble, yes, was the Captain. They call him 'Fly-off' Surtees. A wan smile. Also known as 'Strawberry'. From his complexion.

– *I'd* tell him conditions weren't fit for flying. Wings would tell him the same. But Strawberry – he isn't a pilot –

had always the same reply. 'Get the engines started, the crews aboard. We'll turn into wind and then we'll see.' Once he'd said that, we already knew what would follow. Invariably. As soon as we were headed into wind: 'Fly off.'

– Have you lost many crews?

– That's the extraordinary part of it. He must have the luck of the devil. We've never lost a life through flying in bad weather.

How could I replace Val? Everyone loved him. From the aircrews down through the chiefs and petty officers to the lowliest air mechanic. He departed next morning with the others leaving the squadron. I felt out of my depth. Shit-scared and alone.

Mustn't show it. A week at Machrihanish before embarking. Literally sick with apprehension, not sleeping, couldn't eat. *But mustn't show it.* If I collapse the whole squadron will collapse. Telling the boys we'll be rejoining the ship on Monday. Greeted with a groan. *Now that's enough of that.* We've a job to do and we're damn well going to do it. 'But Strawberry, sir...' You mean Captain Surtees? Well pipe down about Captain Surtees. Did he ever lose a crew to the weather? Grudging silence. Well what's the bloody beef then? Trying somehow or other to pull the squadron together. When I need pulling together. Hostile eyes facing me. I'll do my best to stand up for you but we do what the Captain orders. 'The boss always said...' But I'm the boss for Christ's sake. I don't want to know what the boss said. What Lieutenant-Commander Jones said. We fly on board on Monday. Have some pride in your squadron.

Everyone pissed as hell round the piano every night. But that's normal. At least I know all the songs. Who's that knocking on my door. Cats on the rooftops. The harlot of Jerusalem. The ball of Kirriemuir. Can even teach them some new ones. *But that's not enough* I remember telling myself with unhappy certainty. Knowing the songs is not enough.

Ah Jesus. And it'll be worse, far worse, on board. How the hell can I pull it off?

I chose to fly with the Senior Observer, named appropriately Strong. Due soon for his second stripe, with long operational experience. But not *too* long, no sign of the twitch. Quiet but wholly reliable, George Strong at once impressed me. Steady as Ailsa Craig. So let's get in the air then. Just have a look-see together.

Our Swordfish IIIs the very latest, known to all as pregnant Stringbags from the great bulge in their bellies* to house their ASV Mark X, the best airborne radar yet. They have to be two-seaters, just a pilot and observer, to make room for all the ancillary equipment. No guns of course; what would we want with guns? A further refinement, Rocket Assisted Take-Off Gear, known by its acronym RATOG, making maximum warload possible however light the wind. A rocket under each wingstub. Press the appropriate tit when abeam of the bridge, off go the rockets and you are forthwith propelled skyward. Good as an in-built catapult. And the Pegasus XXX engine, last of the long line of Peggys, better than ever. So here they were in 1945 taking what was basically the same old Stringbag, which had been flying for nearly a decade and was generally believed to have passed long since from front-line duties, still finding it worthwhile to work on her and modify her, giving her such of the latest trappings as she could carry and still sending her forth on the most demanding missions. As I would soon discover.

Flying as much as I could. Whilst getting to know the officers and men I now commanded. And trying to instil some sense of cohesion and pride, some flash of *esprit de corps,* a lifting by its own boot-strings of morale. Leaning heavily on my chiefs and petty-officers who knew everything. Identifying the stalwarts among my aircrews, those who were the trouble-makers and those (the majority) who were somewhere in between, just ordinary honest flyers. Working on all of them as best I could but feeling my best not good enough to have an outfit ready for action the next week.

No trouble with the fighter-boys. They came under my command but operated as an almost autonomous unit, led

* See Plate 13

in the air by Allen Burgham, an already decorated New Zealander. Their Wildcats*, under lease-lend from the States, were relatively modern though not a patch on the latest Spitfires even.

Nairana was one of no fewer than forty-three escort carriers that had now been completed, of which only *Audacity* and *Dasher* had been lost (and *Archer* retired). All but six had been converted in the States. There were also the two new fleet carriers, *Indefatigable* and *Implacable,* commissioned in 1944, and three light fleet carriers, *Colossus, Vengeance* and *Venerable* (the names they chose!), though the last three were only starting their trials. *Nairana,* one of the six British conversions,† namesake of a packet-boat converted to launch seaplanes in 1917, was attached to the First Cruiser Squadron in the Home Fleet, based at Scapa. But now lying at Greenock. My squadron her total establishment. Her last operation set out to be a strike against shipping off Norway but proved totally abortive: it was the night of the full moon, a week after Christmas, but the weather was so unfavourable that, despite Strawberry's reputation, the order to fly was never given. Much moaning because Hogmanay spent at sea on this fruitless mission. Before that a very tough run to Murmansk and back.

I dreaded the time we would join her. Believed all my shortcomings would at once be laid bare. The disembarked maintenance crews had gone overland to Glasgow two days previously. The Wildcats already on board. We took off from Machrihanish on January 22nd, two vics of five Stringbags, one vic of four Stringbags, flights in line astern. Make it good and close boys. Forming up over the sea to westward, then in very tight formation back across the airfield. Ceiling 800 feet. Skirting Arran, skirting Bute. To locate our mother-ship precisely on time in the firth, already turning to windward for us. I signal echelon starboard, we break formation one by one at half-minute intervals to land.

* See Plate 14
† The others were *Audacity, Activity, Pretoria Castle, Vindex* and *Campania.*

And as soon as we landed an immediate change for the better. Contrary to everything I'd expected. I seemed to come alive and all the squadron with me. Such a hustle and bustle. Six times as many aircraft as *Adula* and everyone six times busier. The Wildcats already below-decks in the hangar. The first to land, I am signalled right forward to the port side of the flight deck, my wings already folded before I cut the engine. The second, my number two, wings folded and alongside me within twenty seconds. Thirteen String-bags to be crammed ahead of the barrier before the four-teenth lands. Ground crews at the double to shepherd all in place. The whole operation completed in well under ten minutes.

So now I must face the Captain. Face Strawberry, face Fly-Off, face Captain Villiers Nicholas Surtees, DSO, RN. I make my way to the bridge. On the uncomplex bridge of a MAC-ship, no one but the mate whose watch it is, probably in civvies. Perhaps the ASO. Everything so informal. Nothing informal here. Three or four officers, all in full uniform. Caps, collars and ties! A couple of signalmen. A chief and petty-officer or two. The Captain hunched in front of them all, binoculars raised to eyes, gold-peaked cap pulled down to the binoculars, smaller than the rest, his bright scarlet complexion if nothing else proclaiming his identity.

– Lieutenant-Commander Godley, sir. Come on board to join.

Strawberry hears me. Doesn't lower his glasses.

– Ah Godley. Ah yes.

In his own time turns to see me. Round red face with twisted half-smile. Summing me up. Me bare-headed in fly-ing gear, red silk scarf, helmet and gloves in hand, fur-lined jacket over battledress, Mae West over jacket. I must have looked a schoolboy. Extends his hand to me, welcomes me. Whatever he's thinking he doesn't show.

Is this such a devil incarnate?

I leave the bridge, set out with a petty officer, one of my right-hand men, Landcastle, to begin learning the layout of the ship. The hangar deck, to which one by one my String-bags are being lowered on the lift, then hauled forward by a tractor to their allotted positions, hardly an inch of space between them. Chocked up, securely lashed to the deck, driptrays under each engine. My cabin very far aft, on the deck below the hangar, my suitcase and kitbag waiting to be unpacked. I think a safe haven. 'You'll not sleep here often when we're at sea, sir.' More movement, explains Landcastle, than anywhere else on board. Because so far aft. As it was to happen, I had little time to sleep *anywhere* when at sea. Visiting the messdecks, first the men's, then the petty officers', then the chiefs'. The hierarchy on the lower deck no less evident than in the wardroom. *Nairana* seems ten times bigger than friendly *Adula* though this an illusion. Every square foot utilized, not the wide open spaces above the well decks fore and aft. I hear two bells, make an effort to remember. Yes it must be 1300. So to the wardroom for ginning up. Thank you, Landcastle, as he salutes. I find I've a real appetite for the first time in a week.

We dropped anchor two hours later. Summoned by the Captain. He and I alone together in the austerity of his cabin. As though he wishes to forge a personal bond. He already knows all my background. Makes no reference to my age, my inexperience, my total lack of knowledge of Royal Navy procedures. Takes all that for granted, my petty officers will look after me, what matters is the flying. This is a fighting ship, Godley. And it's your aircraft do the fighting. We exist for one purpose only, to keep them flying. We sail tomorrow night for Scapa, arriving the next evening, the 24th. Now this is for your ears only. The 28th is the full moon. We're going back to Norway. The last full moon, as you know already, we never got off the deck. We could have taken off and landed, but not fly the length of a fjord or attack shipping effectively if sighted. This time we may be luckier.

– What the squadron needs, sir, is one successful op.

– The squadron will be all right, Godley. I rely on you for that.

No mention whatever of shattered morale, of the essential need to rebuild confidence. This too taken for granted. He knows already I must be aware of it. Or if I'm not, nothing he says can make the smallest difference.

We are joined by Commander (Flying), as he is known though not yet a three-striper. He plays the same role in an escort carrier as the ASO played in MAC-ships. The only flyer on board senior to me (though of the same rank), with longer experience in the air, or older. The only intermediary between me and the Captain in flying matters. He will lay down the broad flying requirements, leave me to fill in the details. John Ball has been many months with *Nairana*. Experience going back to Sharks and Seals. Lined and beaten face, tough as leather, someone to help me when I need it.

– Come in Wings. I've been telling Godley our programme. He thinks we need just one success to set the squadron on its feet.

– Maybe next week, says Wings.

– Let's hope so. Well that's all, Godley. Good luck.

Getting the boys together. No, getting my officers together. Telling them we sail for Scapa tomorrow night, no boats ashore this evening. Waiting for the groan. It doesn't come. Now we've got to maintain 100 per cent serviceability just as long as we can. Each of you to work personally on his aircraft tomorrow. Don't just leave it to the men. There'll be night deck landings in the firth after sailing for the new boys. That includes me. A ripple of laughter but friendly. To the open sea by midnight, picking up our escort. Then a Stringbag on defensive patrol, two standing by as back-ups, till after we round Cape Wrath.

The planned programme goes through without a hitch. We sail in perfect weather, a calm sea, frosty air, brightly moonlit sky. The night deck landings are prangless. Our nonpareil batsman, Bob Mathé, soon to become perhaps the only 'bats' to be awarded a DSC – in fact, two DSCs. The luxury of having all of fourteen Stringbags so that continuous single-aircraft cover can easily be provided, if necessary, for over twenty-four hours with no one flying twice. A daylight Cobra with George between Lewis and the mainland. Dropping our hook soon after dark in Scapa.

Someone has written a new song. To the tune of Stand up, stand up for Jesus. We bawl it out round the piano fortissimo, all but the second line. Which is rendered *ppp,* to reach our own charmed circle only.

> *Fly off, fly off for Christ's sake,*
> *For the Captain wants a gong*
> *Fly off, fly off for Christ's sake,*
> *For the Captain can't be wrong...*

Was I wrong in feeling somehow that the last line was sung with less irony than I'd have expected a week earlier?

The hard-pressed enemy was bringing large supplies of vital war material from northern Norway at this time, especially iron ore. Shipped in convoy or independent vessels close inshore. These ships had been attacked by the RAF in daylight using Mosquitoes and had taken to night sailings after suffering heavy losses. It seemed there was nothing, though to us it appeared incredible, that the RAF – whose job it should have been – could send against them at night in the limited airspace available for a low-level attack, the only way of making certain of results. So the Stringbag had once again been called upon. With her absurdly low speed and extremely tight turning circle, she was still, apparently, even in 1945, the only kite for the job.

But the operation ahead of us seems in retrospect so foolhardy, so unnecessary. Our target area was well within range of RAF bases, from which hundreds of modern bombers were being sent out every night, putting only themselves at risk. How could it be that none of these was able for the job in conditions of brilliant moonlight? And to bring two squadrons of obsolete biplanes – 835 in *Nairana,* 813 in *Campania* – to within range of the shipping lane, no fewer than nine warships would sail to within sixty miles of the enemy-occupied coast. In waters where U-boats might be lurking, within easy range of shore-based bombers, even fighters. A cruiser *(Berwick),* two destroyers *(Algonquin* and *Cavendish)* and four smaller warships besides the two carriers. All at risk, very probably for nothing, as four weeks earlier. To fly just one operation against a possibly absent enemy. And in any case no target of real importance expected. Then scuttling back to Scapa.

But ours not to reason why. We sailed at 1900 on January 27th and would take twenty-five hours to reach our takeoff position, which was 140 miles north-west of Bergen and less than half that distance from the coast. The weather perfect, not much swell, maximum visibility. From the small hours of the 28th, we and *Campania* between us kept at least one Stringbag airborne to sweep the sea ahead of us for U-boats. During the few daylight hours – our most northerly latitude would be sixty-two degrees – we also had a pair of Wildcats ranged permanently on the flight deck in case a shadower should find us, but never needed. One of my Stringbags and two of *Campania's* were unfortunately damaged on landing, which reduced our combined striking force to twenty-five.

Briefing at 1830 by Wings, already within 100 miles of Norway. We are to fly off in two waves. The first strike to scramble at 2000, seven Stringbags from *Nairana* and six from *Campania*. Each of these flights to act independently, with its own specified search area. We in 835 to head for the entrance to Rovde Fjord. This isn't a fjord in the usual sense, but an open-ended channel – the route followed by all shipping – between the mainland and a group of offshore islands, a mile or two wide, with mountains rising precipitously up to 3000 feet on either side. We were to follow it for forty miles, attack any targets seen. *Campania's six* aircraft had a similar search area some forty miles to northward.

Wings tells me I can best establish my position by heading first for Ristø, a small offshore island, easily picked up by ASV. Inhabited, he assures me, by nothing more hostile than farmers and cows. Unexplained why, after coming so far, we will be covering only forty miles of the enemy shipping lane. Which will take only half-an-hour. Allowing for ninety minutes to get there and back from the ship, we could have spent at least two hours on patrol, covering four or five times that distance. Even more if on reaching Ristø we split up into subflights, two or three aircraft in each, each with its own search area, whistling up the others if a target sighted.

The second strike, six Stringbags from each carrier, to scramble at 2040. Would orbit safely offshore, in their respective back-up positions, awaiting orders from their leaders who would then be completing their patrols.

I give orders that one aircraft in each strike is to be armed with six bombs, the rest with eight armour-piercing rockets. By 1915, in the most brilliant moonlight, the seven Stringbags of the first strike have been ranged on the flight deck. My own, A for Able, waits in front, facing fore-and-aft amidships. The others, wings already spread, angled inwards in pairs astern of it. We board at 1940, check equipment, start up engines. At 1955 the nine ships turn together into wind so that both flights may scramble simultaneously. *Campania* close on our starboard beam.

At 1959 I get my green light from the bridge, chocks away, open up full throttle, fire my RATOG after eighty yards, am propelled at once skywards into the brilliance of the night. The freezing slipstream blowing in my face. I keep my airspeed below seventy, make a long sweeping turn to port, so that the others can quickly come up with me. (The CO of 813, to avoid any risk of collision, is doing the same to starboard.) In less than five minutes we are in extended echelon formation. I settle down on a course of 042 at a comfortable ninety knots.

I feel perfectly calm and confident. No therapy to compare with commanding an operational squadron! The silvered full moon in a sky without a cloud, so bright that it's nearly like daytime. We can see the great snow-covered mountains of the enemy coast at a range of thirty miles. And Ristø soon visible ahead, not many minutes after George has located it by radar and given me a new course to bring us directly overhead. Where the first excitement awaits us. For reasons I've now forgotten if ever I knew them, my orders are to overfly the little island at cherubs twelve (1200 feet), then use my own discretion. Instead of safely at sea level, remaining so much longer undetected by enemy radar. So I'm leading my six aircraft in open formation, straight and level at ninety knots, between it and the moon at this most vulnerable altitude.

Whereupon two batteries of Bofors guns change all our previous notions of farmers and cows. Streams of multi-coloured tracer come streaking up towards us. At first so slowly, as always, then with lethal acceleration.

We should have been dead ducks. George and I anyway. For most of the flak was aimed at our leading aircraft. And we presented the simplest possible target. But once again our slow speed saved us. Accustomed to Mosquitoes at least three times as fast, the gunners simply couldn't believe that we were stooging in at ninety. For a couple of seconds the tracer came streaming up some thirty yards ahead of us. That was all their chance. Before they could correct their aim, I've put A for Able into a steep diving turn to port, the rest of the boys without delay behind me. In a series of twisting turns to sea level, alternating port and starboard, which the gunners cannot follow. To the safety of the wavetops beyond their range.

But they will have alerted the gun positions ashore. Already before diving I've seen the entrance to our fjord. Now though still several miles distant I see streams of tracer crisscrossing it, from batteries on the mainland and the nearest offshore island. What did they think they were firing at? But knowing for sure that I must lead my Stringbags through this deadly curtain. No way I can escape this. My thoughts at this moment fly to Christopher, four weeks old. Surely not now of all times.

To make matters worse, I see that one of my junior pilots, in the excitement of the moment, has accidentally switched on his navigation lights. He's lit up like a Christmas tree. George to him on the radio: HOPSCOTCH X-RAY, FOR CHRIST'S SAKE DOWSE YOUR LIGHTS. Message not even acknowledged. HOPSCOTCH X-RAY, THIS IS HOP-SCOTCH ABLE. HOW DO YOU HEAR ME? Still no response. We pride ourselves on our radio techniques, but at this critical moment his not working. We send the message by Aldis lamp. The penny drops as we approach the mainland, but our presence now certainly known to every gun position.

Perhaps I'm wrong but I think he'd done us a favour. To the well-guarded fjord entrance, prepared for a hot welcome. In very open formation, flying as low as we dare to avoid being silhouetted. And for some of the time, anyway, the gunners would be unable to fire without shooting at one another. But they never open up. And I believe they must have reached the conclusion, accustomed as they were to ultra-modern aircraft, that this little clutch of single-engined biplanes, dawdling past at under 100 knots, with wheels lowered (of course we couldn't raise them, but how were they to know this?) and lights so boldly flashing, just couldn't be the enemy. Whatever else they might be, perhaps trainees who had lost their way. How else to account for the absence of opposition from these known batteries, which minutes earlier had been firing away at nothing?

Now flying at zero feet up the narrow waters of the fjord. Lights coming on ahead of us in homesteads on both shores as we are heard approaching and men come to their doors, seeming to show us the way. The whole country deep in snow, the white mountains bathed in moonlight rising high above us on either side. Till at last we sight a target. A merchantman sailing towards us on her own. I lead the flight over her, hesitate, decide to fly the last ten miles of our patrol in search of a larger vessel. But the rest of the fjord is empty. Turning back, climbing to 1500 feet, the perfect height for rockets.

I can hardly believe it now, but I had no thoughts whatever for the men sailing in this coaster. Which we were now about to sink. It was nothing compared with the nightly devastation caused by the air forces on both sides. And it was a specific target of strategic importance, not a city where those who suffered most were the civilians. But it amazes me that I never thought for a moment, as I still clearly remember, of the men on board that ship. It was wholly impersonal.

My aim as I banked to dive, absolutely calmly, at the correct angle of twenty degrees towards this doomed vessel, was to strike her with my rockets just below the water level. Flak may have been coming up but I simply wasn't aware of it, I was concentrating solely on my aim. I'd had so much practice and the conditions were so perfect that I expected to be accurate within a very few feet. And I was. Firing my eight rockets in a ripple of four pairs at a range closing from 1000 to 600 yards. Seeing them all striking the water as planned, a yard or two short of the merchantman amidships.

A steep turn to starboard to watch the others. The next two pilots, Roffey and Payne, also score several hits. My own rockets alone would have been enough. Now I know she has no chance of surviving. She is stopped and on fire. I call on the four others to break off the attack, to seek targets ashore. Two of them, Gough and Supple, choose the flak positions at the entrance to the fjord and must have silenced them. In any event they never fired again.

The six aircraft in my flight are soon heading independently back to the ship. I return at low altitude to where the stricken vessel is now low in the water, lifeboats being lowered. And I make one more sweep of the search area. To find two more merchantmen on the point of entering Syvde Fjord, which runs steeply inland to southward. At once calling my second flight, arrived recently offshore. Led by my Senior Pilot, Geoffrey Summers. Three to attack each ship. Waiting for them to approach, then leading them to their targets.

All around me the silent mountains. I can clearly see each cottage on the rock-strewn mainland shore. The steady hum of my Peggy. Summers, Paine and Cridland dive to attack one ship, scoring hits with at least six rockets. Two of my most junior pilots are badly off aim as they swoop down on the other but Provis with his bombs scores a direct hit and two near misses. The first target is on fire but the crew manage to beach her before she can sink. The second is settling rapidly. But I can't stay to observe her. I've been airborne over three hours. Our normal maximum endurance is four-and-a-quarter hours with a war-load and we still have to locate *Nairana* and land on.

We approach her shortly before midnight. I check on my petrol, find I still have nearly forty gallons, enough for over an hour. Well there's a damn good engine for you. The six other aircraft of the first strike have been back for over an hour. Now some of the pilots in the second strike, who think they've been hit by flak or developed engine trouble, are requesting emergency landings. I assure Wings by radio that I've plenty of gas though airborne forty minutes before them, so they are allowed to pancake ahead of me. In the end I'm almost the last to land, at 0017, after four hours and eighteen minutes.

We are already heading home. And quite expecting a counter attack. We had been using radio and the position of warships that included at least one carrier must have been well known to the enemy. But none develops. After a long debriefing, I go below to the hangar to see what damage done. Not a single scratch. And the Stringbag damaged the previous day has been repaired so that all my aircraft are again serviceable.

A couple of hours' sleep. At first light we range the Wild-cats in case of an attack by bombers, a couple of Stringbags for defensive patrols if ordered. Their services not needed.

Back to the hangar to check the aircraft, speak to the men. All spirits high. Great show last night, sir. A piece of cake. But my fitter looks down to me from working on the engine with something less than a grin.

– Do you know how much petrol you had left when you landed, sir?

– Yes, Titchmarsh. That's one hell of a good kite. Over thirty gallons after four-and-a-quarter hours.

– Well sir, I don't know whether to tell you. But I didn't see how it was possible. So I took a reading with a dipstick. Sir, your fuel gauge was unserviceable. You had so little gas it didn't register on the dipstick. Three or four gallons at most.

Three or four gallons. Enough for five or six minutes. A moment or two of silence, then gales of laughter.

– Well, Titchmarsh, for Christ's sake fix that fuel gauge.

– Sir, I've already done so.

– Well for Christ's sake keep it fixed.

Campania's twelve aircraft had flown an inconclusive mission. Apparently they'd carried out an attack but without known results 'in the absence of a flare-dropping aircraft'. It seems strange, it was nearly bright as day, but that's what they reported.

We dropped our hook in Scapa Flow a few minutes after 2000. Everyone in high spirits. By luck we'd had that one success to set the squadron up. Just when we most needed it.*

We spent six days in Scapa. During this time I began to realize what was at the root of all the tensions that had made *Nairana* so much less than a happy ship and were still frequently evident. They had little, I came to see, to do with Strawberry, though as Captain the general antagonism felt by the squadron had become focused on him. In fact he was a great and gallant officer, as air-minded as any of us, who drove his aircrews to the limit but, as the record showed, not beyond it. Or not all that far beyond it anyway. He wasn't a flyer but this was true of almost all captains. The real trouble was the completely unacceptable length of time that some members of the squadron had been kept flying on operations in such perilous, exhausting conditions. Bob Selley, for example, had been in 835 for almost three years without a break. This could never have happened in the RAF, where crews were rotated on a regular, far less demanding basis. The eight who had departed for their 'rest' at the time I joined the squadron, I discovered, had all just been diagnosed as medically unfit to fly – in our language, twitched to bits. And so had come to regard as unreasonable what they would once have seen as a challenge and accepted without question.

There was also the unhappy fact that a majority of the non-flying officers on board, including the Commander, belonged to the old school and still declined to recognize that aircraft had a vital part, let alone a supreme part, to play in naval warfare, even though they were serving in a carrier. Or perhaps *because* they were serving in a carrier. Hence the resentment they felt towards the aircrews, the ship's sole *raison d'être*, especially when all of us were without exception Wavy Navy.

* Long after the war I was able to discover from enemy records that all three ships were in fact sunk – and, happily, not a single crewman killed or injured.

Captain Surtees had none of this. He'd been at pains to make clear to me that he believed what should have been self-evident, that the sole function of *Nairana* was to provide a floating platform from which my squadron could operate. But where did this leave his non-flying executive officers? It left them right in the background, as mechanicals whose main responsibility was to make it possible for us to fly. This they didn't like at all.

My aircrews must have come from every kind of background, I never asked them. They'd won their commissions neither because they'd been to the right schools nor because they knew the right people. But on the sole grounds of being expert flyers. Well reasonably expert. They possessed none of the Dartmouth attitudes of so many straight-ringed officers. And thank the Lord for that. They were just a bunch of kids whose flying for the moment was their life and quite likely their death, knowing nothing whatever of so-called upper-class pretensions and caring even less. That they could successfully operate their outmoded aircraft in nearly impossible weather meant absolutely nothing to their RN fellow-officers (or many of them). Did they have watch-keeping certificates? Could they take charge of a whaler? Did they speak the King's English?

It was ridiculous and in retrospect seems very nearly unbelievable. But it was true. The straight-stripers would so much rather have been serving in a real ship (as they saw it), a cruiser or a destroyer, where a Wavy Navy officer would know his place. Their sentiments overflowed when a senior member of this group described us (and was overheard) as 'all these little buggers masquerading as gentlemen'.

I couldn't take it in silence. Knowing their prejudice was unalterable, I thought the best course was to encourage the squadron to laugh at them. Thus, I hoped, further lifting morale, which such attitudes had done so much to damage, though never before expressed so explicitly. And I wrote a new song, which began with the lines:

We're eight-three-five, masqueraders are we,
Trying to hide our i-dent-i-tee.

And this was the last verse:

So though we may not be quite upper crust,
We'll go on flying as long as we must,
And raise this epitaph over my dust:
He was in eight-three-five.

How we loved bawling this doggerel within all-too-easy hearing of the scowling officer, crimson with rage, who'd made the offensive remark! He knew well we were referring to it but was powerless to stop us, which would have meant admitting it. It was specially good when, as once happened, Strawberry joined us at the piano and we taught him the words, which he thoroughly enjoyed, without knowing their esoteric significance.

Surtees did have shortcomings. For instance his eyesight was so bad that he couldn't make out an attacking torpedo-bomber at 800 yards nor read without spectacles. Moreover he would very seldom wear his spectacles outside the privacy of his cabin, which would have meant admitting to his disability, but ask for signals to be read to him.

Mad however he wasn't. I have to say this because a wild rumour had swept through the squadron some time previously that he might be declared insane – a measure of the resentment he had attracted from some officers in the squadron. The gist of it was that his second-in command, the much disliked F.J. ('Fat Jack') Cartwright, and the ship's senior medical officer, 'Doc' Waterman, had got together when at anchor in Russian waters to consider such a course, *à la* Caine Mutiny, to relieve him of his command, confine him to his cabin (I never heard any actual mention of irons) and set up Cartwright in his place.

I've never been able to determine how much truth resides in this extraordinary tale. But the evidence of insanity put forward is so flimsy that I totally discredit it.

As will be seen, I was able to establish a good working relationship with Surtees. I didn't even find this very difficult. He was a hard man – akin perhaps to Ahab in Moby Dick – but far from impossibly so.

Two days ashore at Hatston for flying practice, with bashes around Kirkwall in the evenings, but *Nairana* never idle long. The day after our return on board, February 4th, Wings and I are summoned to Strawberry's cabin. For the news we are expecting. We are sailing after dark next day with the First Cruiser Squadron to take a convoy to Murmansk. We have to be ready for anything. How's your serviceability, he asks me.

– All aircraft serviceable, sir, except one Wildcat.

– Try and have her ready by noon tomorrow. We're expecting opposition, every aircraft needed.

I go below to my cabin, write a brief note to Penny. I may be away a while, give my love to Christopher. Later singing all the same old songs. But turning in early for my last real sleep till we reached Kola Inlet nine days later.

X

MURMANSK OUTWARD

The convoying of war supplies to our gallant Russian allies, as they were always called in the enthusiastic news bulletins, had begun in September 1941. The only ports open to them were Murmansk, at the head of Kola Inlet, and Archangel some 300 miles to its south-east. To reach them involved sailing deep into the Arctic Circle, often to the southernmost limit of the pack ice. The convoys, for most of the passage of over 1000 miles, would be within range of fast shore-based bombers operating from Norway. U-boats from Norwegian ports needed less than a day to intercept them. And such powerful warships as *Tirpitz, Prinz Eugen* and *Hipper,* also based in Norway, posed a frequent serious threat. Moreover the weather, especially in the winter months, was often so unkind that convoys easily became scattered, leaving the stragglers highly vulnerable.

However the first eleven PQ convoys, as they were originally code-named, went through nearly unopposed, with the loss of only one merchantman.

The picture began to change with the sailing of PQ12 in March 1942. Reconnaissance had shown that the battleship *Tirpitz*, with a strong support group of cruisers and destroyers, had sailed north to Trondheim. The convoy was therefore escorted by almost the whole Home Fleet. Blissfully unaware of this, *Tirpitz* and her consorts ventured forth to attack it, which must have been precisely what the Home Fleet were hoping for, since they were far superior in fire power and numbers. Fortunately for the enemy, bad weather prevented contact being made. On her way back to Trondheim, *Tirpitz* was located by twelve Albacores from *Victorious*, who attacked her with torpedoes but scored no hits.

During the next few months, convoys to North Russia came under increasingly heavy attack. They had virtually no air cover. In mid-1942 there were only five seaworthy carriers and not one of these could be spared. No protection against shadowers and bombers could be expected from shore-based fighters, and the convoys for much of the passage were beyond the effective range of shore-based bombers to keep the U-boats down, because the Russians, with small gratitude, declined to allow the RAF to operate from Lapland, and such air cover as they themselves provided was painfully unreliable. Of the sixty-nine ships in the next three convoys, ten went to the bottom.

But this was only the beginning. By the time PQ16 sailed in May, the enemy had assembled a force of several hundred bombers in northern Norway. To oppose these, the convoy's total fighter strength was a solitary Hurricane in the CAM-ship *Empire Lawrence*, which, it may be remembered, could fly but a single mission. Over a thousand sorties were flown by bombers against this convoy. Seven of its thirty-five merchantmen succumbed. The Hurricane on her mayfly's flight destroyed one bandit and damaged another, the gunners in the escorting warships shot down several more, but enemy losses were relatively low.

The fearful nadir, for which My Lords of the Admiralty were wholly responsible, came with the sailing of PQ17 in June. Its thirty-seven merchantmen had much the same escort as PQ12. It was established by air reconnaissance that *Tirpitz* with two pocket battleships, *Lützow* and *Admiral Scheer*, a heavy cruiser, *Hipper*, and a clutch of destroyers had moved to Alten Fjord, the most northerly anchorage in Norway. On the assumption that they planned to attack the convoy, without even knowing if the enemy fleet had sailed, Their Lordships from their dusty desks in London gave the

fateful order for the convoy to scatter. It is beyond comprehension that they should have taken this decision instead of
leaving it to the Admiral with the convoy. If *Tirpitz* and her
consorts had sailed to attack the convoy, its escorts would
have been hopelessly outgunned. In the event they made no
more than a brief sortie and never came within fifty miles.
But the scattered merchantmen, abandoned by their
escorts, fell easy prey to torpedo-bombers and U-boats. All
but twelve were lost, or over two-thirds of the convoy.

After this disaster, Russian convoys were suspended till
September. By then *Avenger,* the second of the escort carriers, could be made available. Her total establishment
amounted to no more than twelve Hurricanes and three
Stringbags; a 'once-off' Hurricane was again provided, this
time by the CAM-ship *Empire Morn.* These to face several
hundred bombers from their bases in northern Norway.
The convoy, PQ18, lost fourteen of its thirty-nine merchantmen but at least the enemy paid for them: over forty
bombers and three U-boats were destroyed. It is a measure
of the risk involved that this seems to have been considered
a success.

Convoys continued to run the Murmansk gauntlet
through 1943 and 1944. Almost without exception they
came under heavy attack, but losses became 'acceptable' as
air cover was increasingly provided. Not only were carriers
more freely available, so that latterly there was usually at
least one with every convoy, but the Russians from late 1942
at last allowed the RAF to operate from their northern
bases, which was really very considerate of them. Nonetheless, though the convoys to Malta often suffered very serious
losses, the Murmansk run always remained the most hazardous, the most feared.

And this was still true in 1945, though the Battle of the
Atlantic had been won for over a year, when we sailed with
the last but one, JW64.

The twenty-six merchantmen in this convoy left from
Greenock after dark on February 3rd, with an escort of
three destroyers, three sloops, four corvettes and a fleet aux-

iliary. After progressing between the Outer Hebrides and the mainland, they were to rendezvous at 0830 on the 6th, some ninety miles north-east of the Faeroes, with the First Cruiser Squadron (CS1), which would have left Scapa ten hours previously: the escort carriers *Campania* and *Nairana*, the cruiser *Bellona* and eight destroyers. So the merchantmen would be almost outnumbered by their escorts and my thoughts went back to the Atlantic convoy less than a year earlier when four corvettes and two MAC-ships had safely shepherded more than 100 vessels. It was a sign of the times that Rear-Admiral Rhoderick McGrigor, a tough little redheaded Scot, known as Wee McGrigor with affectionate admiration, chose to fly his flag in *Campania*. With 813 still embarked in her and ourselves in *Nairana,* he had twenty-eight Stringbags and twelve Wildcats at his disposal.

We were 200 miles from Norway when we made our rendez-vous, the nearest we would come till forced within half that distance by the southern limit of the pack-ice for two or three days towards the end of the passage. The convoy's initial speed in the favourable conditions was eleven knots, which would have brought us to the safety of Kola Inlet, a distance of 1300 miles, in only five days if we'd been able to maintain it. Our course was almost due north-east and we would hold to it with only minor alterations for the next three days and nights. Thus we would be within continuous range of shore-based shadowers and bombers. A more northerly course would have kept us further from their bases, but would have added a day to our voyage.

The fun wasn't long starting. We and *Campania,* as a rule, were to take turn and turn about to provide cover against bombers and U-boats respectively. If she had her Stringbags ranged for takeoff, we would have our Wildcats and *vice versa.* But all Swordfish in both carriers to be ready to scramble at short notice in emergency at any time, and all Wildcats, which could not operate at night, during the long hours of twilight and the short hours of daylight. On this first day with the convoy, February 6th, we in the Stringbags were flying continuous defensive patrols to keep the U-boats at bay, whilst *Campania's* fighters were at immediate readiness to intercept bombers or shadowers. By bad luck, as we afterwards discovered, we were sighted by a high-flying enemy aircraft on a routine weather flight, and in the evening twilight it was established that our first shadower had made contact and was orbiting the convoy some twenty or thirty miles distant. *Campania* scrambled her fighters within seven minutes, were directed to it by radar, and shot it down. It was a JU-88. Not without loss however. One of the Wildcats failed to return. The cause of loss was never established.

Our position was now known to the enemy. Wee McGrigor held his course. We were again picked up by a shadower in the small hours of the 7th, which kept its respectful distance while reporting our progress to base. To cope with the problem of aircraft shadowing us by night, the unusual step had been taken of embarking a Fulmar in *Campania,* whose pilot was trained as a night-fighter. The Fairey Fulmar, a two-seater, was not quite as antique as the Swordfish, at least she was a monoplane with closed cockpit and retractable undercarriage, but she had been flying since 1939 and was at least fifty knots slower than a Hurricane. However, this also gave her a lower landing speed and it was reckoned she would be able to operate in reasonable conditions when the Wildcats were grounded by night. However at this moment she happened to be unserviceable. The shadower, soon relieved by another, could operate unmolested till first light. The enemy would therefore now know our course and speed as well as our position.

This led us to suppose an attack to be imminent, by bombers or U-boats or both, and in this we were correct. During the night, we crossed the Arctic Circle. The weather was steadily deteriorating: soon a moderate gale was blowing, the ceiling less than 1000 feet, visibility worsening with occasional snow showers. At 0738 on the 8th, in the long pre-dawn twilight, our radar showed aircraft approaching. Our Wildcats were already ranged, their pilots standing by at instant readiness in the ops room. They were at once ordered to scramble.

The enemy striking force, of ten or a dozen JU-88 torpedo bombers, attempted to close the convoy at 0740, three or four minutes before our fighters were airborne. They had almost certainly come from Trondheim, some 300 miles to south-eastward. But their pilots without exception failed to press home their attacks, unwilling to face at close range the outer screen of escorts, who gave them a hot reception. One of them was shot down by the corvette *Denbigh Castle* and others claimed as 'probables'. When they saw our fighters, the survivors turned tail and sought cloud cover before the Wildcats could engage them. Not one of these bombers came within dropping range of the convoy.

A second wave of torpedo-bombers approached at 0930. They were again heavily engaged by the warships in our screen and *Campania* took her turn to send Wildcats in pursuit. Meantime we again ranged our own, in case their support should be needed. But the outcome was much the same as previously. The enemy striking force were compelled by heavy gunfire from our escorts to break off the action without being able to attack, and had found cloud cover before the fighters could reach them.

Within an hour we were again picked up by a shadower. Our Wildcats were still ranged. The gale was now fresh, gusting to forty knots, but they at once scrambled for their second sortie of the day. Much of the cloud had dispersed. The shadower, again a JU-88, was unable to reach cover before they intercepted her and she was shot down in a combined attack by Norman Sargent and Bill Armitage, the latter a young Kiwi.

It is now known that forty-eight JU-88s of Kampfgeschwader 26 were sent to take part in these two attacks, but only about half of them managed to find the convoy and seven of these were shot down, several more than we claimed.

Wee McGrigor ordered an indefinite resumption of round-the-clock Stringbag patrols, whilst from first light the Wildcats were at readiness. However for the moment no further attack developed. By now we were making good only 200 miles a day, an average speed of eight knots, in ever-worsening weather.

The known presence of our fighters was now enough to discourage the enemy from shadowing us in daylight or twilight, but on each of the next two nights bandits were boldly orbiting us. On the first of these, *Campania's* Fulmar was still unserviceable. By the second she was fit to take her chance and scrambled when a shadower appeared soon after nightfall. The sortie was a total failure. Her top speed was probably no greater than her quarry's and her pilot failed to make contact. Moreover on landing he missed all the wires and went full tilt into the barrier. That was the end of our nightfighter for the rest of the round trip.

By 0800 next morning, when we had reached a latitude of 72° 50' and were some 270 miles west-north-west of North Cape, the Admiral swung the convoy to a new course a few degrees north of east. This would bring us ever closer to the airfields and U-boat bases of northern Norway, but we were approaching the limit of the pack ice. It was intensely cold, the wind was constantly gale force, there was much movement on the ship, and for the Stringbags there was a serious danger of icing, not to mention the discomfort of flying in open cockpits, fully exposed to the elements. But we managed to keep flying. In the seventy-two hours between nightfall on the 7th and nightfall on the 10th, over seventy Swordfish patrols would be flown by the two squadrons. Each lasted between ninety minutes and three hours, so on average two Stringbags were continually airborne day and night.

There was precious little day. The sun would rise reluctantly in the south-east, pursue a painful passage, probably unseen, just above the southern horizon, and set in the south-west some four hours after rising. This brief appearance was preceded and succeeded by several hours of gloomy twilight.

I was finding I could manage. Manage but no more. We were all under considerable strain but squadron morale was as high as could be expected. The Wildcat pilots were elated by their success. The Stringbag crews accepted the necessity of each flying a sortie at least once every twenty-four hours and knew that by keeping the U-boats submerged they were preventing an attack. The weather conditions, though bad, were not impossible and I didn't have any complaints. Several aircraft were damaged on landing, but were quickly repaired and I was able to maintain 100 per cent serviceability. I had hardly slept at all since leaving Scapa: either I was flying, or on the bridge, or in the ops room for briefing and debriefing, or in the hangar with the men, supervising repairs and routine maintenance. There was no time for anything else, unless the opportunity came, whether by day or night (it made no difference) for an hour or two of slumber. I would curl up fully dressed, very often in flying gear, in a corner of the ops room or the wardroom. As Landcastle had predicted there was so much movement aft in my cabin and I'd be that much farther from the action if an emergency developed.

But such sleep was always fitful as the ship pitched or rolled through the turbulent Arctic. I found I quickly reached a certain level of fatigue, at which my reactions were only slightly slowed, my ability to fly and work only slightly diminished. Once reached it stayed constant.

I don't think Strawberry ever slept at all. He seemed to be a permanent fixture on the bridge, unless in the ops room for a briefing.

Soon after our alteration of course to eastward, another shadower was detected by radar in the pre-dawn twilight. We at once scrambled our Wildcats. They were speedily homed to it and could carry out a series of attacks before it reached cloud cover. Al Burgham, the flight commander, scored numerous hits and it was claimed as a 'probable'. But we now knew the enemy would be aware of our changed course. And his persistent shadowing was a certain indication that further attacks were planned.

This was confirmed a few minutes after 2000, when two U-boats were detected by HF/DF, one to the south and one to the south-east of the convoy. It was essential to force them down, if possible to attack them. Six of my Stringbags took to the air, two to fly Crocodiles between them and the convoy, two on Lizards round each estimated position.

I flew a night Croc later and it was the most unpleasant flight I ever flew. The temperature was below zero Fahrenheit with a wind gusting to over fifty knots and in our open cockpits we were as exposed as ever to the elements. It was an absolutely pitch dark night and I was forced to fly almost the whole mission on instruments, just as George had to keep his eyes glued to the radar screen. The ceiling was under 1000 feet. I flew as high as I could without entering cloud, though there was little chance of locating the U-boat visually, to give George the best chance of finding her by radar. Just from time to time I'd catch a blurred glimpse of the whitecaps as we buffeted through the night.

Engine failure in these circumstances would almost certainly have been lethal. Ditching at night with such a swell would have been less than a piece of cake. Even if we made it, we could hardly have survived in an open dinghy (if it worked) for many hours. And the gale would be driving us, not towards the nearest shore, but in the general direction of Greenland about 1000 miles to westward. The Admiral could hardly have spared an escort to search for us with U-boats around and so small a chance of finding us fifty miles away in darkness. You in your car, if the engine falters, can pull in to the roadside, lift the bonnet, find out what's wrong. Or in a multi-engined aircraft, if one motor packs up, keep going on the others. No such luck for us. All the time keeping a check on oil pressure and temperature gauge, listening for a change in the engine rhythm that might be a prelude to slow death. But our Peggy hummed on.

Nairana was pitching like crazy when at last we approached to land, but I've seldom seen anything more welcome than the heaving lights of her flight-deck as we came in, guided as ever by Bob Mathé's inspired batsmanship. Our ground speed at touchdown must have been under ten knots and the landing was uneventful.

In the next twelve hours we made good just over sixty miles. We were plunging at walking-speed through the Arctic wilderness. Head-on to the gale, at least we could operate aircraft without leaving station. I knew my turn would soon come round to fly another sortie but sleep was out of the question with a couple of my Stringbags permanently airborne and my men working in the hangar on damaged aircraft round the clock. And throughout those long hours we were continuously shadowed. We were sailing ever closer to enemy bases and the expected attack seemed almost certainly imminent.

George and I were again airborne before sunrise next morning (February 10th). A fresh gale still blowing but better weather. The cloud was in two layers, six or seven-tenths nimbo-stratus at cherubs five to eight (500 to 800 feet) and eight-tenths cumulus and cu-nim at angels four plus (over 4000 feet). Which meant, as for the past three days, no hope of using RPs. Despite the burden of six depth charges, heading skywards within a moment of firing my RATOG with almost half the deck to spare. No HF/DF fixes during the night, so I am to fly a defensive Crocodile, back and forth on alternate tracks to eastward and westward, thirty miles south of the convoy, which would be a quarter of the ever-shrinking distance between it and Norway. Whence any attack would come. Another of my Stringbags on a half-Viper between me and the outer screen of escorts. Keeping as high as I can without losing sight of the ocean. Which means mostly below the nimbus, occasionally soaring higher when I find extensive breaks in it. Much turbulence at the lower altitude and a ground speed of no more than forty knots when heading eastward.

And then an amazing coincidence. For several minutes I've been able to climb to well over cherubs ten. But I see low cloud ahead, dive to get below it, just touching its ragged edges. I am pulling out at cherubs eight when I see, to my amazement, that I'm on a collision course with a squadron of JU-88s, heading northwards towards the convoy at little more than sea level. Ten of them, black crosses and swastikas, in close formation, range a mile.

Two immediate, simultaneous reactions. Warn the fleet and Jesus for some rockets. Within seconds George has sent his signal: BEESWAX FROM TOPAZ ABLE. TALLY-HO TEN EIGHTY-EIGHTS POSITION 180ZZ30. HEADING

FOR CONVOY, OVER. It is briskly acknowledged: ABLE FROM BEESWAX. ROGER, OUT. Thus by this great good fortune we were able to give a detailed warning some two minutes before radar would have revealed that an unknown number of unknown aircraft were approaching. It must have been about a thousand to one against our happening to find ourselves in the right place at the right time.

Two minutes may seem little but it made a real difference. Our Wildcats could get off the deck before the attack developed. And every shipborne gun was manned and ready.

But if only I'd my rockets. This may seem a fanciful wish but was uppermost in my mind. Of course they were intended for use against U-boats or surface vessels and I don't think they were ever fired in an air-to-air attack. But I'd have had a go anyway. The torpedo-bombers were already within range and I was diving straight towards them. My luck at the time was good. Who knows, it might have held. For a single Stringbag to have blazed away with rockets on a squadron of JU-88s, as by pure chance I could have done from where I found myself, would itself have been an achievement. And if I'd just happened to hit one...

But my only armament, defensive or offensive, was a stick of depth charges. So I could only watch impotently as they headed towards the convoy at twice my speed.

This squadron was the spearhead of a sustained series of attacks on the convoy between 1020 and 1050 by over thirty torpedo-bombers of Kampfgeschwader 26. Their pilots, unlike their predecessors, flew in fearlessly over the escorts, despite the attentions of our Wildcats and heavy fire from men-of-war and merchantmen. Those who survived chose individual targets. Many dropped their torpedoes at close range. But ships under attack, whilst firing with all guns, took independent avoiding action to 'comb' the approaching tin-fish and not one of them was hit. *Nairana* herself was lucky to escape. An eighty-eight was shot down by her gunfire when on the point of dropping from a favourable position on her beam. Surtees took no avoiding action 'Enemy aircraft?' he reportedly exclaimed. 'I can see no enemy aircraft. Full ahead.'

In the course of this engagement, two enemy aircraft were shot down by my Wildcats. The victorious pilots were Sam Mearns and Al Burgham. Three were claimed as 'probables' by 813, whilst the escorts and merchantmen destroyed five and damaged eight. Whilst all this was happening, George and I continued our patrol. We'd been expecting to land at 1030 after two-and-a-half hours' flying but the attack was then at its height.

Now another strange encounter. The weather was on the mend, the low cloud was clearing and I'd been able to climb to two or three thousand feet. On the constant lookout for U-boats. Instead I sighted, far beneath me and low above the waves, an isolated enemy bomber heading towards the convoy. Signalled its course and position. Then, just for the hell of it, I made as though to attack, wheeling over towards it in a steep diving turn. This no act of folly. I'd have broken off my dive before coming within close range. The outcome was unexpected.

Out of the corner of his eye, one of the enemy crewmen must have seen me diving towards him and given the alarm. When there's a bit of panic, it's all too easy to make mistakes with aircraft identification, as we ourselves were shortly to discover and as several Wildcats had found already. He may have thought I embodied some dire new secret weapon. Anyway he was taking no chances. He opened up full throttle, went into a steep climbing turn away from me when I was still half a mile distant and headed straight back for Norway. So now we could signal: CARRIED OUT DUMMY ATTACK ON BANDIT. HIS COURSE NOW ONE EIGHT ZERO, SPEED THREE HUNDRED PLUS. We then resumed our Crocodile at a very steady ninety.

Not so funny the next event. When we'd been airborne for over three hours, I was ordered to return. There was an expanse of low cloud ahead of us and I descended through it, emerging at cherubs eight, to find myself in a box of four destroyers. Two of these, cleverly mistaking my single-engined biplane for a twin-engined monoplane, immediately opened up on me with all guns. I headed back into the clouds with some dispatch and George sent a very indignant signal.

When we were finally able to land on, we found we were not the only ones to have come under friendly fire. A Wildcat of 813 had in fact been shot down by a merchantman, the pilot lost. And several more fighters had been damaged, including two from 835.

It was thought the action was over but after a lull of twenty minutes more bandits appeared on our screen. All serviceable Wildcats from both squadrons took to the air; for the time being only six or seven were available between us. These and heavy gunfire from the escorts were enough to dissuade the enemy from pressing home this final attack: again no hits were scored and one bomber was shot down, shared between the Wildcats and shipborne gunfire.

All through the next twelve hours the weather continued to improve. Work without respite on the Wildcats hit by gunfire and Swordfish damaged landing. At noon we were forced by the ever nearer pack ice to a course of east-south-east, which would bring us before long within less than 100 miles of Norway. There was a flap an hour later when an HF/DF fix was obtained on a U-boat not far distant to south-south-east. It is now known that eight U-boats, the Rasmus Gruppe, had been deployed to wait for us here. Two Swordfish were sent at once to investigate. Visibility much improved while they were airborne, the wind always falling till no more than a stiff breeze was blowing. But a new hazard lay ahead.

One of the Swordfish, whose Crocodile had been well ahead of the convoy, appeared overhead an hour before expected. A signal by VHF: DENSE FOG TWENTY MILES AHEAD. REQUEST PANCAKE. A quick word with Wings. As we make our way from the ops room to the bridge, we see the first wisps of fog fluttering over the flight deck. Strawberry turns to us.

– Why is he back early?

– Sir, he reports dense fog ahead. About twenty miles. Requests permission to land.

– Visibility is perfect. Instruct him to resume patrol.

– Aye aye, sir. But we'll have to watch the weather, sir, during the next hour.

Strawberry turns away without a word. For the first time on the trip, a confrontation seems to be approaching. In an hour's time we are supposed to fly off two more Stringbags and receive those airborne. Which for the moment are perfectly safe. We are steaming at eleven knots and it will take nearly two hours to reach the present position of the fog bank. In which aircraft cannot land nor U-boats operate.

The time for takeoff approaches. The two Stringbags ranged. By now we are already passing through patches of fog. I am silent on the bridge. To attempt the patrols would be extremely hazardous and I grimly await orders from the Captain. Ready if necessary to oppose them. At last he half turns to me.

– Can your aircraft scramble?

– Yes, sir. But in less than an hour, if we hit this bank of fog, they'd be unable to land on.

I am expecting the usual peremptory order: 'Fly off.' Instead he asks: 'What do you suggest?' Still only half turning to me.

– Sir, I suggest the two aircraft now airborne should pancake at once. And that we wait one hour before deciding on the others.

– Leaving the convoy without air cover?

– Yes, sir, for an hour. The alternative may be losing two crews and their aircraft.

Strawberry turns away. The night sea now steaming. The flight deck increasingly shrouded. He is weighing up the odds. I know how he hates to cancel a patrol. Suddenly he gives in.

– The two patrols are postponed. Stand by to receive aircraft.

Running aft to the two waiting Stringbags. Takeoff postponed for one hour. Get these two forward ahead of the barrier. The two airborne will be landing as soon as possible.

Within minutes we have turned into wind and both aircraft have landed safely. Half an hour later, the fog is so dense that visibility is no more than fifty yards. There was no question of flying for the next twenty-six hours.

At 0130 on the 12th, soon after our emergence to clear weather and frosty starlight, we alter course for the entrance to Kola Inlet, some 200 miles to southward, less than a day's sailing. At daybreak we make our rendezvous with a small group of Russian warships. An occasional Russian aircraft puts in a brief appearance to help protect us against U-boats. For which they used single-seater fighters, Bell Airacobras, wholly unsuited to such work. By midnight we have reached the shadowed outline of the low-lying coast of Russia. And supposed safety.

But a tragedy to come. We have sailed the whole distance without losing a single ship. But at 0029 on the 13th, when bringing up the rear a mile or two offshore, the corvette *Denbigh Castle* was struck amidships by a torpedo. From one of four U-boats skulking at periscope depth close inshore. Her Captain managed to beach her but she became a total loss.

We had dropped our hook by dawn. I was already fast asleep. In the comfort of my strangely motionless cabin for the first time since leaving Scapa.

XI

MURMANSK HOMEWARD

The half-dozen ships bound for Archangel had been detached with a Russian escort. The rest of the merchant-men steamed on to Murmansk, at the head of the Kola Inlet, to discharge their cargoes. But the men-of-war dropped anchor off Vaenga, halfway up in the inlet between Murmansk and the sea. A road connected this isolated out-post with whatever doubtful delights might have awaited us in Murmansk, but we found on enquiry it was under thirty feet of snow. So our sorties ashore, during the four days and five nights we lay at anchor, were confined to exploring Vaenga. Here's the account I wrote not long afterwards for the *Weekly Review*.

'There was little to explore. A militarized village lying at the foot of barren hills with no sign of life beyond its lim-its. Scattered wooden shacks, a tumbledown barracks and Nissen huts, no bars or restaurants, no places of entertain-ment and only one shop. But most of the boys went ashore at least once, if only to be able to boast of setting foot on Russia.

'On climbing the rickety ladder from the liberty boat to the jetty, we were at once assailed by tattered flocks of chil-dren begging for cigarettes and chocolate. I held out my cigarette case to the smallest little girl, who might perhaps have been five, inviting her to take one. She promptly took the lot, gave me in return a button from a soldier's uniform, ran off delighted. As well she might be. It was next day before I discovered the black market value of cigarettes. This was highest just before the arrival of a convoy, up to 120 roubles for 100 cigarettes; the day after a convoy sailed, they'd fetch less than half that figure.

'We walked up the road towards the RN headquarters in the centre of the town. Everyone in uniform. During both my jaunts ashore, the only adult civilians I encountered were the Russian officers' wives (who alone wore make-up) and the shop-assistants (numbering three). The Army could spare few stalwarts so far from the battle line and all those we saw were either very young or extremely old, shaggy beards with icicles. We called greetings in English and they replied in Russian with a wave and a grin.

'The headquarters were in the only group of stone buildings, looking grand when compared to the others but badly in need of repair. A resident RN Lieutenant was in charge and I wondered what dire sin he might have committed to be condemned to this unenviable appointment. We sought him out to commiserate with him and in particular to ask if he could lend us a few pairs of skis. What else was there to do? I'd been a couple of times to Wengen and wanted to try my hand in the Arctic. And to encourage some of the others to have a go. He plied us with vodka and found three pairs for us, which we bore off triumphantly in search of a suitable practice slope. This we found on the outskirts of the village and spent the rest of the short day tumbling happily down it to the amazement of our allies.

'Next day when we returned to pick up the skis again, we managed to procure some roubles in exchange for cigarettes: "How many would you like?" they said, proffering a bundle. We then descended on the shop, mainly because the story had got around that unused Russian stamps could be flogged at a profit in London. There was very little to be bought beyond the bare necessities of life apart from a shelf of American powdered eggs and such souvenirs as red stars and cap badges. And stamps. I bought a dozen sheets of about 200 each, which I sold a few weeks later to Stanley

Gibbons in the Strand – for just about what I'd paid for them. And our gallant allies were surely confirmed in the opinion already formed the previous day – for how could we possibly want to write so many thousand letters? – that *their* gallant allies must be very strange fish.'

* * * * *

We had arrived in the small hours of February 13th. That evening I'd composed a Valentine to send to the Captains of all our escort vessels, which one of my observers, John Bevan, had written out and brilliantly illustrated, with swastikaed Stringbags and twin-engined Wildcats. It went thus:

The single-engined Stringbag
  Has flown for quite a time,
Its prehistoric silhouette
  Is known in every clime.
How different the eighty-eight,
  With fuselage so slim –
A monoplane with engines two,
  Don't make mistakes with him!

Yet what a metamorphosis
  A bit of action brings,
When Junkers fly at eighty knots
  And grow some second wings;
And Stringbags (clearly nazified)
  And Wildcat sixes too
Become the targets of all guns
  Whilst eighty-eights fly through…

The leopard cannot change its spots,
  Nor I (alas!) change mine;
Remember this, and I'll be pleased
  To be your Valentine.

199

This document we now photographed and made enough prints for distribution next day. I doubt if our *billet-doux* was greatly appreciated, but at least on the homeward run none of us came under fire.

Our luck had been much too good to last. The sinking of *Denbigh Castle* was the first sign that it was changing. It wasn't long before we received further confirmation. Next day the bad news reached us that two merchantmen, *Horace Grey* and *Norffell*, of those on passage with a Russian escort from Archangel to join us for the journey home, had been torpedoed and sunk off the entrance to Kola Inlet, in almost exactly the position where *Denbigh Castle* had been hit. It was therefore all too clear that several U-boats, possibly a pack, were waiting offshore to attack us as we left. In fact, as German records show, there were half a dozen. Our departure was planned for the early hours of the 17th. So, the previous day, a group of five escorts, led by the sloop *Lark*, sallied forth from Vaenga to sweep the approaches to the inlet. They were able to locate and destroy a U-boat (now known to have been *U425*) at 0107 on the 17th and to confirm the presence of others.

We were therefore ready for anything when we weighed anchor a few hours later and headed northwards with the convoy, RA64, which comprised thirty-four merchantmen with the same escorts as before, up the still-dark narrows of the inlet towards the open sea. I had managed to get all my aircraft serviceable but *Campania* was down to nine Swordfish and only two Wildcats, so the bulk of the flying would necessarily fall on us. The two squadrons were ordered to maintain, between them, continuous air cover for as long as weather permitted.

Our task was extremely difficult. Certainly none of the U-boats would venture to the surface, preferring to use their Schnorkels to remain at periscope depth indefinitely. A Schnorkel wasn't big enough to be detected by ASV and was hard to spot visually, even in full daylight, at a range of more than a mile or two. But the sun was up for only four hours a day and in the long twilight we'd have to pass almost directly above the Schnorkel to sight it. Our patrols at night, though hazardous, would in fact be almost pointless.

The first ship of the convoy passed Toros Island at the mouth of Kola Inlet in the morning twilight at 0745. In the twelve hours after we took over the Swordfish duties from *Campania* at 1500, we flew thirteen patrols totalling twenty-six hours. Nonetheless at 1015 an acoustic torpedo from *U968* (as is now known) blew the stern off *Lark* as she swept ahead of the convoy. The two Stringbags nearest to her were diverted at once to her position but the U-boat would have dived deep. A clutch of destroyers spent an hour combing the whole surrounding area but never located the enemy.

Lark suffered casualties but lived to fight again, though not for many months. She was towed by a Russian tug to Murmansk and there repaired.

That was only the start. The convoy made an emergency turn to due east away from the U-boat's position and was still only seven miles offshore when the steamship *Thomas Scott*, close on our starboard beam, was torpedoed by *U968*. A crack like a howitzer and a black cloud from her stern. Though her crew at once abandoned her, she showed no immediate sign of sinking. Re-manned she was taken in tow, but went down before reaching the inlet.

At 1450 on this same eventful day, the convoy was ordered by Wee McGrigor to alter course to due north. He had no possible way of knowing this but it turned out to be a fateful decision. It led us directly to where a U-boat (now known to have been *U711*) was waiting at periscope depth. At 1523 I was again on the bridge and gazing out to westward where the corvette *Bluebell* was some 400 yards distant on our port beam. There was a devastating explosion, a terrible flash of flame, billowing black smoke and the corvette was simply no longer there. She had been struck in the magazine by a torpedo.

Five of her crew were picked up twenty minutes later but only one of them was alive, a petty officer. A group of escorts was at once detached to attack this U-boat, whose position was fairly accurately known, but *U711* had at once dived deep and stopped her engines. Many depth charges were dropped but she survived without damage.*

As soon as darkness had fallen, our escorts began obtaining HF/DF fixes. Soon after 2100 the Admiral ordered an emergency turn to starboard, to avoid a U-boat detected close ahead. More fixes astern of us and it seemed the Stringbags had fulfilled their task of keeping the U-boats submerged. Once they'd had their chance, air cover prevented them from getting ahead of the convoy again.

Except when flying I still spent all my time between the bridge, the operations room, the flight deck and the hangar. Subsisting on sandwiches, cocoa and cigarettes. I was on the bridge when two of our Stringbags were due to scramble at 2330. The weather still nearly perfect though a fresh breeze now blowing and some movement on the ship. As soon as the first Swordfish had come ten yards, I was alarmed to notice that the pilot (I will spare his blushes by not naming him) was heading off-course to starboard. In the few seconds available there was no way of warning him. He fired his RATOG and a moment later, when a foot or two off the ground, struck the island just below me with the last two or three feet of his upper starboard mainplane. Even in a Stringbag he couldn't get away with *that*. The aircraft performed a neat half-roll, dropped upside down into the dark ocean alongside us and rapidly began sinking.

It was a dicey situation. Not only for the pilot and his observer but for everyone on board. The Stringbag carried six depth charges. If dropped in anger, these would go off

*Almost fifty years later, I was telling the story of the catastrophe to a visiting dignitary in the House of Lords guest room. It was overheard at the next table by my friend and colleague Gerry Fitt (the great Northern Ireland politician, Lord Fitt). 'You saw the sinking of the *Bluebell?*' he exclaimed. 'So did I!' Still in his teens, he'd been serving as a greaser in the engine room of a tanker sailing close on her port quarter and had come up on deck for breather just before she was hit. Gerry went on to tell me that long after the war he had been telling the story in a pub when he noticed a man at the next table who was taking a great interest in it. He approached Gerry when he'd finished. 'You mentioned there was only one survivor,' he said. 'You are absolutely right. I was that man.'

on reaching a predetermined depth. There was a safety device to prevent this if they were still attached to the bomb-rack but it was not perfectly reliable. Should it fail at this highly critical moment only a few feet from *Nairana,* she would certainly be severely damaged by the detonation of over half a ton of high explosive and could possibly suc-cumb. To be sunk by her own depth charges would be an ignominious fate. I remember standing on tiptoe, the approved way to avoid the effects of blast, watching the upside-down Stringbag as she vanished beneath the waves. Always hoping for the emergence of the crew if they had survived the impact.

The seconds went by. And the pilot and observer sur-faced, apparently uninjured. For them a new peril: the water was far below freezing point and, despite protective cloth-ing, they could hope to survive in it for only a few minutes. But they were lucky. A corvette had as usual been detailed to take up position close astern of us whilst we were operating aircraft and she picked them up at once. The first Stringbag lost, thirteen to go.

At 0620 on the 18th we made the first of a series of turns to westward, which would eventually bring us to a course of due west when in latitude seventy-three degrees, some 400 miles north of the Arctic Circle. All through the day we con-tinued our patrols in rapidly worsening weather, till at 1530, with a whole gale blowing and darkness falling, the Admiral gave orders for flying to cease till further notice. By mid-night, with the wind gusting to Force 10, the convoy began to be scattered.

Our position was not improved when we were picked up by a shadower before dawn on the 19th. At first light the wind was still over sixty knots. Even Strawberry had to agree that we couldn't operate our Wildcats, though he had them ranged on deck. The convoy remained scattered through-out the 19th and we couldn't fly all day. But neither could the enemy. Until towards midnight we were again picked up by a shadower, who presumably detected by radar that many vessels were isolated and therefore highly vulnerable. Which led us to expect an attack by JU-88s from Norway. Fortunately the weather now at last began to moderate and by 0800 on the 20th there were only four stragglers.

A conference now called: Strawberry, Wings, Al Burgham and myself. If the expected attack developed, would it be possible for the Wildcats to operate? A whole gale was blowing, with a wind over the flight deck of fifty-five knots and occasional gusts to sixty. The wind was dead ahead of us and the ship pitching badly. It was agreed to leave it for Burgham as flight commander to decide, if and when the moment came.

It came soon. We had four Wildcats still serviceable. They were ranged and ready on the flight deck. The chosen pilots at immediate readiness in the ops room. A few minutes before 1000, a force of approaching aircraft detected by radar.

– Come on boys, let's get the buggers.

I climbed to the bridge as the pilots ran aft to their aircraft. The heaving deck seemed to fling them into the sky as at five second intervals they beat their way down the flight deck. But takeoff in these conditions presented no real problem, nor flying once airborne. The real danger – apart from the gunfire of the attacking torpedo-bombers and perhaps of our own ships – would be in landing back on.

The thirty-five JU-88s divided into groups to press home their attacks simultaneously from all points of the compass. So the four Wildcats divided into pairs, to hunt down and harry them as independent units. The enemy bombers began to penetrate the inner screen of escorts where the Wildcats could not venture. Their sinister slim shapes low above the wavetops as with shells bursting round them they fought their way towards us and the convoy. All ships taking violent avoiding action to comb the torpedoes as before. All except *Nairana*. I was on the bridge throughout the action and can say with certainty that Strawberry, again, never once altered course.

Always expecting to see a column of black smoke rising from a victim. But the entire convoy sailed through unscathed. And the enemy bombers, by luck, never sighted the four stragglers, lying at their mercy without escorts far astern of us. And one by one our Wildcats came home. Impregnable Bob Mathé managing somehow to keep his feet in the gale as with imperturbable resolution he signalled them in to land. Not a scratch on any of them, till the very last bounced over the wires and ended in the barrier. George Gordon and Peter Blanco had shot down an 88 between them, seen to fall into the ocean. Norman Sargent and Bill Armitage claimed a 'probable'. The tally from shipborne gunfire was two confirmed, one probable, four damaged.

The Germans later admitted that seven JU-88s failed to return from this mission. The surviving pilots claimed to have sunk two cruisers (we had only one), two destroyers and 'at least eight freighters'. Three U-boats were consequently sent at once to the area, to search for survivors or signs of wreckage, or to finish off disabled ships. Needless to say, they found only the empty Arctic: the sinkings existed only in the minds of the pilots and no ships in the convoy had been hit.

Having beaten off this attack we had twenty uneventful hours. Convoy and escorts ploughed steadily on a WSW course towards the Arctic Circle, still 300 miles ahead of us. Though the wind never fell below Force 8, we could have operated our Stringbags, but with no indication of U-boats the risk was thought unjustifiable. We were shadowed persistently through the long hours of darkness, when our Wildcats couldn't operate, but never again in daylight.

By dawn on the 21st we had been just over four days at sea and had covered only 600 miles – little more than a fast walk. *Campania* had only one Wildcat flyable, so we had ours at continual readiness, whilst sharing the Stringbag patrols to keep the U-boats submerged. Two stragglers came up with the convoy leaving two still missing. We flew off three Stringbags to search for them. One was located twenty miles to the south-west and shepherded safely home. But of the other, *Noyes*, no trace was to be found. Nothing had been heard of her for three days, and it seemed almost certain that she must have been sunk by a marauding U-boat or a detachment of torpedo-bombers.

Darkness fell and the weather began to deteriorate. The wind, which had moderated, had again reached Force 8 when towards midnight HF/DF fixes were obtained on two U-boats, one not far astern of the convoy, the other a greater distance to southward. Somewhere above many thousand feet of cloud a moon must have been shining, but no glimmer of it reached us. The ceiling was 800 feet, visibility half a mile, much motion on the ship. In these conditions our chance of locating the enemy was so slight that Wee McGrigor held the hazards of flying night searches too great to be justified.

We were on stand-by to scramble at first light but the wind was now gusting to force 10 and had veered westerly. The course of the convoy was gradually changed to southward from WSW to SSW. With wind and swell now on our starboard beam, the ship was rolling very severely, which is always more troublesome than pitching. It was becoming increasingly difficult to keep a footing on the flight deck, which was slanting alarmingly and fully exposed to the storm. We still had two Stringbags ranged aft, wings folded and triple lashed. There was no question of flying and the time had come to get these below-decks to the supposed safety of the hangar before they broke their lashings and were swept overboard. It took the combined efforts of twenty men to manhandle each of them to the lift and hold her in position there till she was safely below the exposure of the flight deck.

Just in time. The hurricane struck us at noon. The maximum windspeed our anemometer could register was eighty knots (a little over ninety mph). Its needle reached this point soon afterwards and stayed there for twenty hours. To stand on the bridge and watch this amazing spectacle. As *Nairana* and the battered ships around her, those few within sight of us as the slanting sleet and wave-top spray swept between us in the unending half-light, strove to keep their stations, careering giddily at walking speed through the Arctic. A carrier seeming so top-heavy and her movement always exaggerated by the long straight lines of her flight-deck. So that each time she plunged most steeply with the foam-crested swell to leeward, it seemed certain she must capsize, could never be brought back by the oncoming ocean to an even keel, then only to rear and fall as far again to windward. The flight-deck, now a deserted expanse of glistening steel, swept with frozen sea-spray that the beaten sea drove over it. No man could hope to venture forth to it and survive. He'd be over the side without a word, unable to stand on the unprotected frozen surface as the ship plunged to leeward.

All squadron activity at a standstill. Even in the hangar, no hope of working on maintenance. But my thirteen remaining Stringbags and all six Wildcats still miraculously serviceable.

No respite with night. Rather conditions grew worse and often the windspeed must have exceeded 100 knots. The convoy was inevitably being scattered. Sometime in the early hours of darkness I was on the bridge when a signalman made his way to the Captain.

–Signal from the Admiral, sir.

Strawberry went through his usual ritual. Extended his hand for the signal, then turned away impatiently as though too preoccupied with conning his ship to bother with reading a signal.

–Read it to me, Yeoman.

– Aye, aye, sir. NAIRANA FROM CS ONE. AM TURNING INTO WIND AND HEAVING TO. SIGNAL YOUR INTENTIONS.

Strawberry didn't turn. Just a ghost of a smile, the smallest twist of a lip, as he gazed into the night. For only a couple of seconds. Then without turning:

– Reply as follows. CS ONE FROM NAIRANA. AM STAYING WITH THE CONVOY.

So the escorting warships broke into two groups. *Campania* with three or four destroyers under steerage-way headed westerly into the wind. *Nairana* with the other escorts and the main body of the convoy ploughing southward for home at four knots.

Sometime during those limitless hours of darkness I made my way staggering aft to my cabin where for a couple of nights I'd taken to seeking whatever few fitful hours of sleep were possible. Now with the wind on our beam there was little more movement than anywhere else. No hope of staying in my bunk but I'd made up a bed of a kind on the deck, the mattress wedged somehow in position so that it didn't move about too much as we tossed across the ocean. Deep or prolonged sleep impossible. But I'd drifted into uneasy dream-filled half-sleep when I was wakened during the middle watch by such an almighty crash that I first thought we'd been hit. Yet it seemed to have come from above me. Above me from the hangar deck.

I was already fully dressed. Stumbling to the companionway, clambering somehow up it. Another terrible crash. I entered the hangar, which had been jampacked with my nineteen aircraft. Now a scene of devastation. The yellow tractor used for moving them, weighing nearly a ton. It had been stowed, we thought securely, triple-lashed to the portside bulkhead aft. But had managed to break free. And with terrifying impulse was careering back and forth the full width of the hangar with each roll of the ship. Writing off my Stringbags as it went. I'd been wakened when it first slammed against the starboard bulkhead above me.

I alone on the scene. But joined within seconds by others who'd heard the impact. I tell one of them, for Christ's sake get all the hands you can find. Survey the scene of destruction. Two Stringbags already seriously damaged, probably beyond repair. Two or three more hit, as the maniac tractor carved its way through them. And now, as the ship swings over to port, it careers back thwartships across the deck, striking those hit already and damaging another.

A perilous situation. Hard enough for men to keep their footing anywhere without support. But here the deck is greasy with a fine film of engine-oil overflowed from the drip trays. It's a damned skating rink. A man falls. He slithers towards the bulkhead on his backside. Laughing like a madman till he sees the tractor bearing down on him. Certain death if pulped between tractor and bulkhead. Laughter turning to fear as somehow he scrambles clear of it.

Now I have twenty men. Lengths of rope have been

found. For Christ's sake no one panic and all keep clear of the tractor when it's moving. We descend on it like ants, get a couple of ropes around it secured to the port bulkhead. But not well enough. A moment later the ship rolls over to starboard. Stand clear, everyone, stand clear. The tractor, straining at the ropes, has at once moved out a foot or two. Seems like a living thing. The angle growing steeper, men beginning to fall. We roll through ninety degrees, from forty-five to port to forty-five to starboard, where she seems to stay for ever. Our puny ropes useless. The tractor snaps them like cotton and crashes back among the aircraft.

I find a junior officer. Do the best you can. I'm going to the bridge.

Strawberry there as ever. Hunched gazing out ahead, hands deep in overcoat pockets. Sir, we must turn to windward and heave to. I'm staying with the convoy, holding to this course. Sir, it would be for less than fifteen minutes. I've lost at least two Swordfish, half-a-dozen damaged. Unless we turn, we may lose every aircraft on board.

Not a moment's reflection though now at last he turns to me. Looks me straight in the eyes.

– Godley, take whatever action you think fit. Pipe action stations, get every available hand to the hangar if necessary. Take every yard of cordage you can find, from the ship's boats, anywhere. I'm staying with the convoy.

Aye, aye, sir. Useless to argue. Back in the hangar I find chaos worse than ever. Two more Swordfish already seem write-offs. No need to pipe action stations, I have sixty men awaiting their next chance. With coils of rope and cable. Organizing them into groups of six or ten, each under an officer or chief with its own specific task when the opportunity comes. But for five more minutes we are impotent, as the tractor careers back and forth with the ship, never staying motionless long enough to come near her.

No matter how violent a storm, there is always, sooner or later, a sudden stretch of calmer water. For no more than a few minutes. And now at last this came. The ship rolled violently to starboard, we could get a rope and a cable secured. Not enough. But, as we all stood clear, she came to an even keel, hovered there for breathless moments, then gently rolled back to starboard. The chance we'd been waiting for. Every man descended on her. Two more cables round her, half-a-dozen ropes. Then the ship rolled viciously to port but the tractor moved out only inches from the bulkhead. Next time she came to starboard we finished the job.

Surveying the desolate scene. Four of my remaining thirteen Swordfish battered to pieces. Three others in bad shape. Happily no damage to the Wildcats, which had all been parked forward. A man with a broken leg taken to the sick-bay but miraculously no one seriously injured. I report back to the bridge.

– The tractor is secured, sir. I have six Swordfish flyable and all the Wildcats. It may be possible to repair two or three of the others.

A flicker of a smile on his weary worn face.

– Not too bad, well done. Now pay heed, Godley. The convoy is badly scattered. The weather may moderate. We must be prepared to fly off aircraft at dawn if necessary.

– Aye, aye, sir.

Hardly a thought for aircraft lost, men injured. His single determination to stay with the convoy's main body. Second to that, to be able to fly off aircraft.

Back once more to the hangar. Now for Christ's sake let's clear up this bloody mess. Clear a way to the lift. Get these wrecks to one side. We have to be prepared to fly off aircraft at dawn.

– Aye, aye, sir. Right boys, get fucking cracking.

Not a word of dissent. And we worked through the rest of the night.

But at dawn the hurricane still blowing, though the wind had fallen to seventy knots. We found ourselves in company with *Bellona,* most of the escorts and a dozen merchantmen. *Campania* with her destroyers some sixty miles to westward. The remaining ships of the convoy dispersed astern of us, escort vessels dispatched to round them up and shepherd them home. We were powerless to help them. Till by noon there was at last some sign of a let-up. *Campania* rejoined us soon afterwards, and the Admiral signalled we were to have our Wildcats at readiness. By 1400 the wind only fifty knots. *Campania* scrambled two Stringbags.

Twenty minutes later a despairing Mayday signal from one of the few remaining stragglers, the steamship *Henry Bacon*. She reported she was under attack by nineteen JU-88s. They had been sent to attack the convoy, but on discovering by chance a single unescorted merchantman had chosen to seek no further. Though she was some fifty miles to eastward, we at once flew of four fighters. Who found her on fire and sinking, her attackers already departed. A destroyer was detached to pick up survivors, homed to them by the Wildcats. The ship's gunners claimed two of the Junkers as probables. This was the last ship to be sunk by German aircraft in the war.

By nightfall the wind was again gusting to seventy knots. But all the stragglers except *Noyes,* now missing for five days, were safely back with the convoy.

At first light next morning, February 24th, we had been a week at sea and were just approaching the Arctic Circle, having covered in those seven days just over a thousand miles. But now it would be plain sailing. Our only anxiety came when an RAF Liberator appeared overhead at sunrise and began transmitting R/T signals in plain language to base, giving away our position to any U-boats that might be skulking on the surface within a hundred miles, and to enemy bases in Norway. Wee McGrigor ordered her to pipe down in no uncertain terms.

But no attacks developed. The wind fell to no more than a fresh gale, the sun put in a sudden brief appearance, we were sailing joyously homeward. A few routine patrols. We passed east of the Faeroes at noon on the 27th. Soon afterwards the two carriers and *Bellona* were detached with four destroyers to head for Scapa. We dropped anchor there next morning.

We had given up hope for *Noyes* but two hours later we picked up a signal from her. She was still in latitude sixty-four degrees, some 300 miles astern of the convoy, having sailed on her own for nine days and nights without sighting friend or foe. Two days later, still alone, she reached sanctuary in Loch Ewe.

We had come through the worst weather ever experienced on the Murmansk run – that's official! Twelve of the sixteen destroyers taking part had to go into dry-dock for hull repairs. *Nairana* was unscratched.

We flew ashore to Hatston on March 5th. Wings had told me in confidence that we'd be there a couple of weeks, meaningfully adding that the moon would again be full on the 25th. I took the hint. Re-equipped without delay with five new Stringbags to replace those lost or damaged beyond repair, we put in all the time available practising individual and squadron attacks with new more powerful RPs on fixed and moving targets by day and night.

Squadron morale was reasonably high. And how about my own? I was forcing myself to keep going. That's how I have to put it though I'd have admitted it to no one. No longer the smallest remnant of the old illogical certainty that I'd always return unscathed. Having now flown a total of sixty-seven operations, I felt rather a certainty that I'd run out of luck, that the ace of spades could come up at any time. On the trip to Murmansk and back, necessity had compelled me as the boss to take my turn as it came. Indeed to fly more often than the others. Never looking for pretexts to come home early. But for the first time I'd felt fear with every take-off.

On my early operations, long ago with 811, I would think this is a tough one, we may have losses, but *I'll* come through though I may be the only one. Now just the other way around. Even before a routine patrol, I would find myself thinking there should be no problems. But if one aircraft is lost tonight, it's sure as hell my turn.

At sea I had to keep flying. And I knew this necessity would soon again be present. Safely ashore I could have quietly grounded myself. The excuses ready to hand: administration, paper-work. But I knew I had to keep going, maintain the impetus, or be in danger of collapse. So I drove myself to fly every day, often several times.

I had learnt quickly how to run a squadron, however great my shortcomings, again through pure necessity. But was always aware that through pure lack of experience I could never provide such leadership as I'd known from my own bosses, men like Hayes and Slater, who'd won their wings when I was at school.

But I hadn't far to go with 835. It was March 22nd before we rejoined the ship. For a completely fruitless mission. The First Cruiser Squadron sallied forth three days later so that we and 813 could again try our luck against enemy shipping off Norway. It was dark as hell when we sailed, with driving rain and limitless cloud to obliterate the moon. The weather grew fouler as we ploughed north-eastward, again to within a hundred miles of the enemy-occupied coast. We managed to keep our patrols going almost all the way in search of nonexistent U-boats. And we ranged all aircraft in preparation for the strike as takeoff time approached. But with low cloud there'd be no hope of using rockets. And with visibility less than a mile, the Admiral decided that even Stringbags could not operate in the narrow confines of a fjord. We sailed around for a couple of hours hoping for a let-up but conditions if anything grew worse. Towards midnight the nine ships of the Cruiser Squadron turned on their heels and headed all the way back to Scapa.

To find our Stringbag days were over. We and 813 were the last two squadrons left, apart from 836. There were even now no TBR aircraft more suitable for MAC-ships in the Atlantic and flights from 836 would continue to operate from them till the end of the war in Europe. But Barracudas and Avengers had taken over everywhere else. Now it was our turn. *Nairana* was due for a refit. We were to sail with her to the Clyde where the squadron would be disbanded. On All Fools' Day 1945.

Our last night on board. Drinks flowing freely. Strawberry comes to join us at the piano. His round red face beaming. Well boys you put on a good show. Now how about this new song?

We look blankly at each other. New song, sir? Yes, come on now, let's hear it. The fly-off song, isn't it?

Captains like mothers know everything eventually. The opening bars are played. We come crashing in with the first line:

Fly off, fly off for Christ's sake...

But then silence. Drunk we may be. But no one dares sing the rest in Strawberry's presence.
– Carry on then, sounds a good one. What's the matter with you?
So we take a deep breath and sing it through:

Fly off, fly off for Christ's sake,
  For the Captain wants a gong.
Fly off, fly off for Christ's sake...
  For the Captain can't be wrong.

And then a spontaneous cheer for him. His face more scarlet than ever as he stands grinning with delight.
–That's a good one. The Captain wants a gong, eh? Well he may not be the only one.
It was the last time I ever saw him. Early next day to Glasgow for the train south on leave pending appointment. And Penny meeting me at Portsmouth Harbour station with three-month-old Christopher.

Gongs were awarded liberally, as by now had become the way. Al Burgham had already received the DSC and been mentioned in dispatches for earlier exploits; this time he was left out (wrongly, I think) but three other Wildcat pilots got DSCs, Sam Mearns, George Gordon and Bill Armitage. As, to my great surprise, did I. Bob Mathé, our magnificent batsman, was rewarded with two DSCs – one in the same honours list as everyone else, the second in the birthday honours five days later. George Strong, Norman Sargent, Peter Blanco and Ronald Moss were 'mentioned', and so were four of my groundcrew.
And Strawberry, Captain Villiers Nicholas Surtees, duly received a second DSO, the gong of our doggerel at the

piano. I went on the town with George the night these awards were gazetted. And we must have been pissed as newts because at some stage we thought of Strawberry, found a coin-box in the pub, sent him a telegram, our last signal:

CAPTAIN STRAWBERRY SURTEES DSO AND BAR HMS NAIRANA = CONGRATULATIONS SIR STOP REQUEST PANCAKE = GODLEY AND STRONG

Next day we remembered this with some misgivings and wondered how he'd take it. We needn't have worried. His reply came that evening:

LT-CDR GODLEY DSC AND LT STRONG = THANK YOU BOYS STOP YOU MAY NOW PANCAKE STOP BEST WISHES = STRAWBERRY

XII

NOT WITH A BANG

I was long overdue for my second rest period, after eighteen continuous months in operational squadrons since joining 836 in September 1943. To be perfectly honest, I'd have welcomed a job in an office. That's quite an admission. The alternative would be to take command of a training squadron, and that would mean flying monoplanes. I'd long dreaded the day, sure to come unless I bought it, when I would leave my Stringbag behind and convert to Barracudas or Avengers. These single-engined torpedo-bombers would have been thought slow and old-fashioned, if not obsolete, in the RAF but were all the Navy had to offer for TBR work. And to seasoned old Swordfish pilots their seemingly sleek fuselages, unencumbered mainplanes, high wing-loading, high-powered engines and high stalling speed – all these not only made them seem ultra-modern and sophisticated but combined to spell out danger.

We were ham-handed as hell after hundreds of hours (in my own case 729) flying Stringbags to their extreme limits, as a pilot must to be worth his keep. Acquiring habits admirable in biplanes, that could be fatal if practised in so called advanced aircraft. I don't know how many Stringbag boys, having survived one or more operational tours, killed themselves far from battle in Avengers or Barracudas by carelessly reverting to old ways through force of habit, yank ing the stick over at too low an airspeed and spinning off the turn, or leaving the pull-out too late in a steep dive.

The US-built Grumman Avenger was always more popular than the Fairey Barracuda, the least-liked aircraft in the service. The Barra, a high-wing monoplane,* had so many teething troubles that it didn't reach the squadrons till 1943, two years later than planned. Its performance was at once found in every way inferior to the Avenger's. And it was riddled with gremlins: apart from being easy to get into a spin and difficult to get out of one, its wings had been known to fold without warning in level flight, a most deplorable tendency. And Barracudas on routine flights over the sea had simply disappeared, nothing more ever heard of them. However the supply of Avengers was limited and by 1945, like it or not, the Barra was being flown by the majority of front-line TBR squadrons.

Penny and Christopher were still at Brookfield and we decided to spend my leave there. Her father, the admiral, had just won a hard-earned knighthood for his five-and-a-half post-retirement years at sea as Commodore. The household was completed by her mother and by her grandmother, known to all as Gar. Dear ancient Gar, in her beads and hats and long dresses, who belonged to another era. Gar who had commented, when told of the invention of jet aircraft, that she'd always thought it was *such* an ugly stone, she was glad they'd found a use for it. We had quiet family days, a couple of sorties to London, waited for my appointment.

It came at the end of April. After a three-week Monoplane Conversion Course, as they were pleased to call it, I was to take command of 714, a training squadron based at Crimond in Aberdeenshire. Teaching kids who'd just won their wings to fly operational aircraft. Barracudas.

I felt a dreadful apprehension. It wasn't only that I hadn't yet learnt to fly the things myself. But just as I had kept hanging to that dinghy in mid-Atlantic far beyond my natural powers. And then lost consciousness as soon as it was

See Plate 17 for portrait of Barracuda in typical position.

no longer necessary to hold on, the moment those strong arms embraced me to safety. So I had kept flying when compelled by the moment's necessity. Now I was in safety, the necessity behind me. Yet I to whom flying had been a joy and a delight. Since faraway schoolboy days at Croydon or Brooklands. Finding myself in fear of it. Admitting it to no one but my already impaired confidence disintegrating. Luck had been with me all these years again and again. On such varied occasions, in such strange ways. Which I had simply taken for granted. And now feeling a certainty that at last it had run out. I'd pushed it too far already. Always nearer the death card. Though now no Arctic wastes but green friendly fields beneath me.

I don't want to fly any more. It was now I first admitted it though only to myself. But there was no way of getting out of it. How would I get away with it?

My conversion course was at nearby Lee-on-Solent, the FAA headquarters where I'd joined 811 in far-off 1941 and had returned to serve on the staff of RANAS in 1942. HMS *Daedalus*. Daedalus, father of Icarus who had bought it flying recklessly, flying too close to the sun. And the wax in his wings had melted. And they'd folded in mid-air, just like a Barracuda's. Well *this* Icarus intended to be very much more prudent. Not as in those Chesapeake days. When I took survival for granted. Now everything was different.

It turned out that my instructor was Phil Blakey, Phil who had been my flight commander when first I joined 836. He still a Lieutenant, I now his senior officer. But that was irrelevant, we were old pals. Not such old pals however that I could open my heart to him. Far too dark a secret.

Three flips in a dual-control Miles Master with him, in separate cockpits one behind the other, to get the feel of a monoplane. Whilst the Barracuda awaited me. And so light were the controls of this simple trainer that she seemed totally unstable. Each time I touched the stick, she climbed or dived or banked about three times more steeply than I'd intended. Hating every minute of it. Jesus, Phil, it isn't like flying a Stringbag. A cheerful laugh from him, you'll soon get the hang of it. Now try a steep turn to starboard. Hesitantly with stick and rudder, then back with the stick. To plunge earthwards in the turn. An elementary error, not enough top rudder. And then over-correcting, the Master slewing sideways across the sky.

– Hold on a second, I've got her.

For God's sake, making a hash of a steep turn. Phil straightens her out. Now try again, John. Going into it so slowly. Eyes glued to the turn-and-bank indicator on my instrument panel. Keep the top needle central. I who could fly a Stringbag through any manoeuvre in the book, in almost any weather, without a glance at my instruments.

That evening at Brookfield. Well how did it go, darling? Oh fine, just fine. A piece of cake, that's what it was. Just a piece of cake.

We progress to circuits and bumps. No trouble with take-offs. Propeller to fine pitch. Ten degrees of flaps. Check all instruments and controls. Turn her into wind. Full throttle and keep her straight. It's like being back at Luton. The airfield drops away beneath me. Now raise undercart. Climb (but not too steeply), raise flaps, coarsen pitch to climbing revs. A slow steady turn and straight round for landing; not so easy. Lower undercart, prop to fully fine, throttle back to lose speed before lowering flaps. Making such a long straight approach. Afraid of stalling, my eyes back and forth to the ASI, keeping ten knots in hand. All the time flying scared.

– You're a good bit too fast, John. Eight or ten knots. Throttle back, keep the nose up.

I let her lose five knots. *You're still too fast.* But now we're at fifty feet and well past the perimeter. I close the throttle, we float and float.

– Here, I've got her. We'd better go round again.

Better go round again. For the love of Jesus I could land a Stringbag on a sixpence. On a bloody MAC-ship flight deck as it heaved and pitched across the ocean. Couldn't put down a Master on an airfield.

Three more circuits and landings. Which I manage fairly successfully. But Phil gives me a look as we climb from our

219

cockpits. You're just a wee bit rusty. But you'll get used to it. Oh sure, sure. I'll soon get used to it, just a wee bit rusty.

Next day aerobatics. We climb to 5000 feet, this time in a Harvard. Try a slow roll, says Phil. I've forgotten how to do it. Three years since my last slow roll, in a Chesapeake. I get her banked a bit more than ninety degrees, she begins to fall out of it, we are losing height in a sharp diving turn, less than half the roll completed.

– OK, John, I've got her. We'll go through it together. You must get the stick forward. Here we go now.

Over and over. In a moment upside down, hanging on my straps, the dust from the floor of the cockpit in my eyes as Phil shows me the way. On round till we're once more straight and level. Jesus, I'll never be able to do it.

Rolls, loops, spins. I get through the hour somehow. In a cold sweat but manage not to disgrace myself again.

– Fine, says Phil when we've landed. Now how about the Barra?

– The Barra. Sure, why not.

And so, that same day, I first flew a Barracuda. The moment I'd been dreading. It wasn't mainly that it was so much more complex and powerful than a Stringbag, with so much more to remember, though that was part of it. It was its relatively high stalling speed, its relatively vicious stall and its propensity for spinning. And all its known and unknown gremlins. I'd have been far happier taking a Stringbag on an op than a Barra on my first solo.

But for God's sake you're a highly experienced pilot. Veteran with over a thousand hours. Two-and-a-half stripes. Flown day and night in all weathers. And at least you'll be on your own. So take it very easy. No one ever buys it on a first solo. So leave the widest safety margins. And take it fucking easy.

So I taxied this bloody great Barra (so it seemed) round the perimeter for takeoff. Still no runways. Spent a full five minutes on cockpit drill. Twice checked flaps correctly lowered, prop to fully fine, engine temperature, oil pressure, hydraulic pressure. Ran her up, this Merlin 32, twice as powerful as any other engine I'd flown behind. Tested magne-toes, all OK. So this is it, turn to windward. Turn into wind, you bugger. Now full throttle but holding her on the brakes till maximum power reached. Brakes off, surging forward. Just wait for it, nothing you have to do. Except be prepared for engine failure.

In a Stringbag by now I'd be airborne. But bloody wait for it. Such a damned long takeoff run. Now she should come unstuck. So gently back with the stick. Ten feet up, right keep her there, don't be in a hurry. Now a good twenty knots above stalling speed, so lift her into the sky and up with the undercart. Waiting for the safety of well over 1000 feet before raising flaps, throttling back, coarsening the prop to climbing revs. A long shallow turn still climbing.

This 'familiarization' flight was scheduled to last an hour. So I sped out of sight towards Winchester, staying good and high so that I could safely bale out if any expected disaster struck me, and pottered around familiarizing myself. Which meant a series of very gentle turns in level flight waiting for something to go wrong.

– How were things today, darling?

– Oh I had my first flight in a Barra. No problems, just a piece of cake. Now where's that son of mine?

During the next two weeks I made ten more flights in these damned Barracudas before being adjudged proficient, with less than fourteen hours' experience, to show rookies how to fly them. Which I most certainly was not. Try as I might, I simply could not bring myself to drive them much more than halfway to their limit. And this I couldn't conceal. Several of my flights were what we called 'Chase-me-Charlies': the instructor in one Barra, his pupil astern of him in another, supposed to follow him through every manoeuvre made. Phil would go into a steep turn at low speed and I just couldn't force myself to pull back hard enough on the stick to stay with him. Or in a soaring high-speed climb he would perform a barrel roll and I, if I tried to do the same, would inevitably fall out of it. But more probably wouldn't try, hoping he might not see this in his rear-view mirror.

And on May 18th, when VE-Day had come and gone, I set

forth on the long train journey from Portsmouth by way of London to Aberdeen, to take up my last appointment. There were two or three training squadrons at Crimond. I had fifteen Barracudas in 714 and four or five instructors. Our task was to take batches of young pilots, who'd just got their wings after little more than 150 hours, and teach them to fly operational aircraft. Much the same as it had been for me long ago at Crail but we did no torpedo training. The kids, almost all under twenty-one and many of them midshipmen of nineteen, had done all their flying on monoplanes and no dual instruction was necessary. We just gave them a manual to study, showed them round the cockpit and off they went on their solos. Then a month of formation flying, divebombing, low-level bombing, navexes, night landings. They were as keen as mustard, their flying was their life as once mine had been, they knew no fear and were ready for anything. From 714 they would go on for their torpedo and deck-landing training, then the best of them to the Pacific. Which couldn't come soon enough.

Apart from my fear of flying, or more probably as a product of it, I was beginning to feel a presentiment, totally unjustifiable but growing ever stronger, of certain impending disaster. Disaster to myself. I carried this with me every day. And every night as I lay sleepless, living through each imagined peril that lay ahead of me. Yet there were no perils. Never like this when flying daily over the Arctic or Atlantic, or earlier along the flak-ridden coasts of France and Holland. But now when commanding a squadron in peaceful Scotland I felt this growing certainty that death was round the corner.

My shattered self-confidence was in no way helped when soon after my arrival a pilot was killed in the way that I most feared. And I saw the whole thing happen. He wasn't one of my boys, he was with a visiting operational squadron, and yes it turned out that he had just converted to Barras after hundreds of hours on Stringbags. So vividly still remembered. On my way by motor-bike from my office to the mess. Watching this Barracuda out of the corner of my eye as it came in to land, seemed to be flying so slowly, banked steeply to port on its last turn for landing and at once whipped into a spin. At less than 400 feet the pilot hadn't a hope. The Barra had hardly time to complete a revolution before falling vertically into a field beside the mess. Not a hundred yards from me. The first flames sprouting at once from the half-buried engine.

I was first to reach the scene ten seconds later. Remember every moment. The group of young Wrens laughing as they ran to it, such a joke to have a prang so close beside them, then mutely blanched with horror as it came home to them that a man's mangled body was inside that twisted wreckage. Forcing myself to walk right up to it (the only one to do so) to confirm that the pilot was dead. As was absolutely certain. A great crowd of men and girls, all those nearby, in a speechless circle round the dead man's pyre, venturing no closer. But in fact there was as yet no danger from the flames. And I will now admit another never admitted fact. I looked though the crumpled glasshouse into the tangled cockpit. Gazed for ten or fifteen seconds as the flames grew stronger. There had to be a pilot in there, or his remnants. *But the damned cockpit was empty.* I never saw a body in that wreckage. Walking calmly back to safety as flames enveloped the cockpit and spread towards the petrol tanks.

– Well sure as hell there's no point trying to get *him* out.

The wrecked Barracuda burning fiercely as the fire tenders reached the scene. And long afterwards the cremated body of the one-time Stringbag pilot extracted piecemeal from his cockpit. A job I didn't help with. The body that could have been my own. Which my eyes had refused to see when they gazed at it, seconds after death, foreseeing my own.

Penny and Christopher soon joined me. I'd found rooms in the nearby village of Strichen, where Miss Fraser regaled us with porridge and cream, with oatcakes and fresh herrings, with baps and even occasional steaks. Suitably cooing about the braw wee bairn. I went back and forth to the air station on my motor-bike. Soon after arriving I'd made it clear to my officers that I held it no part of my duties as C.O. to do any flying instruction. As I explained, I just didn't have the time. So many administrative duties. An occasional air test perhaps. I hadn't flown at all for the first week or two. Too busy getting settled in, getting to know officers and men, drawing up new training schedules, dealing with a backlog of correspondence. So many good excuses. And in five weeks I'd fly only ten times, a total of less than five hours.

And the presentiment growing. Of impending personal disaster. Deepened by losing one of my young pilots. A red-haired midshipman of nineteen. Who panicked on a night flight when mist swirled over the airfield. I in the control tower trying to give him confidence by R/T. THE MIST IS EXPECTED TO CLEAR SOON, DO NOT ATTEMPT TO LAND. But no reply. COXCOMB TANGO, HOW DO YOU HEAR ME? His wireless unserviceable. No reply as he tries to make it. But then mistaking the lights in the control tower for those on the duty runway. And coming straight at us, at the last instant realizing his error, swinging away at fifty feet, but still catching our aerial in his propeller. Careering down out of control through this sudden loss of power to plough headlong into a line of my Barras waiting parked at their dispersal point. A dull explosion, a blinding spurt of flame from them. Racing to the scene. The dead boy strapped in his cockpit, the great heat of the enveloping flames jerk his corpse into movement as though suddenly alive again. Five Barras burning.

So two men killed within four weeks. Though none so much as scratched in my previous eighteen months in the front line. What's the French superstition – *jamais deux sans trois*.

Sometime at the end of May they found out what must have been the cause in many cases of Barras vanishing without trace. An Admiralty Fleet Order. All Barracudas to be equipped as soon as possible with oxygen. Once so equipped, no pilot to fly a Barra without an oxygen mask even on circuits and bumps, though not normally required except for high flying. And the reason was that a weakness had at last been traced in the hydraulics system. The pressure gauge was located between the pilot's feet, inserted into the feedpipe that conveyed the hydraulic fluid to raise or lower the flaps and wheels. Now this fluid contained ether, so was a very effective anaesthetic. And a post-mortem on a pilot killed in a recent accident revealed he had been anaesthetized. Examination of the wreckage had shown the feedpipe had fractured at the point of entry to the pressure gauge. From which it was inferred that the cockpit had quickly been filled with this potentially lethal fluid. The pilot had been put to sleep at 7000 feet and never woke up.

One more ever-present peril to add to those already threatening me each time I thought of flying. For no oxygen equipment, which would at once remove this threat, was immediately available. But of course the fear was irrational like all the others. OK now it was known that a number of previously unexplained deaths had been caused by pilots simply passing out. But the odds against it happening on any given flight were thousands to one. Just as they were against the wings folding. Or spinning off a turn. Or whatever. But if it happened to anyone, it would surely happen to me.

By June 7th, though how was I to know it, I had only five more flights left as a pilot in my life. After a week on the ground, I persuaded myself to fly an air test of twenty-five minutes. Big deal. On the tenth I took up two young pupils for half an hour as passengers to familiarize them with the area. On the fifteenth a twenty-five minute test flight. I then managed to stay ten days on the ground until, running short of pretexts, I had to fly to Banff and back.

It happened at this time that we somehow ran short of instructors and there was therefore some difficulty in carrying through our programme. Only a couple available and three required. One to lead a flight of rookies on a dive-bombing exercise, two as leaders for formation flying. Discussing it with my senior pilot.

– I suppose you wouldn't take one of them, sir?

– I'm afraid it's not possible, Bridgeland. I have this report to finish. So look we'll scrub the bombing.

And Bridgeland as he left my office hardly bothering to hide the contempt he felt. 'I'm afraid it's not possible.' Much more to the point if I'd just said 'I'm afraid'.

So to June 28th. For my last ever flight as a pilot. And the last of so many days (as I leaf through my logbooks) on which I really should have been killed. The last time I'd ever sit proudly in a pilot's seat, my feet on the rudder bar, my right hand on the control column, my left hand free for throttle or trimmer or flaps. Oh how once it had been. The world ahead of me, the clouds my playthings, the sun and stars my guide. Not any more.

Another routine test flight, half an hour in a Barra that had been in for overhaul. Everything routine. Weather conditions perfect as I soar into the breathless sky above those pacific fields. Climbing to two or three thousand, banking and gliding in the sunshine. Yet all the time, as always now, waiting for disaster. But everything seems normal. And so returning homeward, losing height to prepare for landing. Below a thousand feet now. And downwind nearing the airfield when God Almighty it happened.

Without any warning, a fine spray of liquid in my face. At once my eyes to the hydraulic pressure gauge. And Christ that's where it's coming from. Hydraulic fluid. *For God's sake it's happening*. My long-felt presentiment finally justified. The spray becoming stronger, my brain singing. For the love of Jesus shove back the glasshouse roof, get your bloody head out, as far as possible into the slipstream. How many minutes or seconds left of consciousness? In which to get her down. For no hope of baling out at such low altitude. Oh try now to think calmly. No time to get her to leeward, to make an orthodox landing on the duty runway. *Just get her on the deck*. Now my head is reeling as the ether fills the cockpit. No aircraft in the circuit, none preparing for takeoff. So go crosswind, across the runways, it doesn't matter. Firing a red Very light, throttling right back, lowering flaps and wheels for which just enough pressure left. Whilst diving and steeply turning to make my last approach. Keep way out in the slipstream, breathe all the air you can. A couple of hundred feet. Holding my breath to look back into the cockpit for a final check of my instruments. The gush of fluid in my face. I'm a bit fast but better than being too slow. Everything else OK. So go on ahead, get her down for Christ's sake. A bit less throttle, come to starboard. As I feel my senses leaving me. The grass of the airfield twenty feet below me, now back with the stick. I strain out into the slipstream but feel myself overpowered. Throttle fully closed, we float for an eternity, then at last the firm ground under me. Now just keep her straight just keep her straight just keep her...

That's as far as I could remember. Coming round in the ambulance. Within seconds of touching down, I'd slumped back into the cockpit. And the Barra had rolled on alone, carrying me the last fifty yards of my flying career, me unconscious at the controls, till it came to a standstill of its own will, undamaged. Close to the perimeter ahead. And the crew of the fire tender had lifted me from the cockpit and stretched me out on the grass. And the ambulance had reached the scene whilst I lay there peacefully sleeping. In the warm summer sunshine. With the skylarks high above me. And in the ambulance slowly remembering. And knowing with absolute certainty that my days as a pilot were over.

Of the next four months I have very few recollections. I must have been going through the motions of commanding 714. I don't know if I ever came out with it and said to my instructors, look boys I've had it, I'm not flying any more. I don't think so but it must have been understood. And I must have kissed Penny and Christopher goodbye every morning, taken my motor-bike from Strichen to the airfield, made out the flying schedules, dealt with the paper-work, seen defaulters and requestmen, done everything I had to do. Everything but fly. I do remember that all aircraft were equipped PDQ with oxygen equipment, which magically materialized soon after my escape was signalled urgently to FONAS, repeated Admiralty. And I remember thinking, Jesus, if that AFO hadn't been promulgated just a few days earlier, I wouldn't have known at once what was happening, would have kept the glasshouse closed and certainly lost consciousness at several hundred feet. 'For reasons not ascertained, this experienced pilot was seen to make a steep diving turn when preparing to carry out a normal landing after a test flight. He appeared to have lost control as the aircraft fell to the ground and exploded. The fire was soon brought under control but the Barracuda was totally destroyed so that evidence of mechanical failure (if any) was unobtainable. The pilot's body was incinerated so that no meaningful post-mortem was possible.' Imagined extract from my posthumous accident report, neatly made out on Form A25 by Commander (Flying), countersigned by the Captain.

I'd get by at Crimond somehow but what would follow? In another few months, perhaps as soon as October, my rest period would be over. I had always assumed that I would then be given a front-line squadron, almost certainly Barras, operating from one of the new fleet carriers in the Far East. From which there would be no escape.

But deliverance was at hand. In early August came the A-bombs. Then unconditional surrender. And a month later, with the war over, I could at last do what I'd long known I'd have to do in the end. Go to the Surgeon-Commander.

He was very sympathetic. As though he'd been expecting me. So I hadn't flown at all since that very unpleasant incident two months ago? Well, you know, it isn't really surprising. And only five hours since April. We're always getting cases like this, it's nothing out of the ordinary. Tell me more about your flying, John. Well, over three years in front-line squadrons, Doc. And sixty-seven ops. And four total engine failures. But worst of all, Doc; these fucking Barras. I was a Stringbag boy, Doc, bring back my Stringbag (a song we used to sing) and I'll fly it, but not these gremlin-filled Barracudas which will spin as soon as look at you, their wings folding in mid-air, and now they fucking anaesthetize you for God's sake. And if I don't kill myself I'll kill someone else, Doc. Maybe one of these kids and, Jesus, I can't take it any more, I'm just twitched to hell, I've had it.

Sitting there with my DSC ribbon and the ribbons of all the campaign gongs that had just been dished out to everyone. And this torrent of fears, which pride or self-deceit had so long kept dammed inside me, pouring forth once the first crack had been opened in the gates to this silent concerned hearer.

Who still sat unspeaking as I faced him, or rather couldn't

face him. Till at last he said, now listen, John, a father to a son, the strong consoling father I'd never had for Christ's sake, now John it's not a question any more of whether you want to fly or not. Because you've flown too far already and I'm grounding you forthwith. Do you understand me, I hereby officially ground you. You are hereby forbidden to fly. You'll be due for demobbing about December? Well I'll see the Captain and recommend you be sent on indefinite leave forthwith pending discharge. Now take a couple of these, just sit there and rest awhile, or lie down if you like, just take it nice and easy. You'll never fly again.

So I lay down, laid down everything. And a few days later, leaving Crimond for the last time, I made the last entry in my log, those lines of T. S. Eliot's that were so entirely appropriate:

This is the way the world ends,
Not with a bang but a whimper.

* * * *

During the last weeks at Crimond, the new Labour Government had announced the Further Education and Training Scheme, which would provide grants for servicemen whose education had been interrupted, to enable them to complete it. I'd never given a thought to what I'd do after the war if I survived it. There could have been no question of going back to Balliol, even if I hadn't a wife and son to support, with hardly a penny to my name. But now it seemed certain that I'd qualify for a FETS grant, which would give me time to catch my breath, to look around and make decisions. I applied and was successful. So after Christmas, having been released from the service on December 1st, I found myself back at Oxford on a munificent grant, including marriage allowance, of something over £400 a year. With such few friends, including Angel, who'd also managed to survive.

Plato and Virgil seemed more irrelevant than ever and instead I read PPE.* It was a two-year shortened course, I didn't work much harder than before, but I found PPE easy and took a respectable second at the end of 1947. My brother Wynne, though six years younger than me, was approaching his final year at New College when I went up. He took a first six months before me. Aged nearly twenty-one. Which I didn't resent in the least. He had just been young enough to miss the war and it seemed all in the natural order of things. I'd had something (I told myself) that he could never have: the comradeship of service life, the power and the glory, the responsibility of commanding men, of leading my squadron in action, of flying free across the world. I hadn't yet come to realize that all these were absolutely valueless. Or worth so much less than I'd paid for them, than we'd all paid. All those lost years. Which I found as I grew older had so profoundly destabilized my life, setting it askew, had consumed all my early manhood. To be always six years behind, six years astern of station. With so many hundreds of thousands of others.

And all for nothing. Foes turn to allies, allies become foes. Unless, because I came to see it was all for nothing, to learn the total futility of violence. Which I have long since repudiated in any form whatever. By luck it happened that almost all my operational flying was to protect convoys, to keep off the U-boats that preyed on them. But I may have killed men with the mines I laid, the RPs fired, the torpedoes dropped. I may but there's no way of knowing. There can never be any proof. And if I did I'm sorry. Hypocrite, hypocrite. What good being sorry? If they're dead, they're dead.

Five years before I could bring myself to fly even as a passenger. It was 1950, my divorce had just come through, I was on my way to New Zealand with Marigold, the start of thirty years of wandering. Never settled down after my service in the Navy. We'd gone overland in a borrowed Morris Oxford from Calais to Calcutta, whence came the chance of a free

* Philosophy, politics and economics – in my case mainly economics.

flight with KLM by way of Djakarta to Australia. In a converted Liberator. Hating every moment of it. Worst of all having no parachute. And the torture of not knowing what was going on up-front, clinging to my seat. Why is he making this turn? What's his airspeed? And the weather ahead? Has he remembered his flaps? A thousand imagined perils in every hour.

Gradually I overcame my fear of flying. During the next five years, though I was travelling extensively, I never flew unless it was inescapable. Even to spend three days in Venice with all expenses paid: boat and train all the way out from Killegar, boat and train all the way home. Or by train from Miami to Minneapolis. And Atlantic crossings time and again in the *QM* or *Ile-de-France* rather than face twelve hours in the air.

Slowly the remaining fear became less important than the inconvenience. And in the last four decades I've flown everywhere. To Peking and Aden and Lourenço Marques. To Moscow, Bogota, Baghdad. To Teheran, Tegucigalpa, Jiddah and Havana. By Russian helicopter through Kurdistan. By Jumbo to Amman. So many times to the States, and within the States from New York to San Francisco, from Dallas to Grand Rapids. Shuttling back and forth between Dublin or Belfast and London. It has never stopped. Always seeking something I'd never find.

And the great four-engined airliner never turns for a night takeoff from the international airport but I remember the dimmed lights on the swinging flight-deck as I wait in my Stringbag for the quick green signal from the bridge. Never sit a passenger strapped impotent in my seat but I'm alone at the controls, the whole world before me. Never make the long approach to land on a great runway but I see that foam-glistened platform in mid-ocean. Never climb sedately through the overcast but I am once more playing with the clouds, diving and soaring free.

Appendix 1
Wing-Commander Neville Usborne RNAS

Amongst my mother's papers I came across a claim submitted in 1925 to the Royal Commission on Awards to Inventors on behalf of Rear-Admiral Murray Sueter and the executors of her late husband, Neville Usborne, setting out the circumstances under which they had invented the so-called SS3 (Submarine Searcher) non-rigid airship, which became known as the Blimp.* In his book *Aircraft and Sea Power*, Admiral Hezlett mentions that the first of these was produced 'in the remarkably short time of three weeks' from the time such a craft was demanded by Admiral Fisher. The following is an extract from this claim, which though written mostly in the third person was drafted by Sueter himself in his handwriting.

'Early in 1915 the submarine menace to our shipping started to increase. Lord Fisher summoned an important conference to consider the proposal of Mr Holt Thomas to build a large number of small airships for submarine patrols. Until then the Admiralty airship officers could get practically no support. But with Lord Fisher's powerful support, airship work was given a new lease of life.

'Mr Thomas was given an order for a small airship of Willows design. To compete with this, Commander Usborne was given instructions to develop a small envelope of 60,000 cubic feet capacity. Admiral Sueter suggested, as he had some BE2C aeroplanes, which the pilots did not like

* See Plate 2. The word "blimp", which has passed into the language (with two quite different meanings), was coined from a phrase in a 1915 flying manual: Airships are two kinds: (a) rigid and (b) limp.

because Commander Samson had sent in an adverse report about these machines, that the chassis of one of them should be tried with one of the old envelopes of the Army airships. The result of tests with this machine promised well and a two-ply envelope was ordered from Messrs Shorts. Commander Usborne had to develop the whole of this envelope work.

'At first we had very considerable trouble with dopes because of very small holes in the dope. But Commander Usborne had developed Ioco dope for the first rigid airship [*Naval Airship No. I*] and brought his great experience to play and gradually the dope became so good that he managed in later airships to save much weight by using single-ply fabrics. These were lighter than rubber-proofed fabrics.

'When the new Shorts envelope was fitted to a BE2C chassis it was christened "SS3" – Submarine Searcher No. 3. The first experiment was SS1. The Holt Thomas airship was called SS2 and comparative trials were carried out with the two airships. The Willows airship [i.e. SS2] was a failure: the seams of the envelope were doped over and over again but the aeroplane fabric was a poor holder of hydrogen. The Sueter-Usborne airship [SS3], after some difficulty in determining the best position for slinging the car and the best position for fins and rudder, was an undoubted success. Many of these small airships were ordered and none differed very much from the original ...

'The part played by our flexible [i.e. non-rigid] airships during the war in protecting our merchant ships made an exceedingly valuable addition to our naval patrols. Admiral Sueter desires to place on record his high appreciation of the hard work and devotion to the airship cause that was displayed by Commander Usborne. Far into the night and early hours of the morning, this scientific officer worked to make these airships a success, and to him in large measure their wonderful success is due... No submarine ever sank a surface ship where there was an airship patrol.'

Usborne continued his pioneering research and met his death the following year (1916) flying the prototype of a revolutionary anti-Zeppelin craft that he himself had designed.

The facts are worth recording. Zeppelins were a very serious menace: they came in over London above the range of ack-ack, and fighter aircraft could seldom climb quickly enough to intercept them. Usborne's plan was simple: to attach a fighter aircraft underneath a balloon, which would then rise quickly to above the Zeppelin height. The fighter's engine would have been ticking over since before take-off and the pilot would then operate a release mechanism separating the two craft. The unmanned balloon would float off on its own. The fighter, having no forward momentum, would drop vertically in a stall till it attained flying speed. Then shoot down the Zepp – easy.

Tests proved satisfactory using once again a B2C fighter and a demonstration was arranged in front of the top brass. No-one ever knew what went wrong but the release mechanism malfunctioned and the B2C with its two occupants, Usborne and his co-pilot, fell vertically to the ground from several thousand feet. No parachutes.

My mother told me how, lying beside her husband three nights beforehand, she had dreamt she saw a black car waiting in the sunshine outside their London house and knew its occupants had come from the Admiralty to tell her of Neville's death. On waking she told him and asked him to postpone the test. He wouldn't. When the day came, she determined to stop the dream coming true by leaving with him first thing and not returning till after midnight. But at midnight the black car was waiting.

Appendix 2
Stringbag History

One of many remarkable facts about the Stringbag is that by all the rules it should have been very nearly obsolescent not long after reaching the first front-line squadrons in 1936, yet was still operational nearly a decade later.

It was largely designed to meet a specification issued by the Air Ministry (who then controlled the Fleet Air Arm) in October 1930. This resulted in Fairey's designing the prototype S 9/30, for which they received a go-ahead less than a year later. The aircraft closely resembled the Swordfish apart from its liquid-cooled Rolls Royce Kestrel II engine, which gave it a pointed nose. It first flew in February 1934.

Meantime Fairey's had been working on another prototype, known as TSR I, which was intended for the Greek navy. With its Bristol Pegasus II radial engine, it was even more like a Stringbag. Though work on 'the Greek machine', as it became known, started after that on the S 9/30, it flew nearly a year earlier, in March 1933. It promised well but one little design fault came to light. In September Fairey's chief test pilot, C. S. Staniland, took it up for spinning trials.

He experienced great difficulty in getting TSR I to spin, as would later be the case with the Stringbag, but once he succeeded the aircraft went into a flat spin (with the nose only slightly below the horizon) and simply wouldn't come out.

After completing a dozen revolutions, Staniland decided to jump, but only jumped as far as the observer's open cockpit behind him. He thus became probably the only aviator to bale out twice from the same aircraft. S 9/30 was smashed to pieces.

Instead of persevering with this prototype, the Fairey design team under Marcel Lobelle now combined the knowledge gained from S 9/30 and TSR I to produce a new mark with a Pegasus III engine, at first christened TSR II. This historic aircraft, No. K4190, the first Swordfish, made its initial flight in Staniland's hands on April 17th 1934. Apart from its two-blade wooden propeller, it was virtually identical to the Stringbags I was flying in 1941.

The Air Ministry soon afterwards placed an order for eighty-nine Swordfish, which began to reach the squadrons in July 1936. The first to be equipped were 825 in *Glorious* and 811 in *Furious,* which had previously been flying Fairey Seals and Blackburn Baffins respectively. By the outbreak of war thirteen squadrons had been equipped with this 'new' TBR aircraft, which, however, already looked like an escapee from World War I by comparison with those being delivered to the RAF, whether fighters or bombers.

A total of 692 Swordfish had been built by early 1940. Now Fairey's went over to producing Albacores exclusively. This was the 'improved', cleaned-up version that was intended to replace the Swordfish but never managed to do so: the Albacore was no more than an unhappy memory when the Stringbag was still very much in the front line. Production of the latter was continued by Blackburn's, who had built 300 by 1942.

A modified version, the Swordfish II, was then introduced with a strengthened lower mainplane to enable RPs to be fired. Blackburn's built 1080 of these. In the later ones, the faithful Pegasus III engine was replaced by the more powerful XXX.

By 1944 this in turn had been superseded by the Swordfish III (known to us as the 'pregnant Stringbag' – see page 166), also powered by the XXX. A total of 320 Mk IIIs were built by Blackburn's, making a grand total of 2392 Stringbags. Two of these are still flying.*

* For a more detailed account, see *Fairey Aircraft* by H. A. Taylor, from which most of the above has been gleaned.

Appendix 3
The Merchant Aircraft Carriers

Name	Entered service	Tanker or grainer	Displace- ment (tons)	Flight deck (ft)	Converted by
Empire MacAlpine	4/43	G	7950	414 x 62	Burntisland
Rapana	7/43	T (AS)*	8000	462 x 62	Smith's Yard
Empire MacAndrew	7/43	G	7950	423 x 62	Denny Bros
Amastra	8/43	T (AS)	8000	462 x 62	Smith's Yard
Empire MacRae	9/43	G	8250	424 x 62	Lithgow's
Acavus	10/43	T (AS)	8000	462 x 62 } No record	
Ancylus	10/43	T (AS)	8000	462 x 62	
Empire MacKay	10/43	T (BP)*	8908	460 x 62	Harland/Wolff
Empire MacColl	11/43	T (BP)	9133	461 x 62	Cammel Laird
Empire MacCallum	12/43	G	8250	424 x 62	Lithgow's
Empire MacKendrick	12/43	G	7950	414 x 62	Burntisland
Empire MacMahon	12/43	T (BP)	8856	462 x 62	Swan Hunter
Empire MacCabe	12/43	T (BP)	9249	462 x 62	Swan Hunter
Alexia	12/43	T (AS)	8000	462 x 62 } No record	
Miralda	1/44	T (AS)	8000	462 x 62	
Adula	2/44	T (AS)	8000	462 x 62	Silley Cox
Empire MacDermott	3/44	G	7950	423 x 62	Denny Bros
Gadila†	3/44	T (AS)	8000	462 x 62	Smith's Yard
Macoma†	5/44	T (AS)	8000	462 x 62	No record

* AS indicates Anglo-Saxon (Shell); BP indicates Bntish Petroleum.
† Air party provided by the Royal Netherlands Navy.

Index